CULTURAL STUDIES 1983

Stuart Hall: Selected Writings

A series edited by Catherine Hall and Bill Schwarz

CULTURAL STUDIES 1983

A Theoretical History

Edited and with an introduction by
Jennifer Daryl Slack and **Lawrence Grossberg**

Stuart Hall

DUKE UNIVERSITY PRESS | DURHAM AND LONDON | 2016

Library of Congress Cataloging-in-Publication Data
Names: Hall, Stuart, [date], author. | Slack, Jennifer Daryl,
editor. | Grossberg, Lawrence, editor. | Hall, Stuart, [date].
Works. Selections. 2016.
Title: Cultural studies 1983 : a theoretical history / Stuart
Hall ; edited and with an introduction by Jennifer Daryl
Slack and Lawrence Grossberg.
Description: Durham : Duke University Press, 2016. | Series:
Stuart Hall, selected writings | Includes bibliographical
references and index.
Identifiers: LCCN 2016020794 (print)
LCCN 2016022037 (ebook)
ISBN 9780822362487 (hardcover : alk. paper)
ISBN 9780822362630 (pbk. : alk. paper)
ISBN 9780822373650 (e-book)
Subjects: LCSH: Culture—Study and teaching. | Critical
theory. | Social sciences—Philosophy.
Classification: LCC HM623.H365 2016 (print) |
LCC HM623 (ebook) | DDC 306—dc23
LC record available at https://lccn.loc.gov/2016020794

Cover art: Photo of Stuart Hall by Dharmachari
Mahasiddhi.

CONTENTS

Lawrence Grossberg and Jennifer Daryl Slack

The lectures in this volume were delivered by Stuart Hall in the summer of 1983 at the University of Illinois at Urbana-Champaign as part of the teaching institute (which was followed by a conference) called "Marxism and the Interpretation of Culture: Limits, Frontiers, Boundaries," organized by Cary Nelson and Lawrence Grossberg. Both the teaching institute, June 8–July 8, and the conference, July 8–12, have been extremely influential in shaping the development of cultural theory in and across a variety of disciplines, including Cultural Studies, Communication, Literary Theory, Film Studies, Anthropology, and Education. The teaching institute consisted of seminars taught by Perry Anderson, Stuart Hall, Fredric Jameson, Julia Lesage, Gajo Petrovi, Gayatri Spivak, and University of Illinois faculty A. Belden Fields, Lawrence Grossberg, and Richard Schacht. Participants were students and faculty from across the U.S. as well as from several other countries. The conference, with an audience of over five hundred students and faculty, resulted in a book of essays and exchanges (Nelson and Grossberg 1988) that reflects the event's many interdisciplinary exchanges and includes Hall's "The Toad in the Garden: Thatcherism among the Theorists" (35–73). The shape of cultural theory—its interpretation, directions, scholarship, and teaching—in the U.S. today can be credited in part to the events of that summer and the book, the extensive interaction of established and young scholars in the seminars and conference, and the cultivation of a collective sense of the vitality and diversity of Marxist contributions to cultural theory at the time.

These events have been hailed as a particularly significant moment in the history of Cultural Studies, for although a few people were writing about and practicing Cultural Studies in the U.S. (and other places outside of Britain) at the time, and although Hall had given occasional lectures in the U.S., the teaching institute provided the first sustained exposure for many intellectuals to both Hall and British Cultural Studies. At the seminar's beginning, only a few people knew of Hall's work and the work of the Centre for Contemporary Cultural Studies, but very quickly, as news of the exceptional nature of these lectures spread, Hall attracted hundreds of students and faculty, many driving for hours to attend. The lectures were riveting, and the mood during the lectures was electric. We had the sense of being part of theory being developed, of Cultural Studies being made. The lectures were contributing to invigorating Cultural Studies in the U.S. in both subtle and dramatic ways.

Hall had been the first person Richard Hoggart hired at the Centre for Contemporary Cultural Studies at Birmingham University. When Hoggart left to take up a high-level position at UNESCO in 1969, Hall became the new director, where he remained until 1980, when he was appointed Professor of Sociology at the Open University. By the summer of 1983, the work of the Centre and Hall's important contributions were gaining visibility in what were largely minor disciplines (e.g., Communication Studies and Education) at a number of respected public universities rather than elite private schools. The Centre's early work on working-class culture, media, news and popular culture, subcultures, ideology, and semiotics, as well as the now classic study of racism and the new conservatism (notably a book that predicted the rise of Thatcherism, *Policing the Crisis* [Hall et al. 1978]), was neither well known nor widely available outside the U.K. But while Hall had already become the leading figure and the most articulate spokesperson for the project of Cultural Studies, few people outside the U.K. knew of either Hall or the project.

What Hall presented in this series of eight lectures was a personally guided tour of the emergence and development of British Cultural Studies as seen from his own perspective. These lectures are, in fact, the first serious attempt to tell a story about the emergence and development of Cultural Studies at the Centre. Yet they are both less and more than this, as the 1988 preface he wrote some years after the lectures makes clear. They are not in any sense a history of the Centre. They underplay the crucial empirical studies and contributions of the various research groups that formed the heart of the Centre in the 1970s. They largely bypass the Centre as a space of administrative and organizational experimentation that provided the condition of possibility of its intellectual experimentation. They put aside the crucial and often heated political debates and diversity that constituted a vital part of the everyday life of the Centre and often connected it with political and artistic activities in Birmingham (and to a lesser extent, in London and elsewhere).

The lectures offer instead a history of theory. Even then, however, they could not possibly be a comprehensive account of the rich theoretical sources, confrontations, negotiations, and paths taken up and rejected, as well as advances that constituted the formation and history of British Cultural Studies. For example, it is difficult to miss the lacunae of women's voices in this story, when by 1983 there had been significant theoretical challenges to the influence of patriarchy on subcultural theory and significant contributions by feminists to theorizing articulation. The reality of even Cultural Studies' theoretical history was already then too messy, uneven, and contested at any and every moment—paths were taken up and rejected, some coexisted, and others confronted each other with open hostility—for one person to tell the story adequately, even when that one person was Stuart Hall. In addition, these lectures were further inflected no doubt by the challenge to contribute to the overall theme of the teaching institute and conference: Marxism's contribution to the interpretation of culture.

This collection is also a history of what John Clarke once called "the diversity that won" and in that sense, it is a history of what had already become the dominant trajectory of British Cultural Studies. It is the beginning of a story that has Hall's own development at its center, and, at least up to the point at which this version of the story ends, it is a story not so much about Marxism as about the Centre's history, to use Hall's description of theoretical work, of "wrestling with the angels" of Marxist theory. But it is an encounter with Marxism avant la lettre in a double sense. On the one hand, Cultural Studies' roots—both intellectually and politically (in the New Left)—were explicitly defined by a rejection of the politics of the dominant forms of Marxist theory and politics, and both the New Left and Cultural Studies were seeking another sort of critical materialist practice and socialist politics. On the other hand, insofar as the first significant theoretical engagement was with the work of Raymond Williams, it was Williams before he came out of the Marxist closet as it were, before he knew that there were other ways to do Marxism.

Hall obviously knew all this; he knew that he was constructing a story, making it up as it were, paralleling the efforts of those at the Centre to make up Cultural Studies as they were claiming to do it. It is in this sense as well that he describes it as a "theoretical history," a history that self-consciously understands that it is "fictioning the real." It is also a narrative that ends before its time, for it ends not at the time of the lectures but at the slightly earlier moment when Hall left the Centre. Thus, when we started to talk with Hall about publishing these lectures, he suggested that he would want to update and extend the story, suggested that he had come to some sort of terms with developments in Cultural Studies that postdated where the lectures left off—particularly chapters on post-structuralism, subjectivity, and the engagement with feminism. It should be noted that later he did extend the narrative—and in the process changed it significantly—in the lecture he gave at the conference "Cultural Studies Now and in the Future" in 1988, subsequently published as "Cultural Studies and Its Theoretical Legacies" (Hall 1992).

All of this raises the interesting question of why it has taken over thirty years for these lectures to see the light of day or, to be more morose, why they are appearing only after Hall's death. When we approached Hall about the possibility of publishing the lectures, he was, to say the least, uncertain and finally agreed only if they could be presented as a historical document, the product of a particular moment, as a story constructed at a particular moment and from a particular perspective about developments that by the very act of being narrated were being artificially closed, as if they were finished, or their trajectory already guaranteed. It is no secret that Hall was an essayist. Essays are interventions into specific intellectual debates, and into specific historical and political contexts. They do not create fixed and universal positions; they are not finished statements, for they are always provisional, always open to revision as new intellectual resources become available, as historical contexts change, and as the relations of power (domination and resistance, containment, and struggle) face new challenges. This was Hall's mode of thinking. The temporality of books is different: It suggests closure and a certainty that Hall eschewed. The only books that bear his name are either collaborative or edited, with one exception: Hall was persuaded (largely by his friend, Martin Jacques, the editor of *Marxism Today*) to publish *The Hard Road to Renewal* (1988), a collection of his essays on Thatcherism as an intervention at a precise moment with the precise intent to open up debates about future directions of the Left and of the Labour Party more generally.

This is a crucial point, for while many intellectuals are comfortable with the necessary contextuality of empirical accounts, it is more difficult to accept that theories (and concepts) have to be approached similarly, as contextually specific tools or interventions. Hall was particularly wary of this in the light of what he sometimes described as the tendency to fetishize theory in the U.S. academy, to believe that one's critical intellectual work could be understood as the search for the right theory, which, once found, would unlock the secrets of any social reality. This contextuality of theory is what he so elegantly tried to emphasize in (and why we believe he insisted on writing) the preface to these lectures. He did not want readers to think that he was suggesting that he was proposing the right theory, even for Cultural Studies, even for Cultural Studies in Britain. He did not want readers to think that he was telling them what Cultural Studies really was, what it should look like, the theoretical resources it should utilize, or the theoretical paths it should follow. Rather, he was describing a project that he could not specify apart from the way it was actualized and developed in the British context. Let us be clear. He was not saying that Cultural Studies was and could only be a uniquely British field; only that he could only describe the way it came to be articulated in the British context. He was not saying that these are the necessary theoretical components of Cultural Studies; only that these were what was taken up from the field of theoretical resources that were available. He was not saying that these particular debates are necessarily constitutive of Cultural Studies; only that Cultural Studies constitutes itself in a process of continuous theorizing, always responding to the political challenges of what he called a "conjuncture." He was not saying that this is the final shape of Cultural Studies, even British Cultural Studies; only that this was as far as the story went, or at least, as far as he was able to narrate a story at the time of the lectures. And he was not saying that the story (and its ending) could be picked up and "transferred wholesale" into another geographical/intellectual/organizational/political context. One has to treat his ideas of Cultural Studies—and the theoretical moves on which it has been constructed—with the same care he would later describe in his own relation to Gramsci's concepts: "they have to be delicately dis-interred from their concrete and specific historical embeddedness and transplanted to new soil with considerable care and patience" (Hall 1986, 6–7).

Given the unique status of this book as a historical document, as a record of Hall's lectures delivered over thirty years ago, we have been faced with some rather unusual choices as editors. We have left the structures of the lectures relatively intact, for they embody Hall's own logic and structure, although his later writings might suggest other possible organizations. We considered adding chapters, based either on published works or other lectures, recognizing Hall's own desire, expressed years after these lectures were given, to update the story as well as to offer a more elaborate description of his own engagement with both Marx's theory and with other Marxist theorists—given in a series of brilliant but largely unknown essays including "Rethinking the 'Base-and-Superstructure' Metaphor" (1977b), "The 'Political' and the 'Economic' in Marx's Theory of Classes" (1977a), and "Marx's Notes on Method: A 'Reading' of the '1857 Introduction to the Grundrisse'" (2003). But we decided that these lectures, which had such a profound influence on those who heard them and who often carried their lessons to their own work and institutions, that this version of the story was worth having in itself, and in its own right. Because we view it as much as a historical document as a valuable contemporary contribution to Cultural Studies, we have chosen to use the time and tense of the lectures in order to stay within the moment, although this may read somewhat strangely (especially now that some of the authors discussed in the present tense are deceased). We have also tried to retain some of the personality of the lectures by leaving in some of the stylistic quirks that marked Hall's speaking style, unless they made the text significantly more awkward. We have also added references when they seemed called for, and we have tried as much as possible to use the references that Hall would have used at the time. The most difficult decisions resulted from the ordinary practices of the academy. A number of these lectures became templates for later publications, some of which we assisted with. Material in lectures 5 and 6, in which Hall addressed the Althusserian break, ideology, and articulation, was reorganized into the now widely cited article, "Signification, Representation, Ideology: Althusser and the Post-Structuralist Debates" (Hall 1985). It is in the original lecture where, for example, Hall first elaborated the multiple ways of being hailed as "black" to powerfully illustrate the work of ideology and articulation. The publication of this article was specifically meant to introduce Hall and the generative possibilities offered by Cultural Studies to a broader North American audience. Material on Gramsci, ideological struggle, and cultural resistance from lecture 7 was later integrated into "Gramsci's Relevance for the Study of Race and Ethnicity" (Hall 1986), another central essay in Hall's oeuvre. In fact, there are echoes and resonances of the lectures presented here in many other essays Hall authored in the mid- to late 1980s. We did not reconcile these lectures with later published versions, except in cases where brief corrections or elaborations were necessary for either accuracy or clarity. We decided to remain true to the original lectures as much as possible, to honor both the theoretical moment and the characteristic rhythms of Hall's oral delivery.

That these lectures were recorded and saved is remarkable. Jennifer Slack, enthralled to meet at last the teacher of her teacher (Lawrence Grossberg), decided and received permission to record the lectures. She sat in the front row of the lecture hall with a small portable cassette recorder, flipping over cassettes as necessary. Once Hall realized that words were lost when cassettes were turned over, he would generously pause his lecture until recording resumed. After several weeks, when it became clear to all those in attendance that these lectures were a monumental contribution to Cultural Studies, and we began to contemplate the importance of concepts such as articulation unfolding before us, we began discussing the possibility of publishing the lectures. Were it not for the reasons discussed above, this would have happened in the 1980s. After the teaching institute and conference, we transcribed and typed the lectures (there was no help from computers back then), at both Purdue University and the University of Illinois, with assistance from an undergraduate student at Purdue and a couple of graduate students. The technology was clunky and the process labor intensive. Hall read all the transcripts and was engaged in editing them when the project was halted in the late 1980s as a consequence of Hall's reluctance to publish. The partially edited, typed, and yellowing manuscript has been stored in a box until recently. And the original cassettes still sit on Jennifer's desk, except for the first one, which has been lost to time.

Hall, as anyone who met him can attest, was a profoundly generous scholar. His reluctance to police the boundaries of Cultural Studies by telling his story of Cultural Studies as though it were the story of Cultural Studies kept this story from being widely shared until now. It is a good story, a helpful story, and a story that will still contribute significantly to—perhaps reenergize—ongoing conversations about what Cultural Studies has been, is, and can be. These lectures still have much to contribute to understanding and engaging relations of power, to understanding and engaging relations of cultural domination, struggle, and resistance. We are deeply grateful to Catherine Hall, who has granted us permission to share these lectures now.

References

Hall, Stuart. 1977a. "The 'Political' and the 'Economic' in Marx's Theory of Classes." In *Class and Class Structure*, edited by Alan Hunt, 15–60. London: Lawrence and Wishart.

Hall, Stuart. 1977b. "Rethinking the 'Base-and-Superstructure' Metaphor." In *Class and Party*, edited by John Bloomfield et al., 43–72. London: Lawrence and Wishart.

Hall, Stuart. 1985. "Signification, Representation, Ideology: Althusser and the Post-Structuralist Debates." *Critical Studies in Mass Communication* 2 (2): 91–114.

Hall, Stuart. 1986. "Gramsci's Relevance for the Study of Race and Ethnicity." *Journal of Communication Inquiry* 10 (2): 5–27.

Hall, Stuart. 1988. *The Hard Road to Renewal*. London: Verso.

Hall, Stuart. 1992. "Cultural Studies and Its Theoretical Legacies." In *Cultural Studies*, edited by Lawrence Grossberg, Cary Nelson, and Paula Treichler, 277–294. New York: Routledge.

Hall, Stuart. 2003. "Marx's Notes on Method: A 'Reading' of the '1857 Introduction to the Grundrisse.'" *Cultural Studies* 17 (2): 113–149.

Hall, Stuart, Chas Critcher, Tony Jefferson, John Clarke, and Brian Roberts. 1978. *Policing the Crisis: Mugging, the State, and Law and Order*. London: Macmillan.

Nelson, Cary, and Lawrence Grossberg, eds. 1988. *Marxism and the Interpretation of Cultures*. Urbana: University of Illinois Press.

The history of Cultural Studies and the terms in which it is presented here overlap in part with my own biography. I am giving the story as I understand it. This obviously has both advantages and disadvantages. On the one hand, I know the story quite well; on the other hand, I'm addicted to a particular version of it. I will not, in what follows, attempt to offer a survey of cultural theories in general. There is no point in even trying, as if I could, to cover the whole field. What I want to talk about is the evolution of theoretical work in the field of Cultural Studies as I have experienced it. Cultural Studies has evolved in England in a particular way. I will outline that way, speaking as it were out of my own experience. But by speaking analytically and conceptually about this history, without offering that experience as the last word in Cultural Studies, I hope to bring forward concepts from that tradition which might be of use to other traditions or in relation to concrete interests other than those which defined the particular British evolution. Hence, the title *Cultural Studies 1983: A Theoretical History*. These lectures are meant to provide a history of the theoretical underpinnings of Cultural Studies, but at the same time they try to recognise and acknowledge the perspective they take on that history, a perspective defined in part by my own theoretical position as it has evolved; thus it is of necessity something of an idealised—theoretical, as it were—history.

ot mean to suggest that this strategy is merely a necessary com-
sort of pale reflection of what it ought to be. Actually I think
what theorising is actually like; it is a continuous engagement
dialog between positions in which clarification is a mutual process.
The notion that theory progresses by a sudden epistemological rupture
with all the bad theories that preceded it, by a sudden leap into science
which only requires that one now unfolds the concepts in all their rigorous purity, without any further need to think again for another epoch,
is the summit of the rationalist illusion. And of course, this isn't actually
what thinking is like. So these lectures are an attempt to engage in a little
practical theorising.

I want to frame this history of Cultural Studies by reminding you that
it is always important to understand the historical context of theories,
whether of Gramsci, Althusser, Lévi-Strauss, et cetera. This doesn't mean
that the history explains the theory, nor that it can provide a warrant
for the scientific accuracy of the theory. History and theory are two
interlocking but not entirely coterminous fields. Ideas always arise in
particular concrete historical locations which inflect the ideas in certain
ways. The ideas arise in part because of the history. But having established the context, one needs to look at the internal coherence of the theory which is being elaborated and at the way in which it constitutes itself
in response to the problematics which it defines. This is bound to involve
a work between history and theory, rather than either the unfolding of a
logically and conceptually clarified theoretical line of thinking or simply
the deconstruction of theory into its historical conditions.

Cultural Studies addressed questions in an English context, where
particular political problems were pressing and particular theoretical resources available. One always begins to grapple with and analyse difficult
political situations using one's experiences and understandings. But one
draws upon theories to break into experience, to open up to investigation the problematic nature that such political situations present to us
in order to better understand what is going on and how to respond.
Cultural studies emerged at just such a moment, but there are always
other such moments, confronting people with a major historical shift,
a change in the tempo and texture of society, the emergence of a new
set of relations. And it is that which is problematic and which defines
the theoretical and political problematic as well. It is in the face of such

real problematics that old theories prove themselves inadequate. Then new theories have to be generated in order to take one further towards that point which we all affirm as if it already existed but which in fact is the point towards which we hope we are travelling: the unity of theory and practice.

This theoretical work always operates on an already occupied theoretical terrain. You never simply begin to speak a discourse which has no relation to the other discourses already in the field. Theoretical development is in part the displacement of at least some parts of other inadequate theorisations for more adequate ones. And so one must begin by describing the existing terrain of theoretical discourses which have attempted to think in this area, for it is out of these that, initially, some synthesis had to be made, and against which some new positions had to be advanced. There is a theoretical interdiscourse always at play among a set of discourses, and this affects how thinking goes on in a particular social formation. It is very difficult in a particular intellectual milieu to think outside of the dominant philosophical discourses with which you have to engage. For instance, understanding the influence of Raymond Williams (lecture 2) involves in part understanding the particular character of the English empirical mode of thought. This is not to claim that Williams is a classical empiricist but it does mean that in engaging his work, one has to acknowledge the dominance of a highly empirical and pragmatic discourse in English thought. And of course, if one thinks about Cultural Studies in a different situation—such as an American one—you will find that it will have to engage, in its own ways, with its own other discourses if it is to displace them. Thus, for example, when I talk about American sociology (lecture 1), I will not tell you how Cultural Studies in an American context would have to engage the sociological tradition but rather explain how we in England had to engage with it, how American sociology appeared in our intellectual milieu in a particular form and had to be accepted, modified, opposed, or transformed.

I also want to emphasise the importance of the institutional moment, which is separate from the bringing together of a set of intellectual discourses. Something additional happens when a set of discourses and practices are institutionalised: They are concretised in a particular form, in a program of activities and a specific socially composed group of people. They are directed to certain targets and projects. In another place, on the basis of a different kind of institutionalisation, different practices emerge. While I will emphasise the fact that the Centre for Contemporary Cultural Studies appeared at a certain moment, in a certain place, I also want to make the more general point that what happens in the evolution of a new field of study must be partly understood in terms of the forms in which those studies are institutionalised.

Finally, I want to point out that it was partially fortuitous that the field was organised around the concept of culture, which is exceedingly slippery, vague, and amorphous, with multifarious and diverse meanings. As director of the Centre for Contemporary Cultural Studies for a long time, the invitations I feared most were those which expected me to explain what culture actually meant. It is one of those concepts which, unlike the State, tends to wither away and disappear the more you work on it. But it is not just that it is a very difficult concept to get hold of. Even more important is the fact that to work in Cultural Studies does not necessarily mean that you think the entire world can be explained from a cultural point of view. Indeed, I sometimes think that working in Cultural Studies is rather like choosing to work in a displaced field, because so much of what one requires to understand cultural relations is not, in any obvious sense, cultural. In that sense Cultural Studies is an interdisciplinary field. It draws on and is fed by other disciplines which intersect it. In fact, Cultural Studies appears and remains on the scene as an intellectual and political space between a number of intersecting, intellectual, and academic disciplines.

The Formation of Cultural Studies

The problematic of Cultural Studies appeared in British intellectual history in the 1950s and early 1960s. It is important to understand that the concept of culture was proposed, not as the answer to some grand theoretical question, but as a response to a very concrete *political* problem and question: What happened to the working class under conditions of economic affluence? The post–Second World War decades in Britain, especially the fifties and sixties, was a period of an unusually high level of economic affluence and sustained economic growth such as the British economy had not seen in this (twentieth) century. It was, comparatively, quite a remarkable period, and its impact on social relations and cultural attitudes was profound. Of course, these broad changes were not just the result of the economic changes, but also of the exceptional conditions of the war itself. War quite frequently disrupts the chain of normal relations, including class, in a society. And while it doesn't create new trends from nothing, ab initio and ex nihilo, it does provide the circumstances in which trends already lying deep within the society can, as it were, move at an accelerated pace, enabling them to appear and break through the resistances of normal life more easily and rapidly than under normal conditions. It is clear that significant changes began during the war itself and continued, at an increasing rate, immediately after the war in Britain. It was the period during which, to everybody's surprise, Labour achieved a large majority (perhaps the last major Labour victory we are likely to see, but that may be too pessimistic) and initiated the welfare state, which, by itself, would make this a major historical moment. But then, on top of that so to speak, comes a powerfully led consumer boom which itself had a very considerable social and political impact. This is especially so because, when Labour loses power in the mid-fifties, the period of high affluence is led, even dominated by the Conservatives, and the cultural definitions of affluence are given to the British people under Conservative hegemony. Harold Macmillan [British prime minister, 1957–1963] is one of those Edwardian wizards—perhaps the last— who simply didn't bother about the economy. It ran itself and every now and again he reminded the electorate of how well it was doing. His slogan was "You've never had it so good; make sure you go on having it as good." There was a sustained attempt to identify economic affluence, the coming of mass society, with the political hegemony of the Conservative Party.

This is the "American phase" in British life. Until then, people, especially Marxists, thought—knew—that Britain was the first paradigm industrial society, that everything, from expansion to the tendential decline in the rate of profit, happens first in Britain. But in the postwar period they have to confront the fact that the paradigm case, for all of Western Europe, suddenly becomes the United States. As far as the population was concerned, it was all going extremely well here and there. But significant changes in the patterns of social life were taking place that, in a very rough way, seemed to mark off the postwar from the prewar period, changes which can be identified with American culture's taking the historical lead in a global context: the diminishing sharpness of class relations; the drifting and incorporation of sectors of the working and lower-middle classes into the professional and nonprofessional commercial classes; the beginnings of mass cultures; the massive penetration of the mass media and the beginnings of a television age; the rapid expansion of a consciousness led by consumer advertising, et cetera.

Consequently, British intellectuals and politicians alike had to confront questions about the nature of mass culture and mass society, about the changes taking place in an affluent, capitalist, developed, industrial society, and those questions had to be seen in American terms for the first time. When the Labour Party lost for the second time in the 1959 election, people were predicting that the Conservatives would be in power for a hundred years (thankfully they weren't, but it looked endless). The leader of the Labour Party, trying to explain what had gone wrong to the 1959 Labour conference, reached into his analytic tool bag and blamed the telly, and the fridge, and the secondhand motorcar, and the women's magazines, and the disappearance of the working-class cloth cap, and the fact that people didn't go to the whippets anymore. The breakdown of cultural life explained what had gone wrong! Consequently, the next question that had to be faced was "Must Labour lose?"—not coincidentally, the title of one of the most popular books of the period (Abrams and Rose 1960). And the answer was clearly "yes!" insofar as Labour was identified with a particular kind of traditional industrial class culture that was being undermined by the sweeping affluence of mass society. For in that kind of society, it was thought, class would necessarily be eroded and the society would come to look and feel like, would come to take on the character and shape of, American society. And as a consequence, politics would have to change.

This all too brief sketch may hide the fact that these changes presented enormous problems of analysis for those looking at the society. On both sides of the Atlantic, people are talking about the "postcapitalist" society, about the decline and disappearance of traditional class-oriented political ideologies. Some people, of course, even went so far as to talk about the "end of ideology" [notably Daniel Bell 1960]. But while there were economic and political questions about the nature of this socioeconomic system, which looked so different from British societies in the past, it was also perfectly clear that the major transformations were not so much political and economic as cultural and social. But that raised yet another fundamental question: Namely, what are the tools with which one tries to understand the nature of subtle and often contradictory cultural change? And it also assumed, very importantly, that if you can understand the changes that are taking place in the culture of the society, you will have a very important strategic clue to understanding broader changes in society's nature and how it is working.

I have begun with this history to separate myself from those who would read the birth of Cultural Studies as an intellectual project, while I want to insist that it is in fact born as a political project, as a way of analysing postwar advanced capitalist culture. Not surprisingly, then, the emergence of Cultural Studies is intimately connected with the birth of the New Left as a distinct political grouping, and for some time, the two movements remain very closely bound together, running parallel with one another. The New Left in the mid-fifties, its first incarnation, was committed to the project of a radical analysis of the nature of society having recognised (unlike the traditional—including Marxist—Left) that things were indeed changing, and that many of the available theoretical and analytic tools they had inherited were not very effective for the task. The New Left recognised the importance of cultural change in this period, but found little help in the existing Marxist bag of tricks; for the most part, the concept simply didn't appear. I will return shortly to the question of the early forms of Marxist thinking about the problem of culture.

My point, however, is not to focus on the New Left itself but rather to point to the connection that existed between it and the formation of Cultural Studies. Many of the founding figures of Cultural Studies were positioned in the orbit of the early New Left and the kind of political thinking which nurtured it, including Raymond Williams and, to some extent, Richard Hoggart. And others who were actively involved in developing Cultural Studies, myself included, were even more strongly identified with it, actively writing for *New Left Review* and other journals, and actively engaged in the political movement. There's a real sense of shared personnel between the two developments at this early stage.

One of the people who attempts to chart the nature of the cultural changes taking place is Richard Hoggart (1957) in a book called *The Uses of Literacy*. Hoggart's background is northern working class; when he writes the book, he was a teacher in adult education; he later became Professor of English and the founder of the Centre for Contemporary Cultural Studies at the University of Birmingham. He is in a sense steeped in the English literary critical tradition. That is to say he is formed, as almost all of us were who went through an English degree at the time, by the ideas of and a contestation with the spirit of F. R. Leavis, to whom I shall return. Thus, when Hoggart writes about culture, he is writing therefore as a literary critic, attempting to do the kind of analysis or reading of real social and cultural life that he would do on a poem or a novel. He is trying to recall the kinds of lives which he and people like him lived in the traditional industrial working class before the war. He sees inscribed, not so much in the political and economic conditions, but in the social and cultural aspects of working-class life in that period, a certain pattern of culture, a certain set of values, a certain set of relationships between people. He sees how people who didn't have access to a great deal of the material goods made a life for themselves, how they created and constructed a culture which sustained them. Of course, it sustained them in positions of subordination. They weren't the masters and mistresses of the world. They weren't people who were going to lead anything, but they were able to survive. And they survived with dignity.

Their lives constituted a pattern of culture: not the authenticated, valorised, or dominant pattern of culture, not the literate and "cultured" pattern of culture, but something he wants to call "a culture" nevertheless. He evokes that early traditional working class—which the leader of the Labour Party has said is disappearing forever—and he tries to "read it" in the same way he would read a piece of prose. He describes the kind of working-class home in which he was raised; he looks at how they arrange their living rooms, at the fact that even if the house is going to rack and ruin, there is always one place in it for visitors. Nobody else in the house ever goes into it. They may be sleeping four in a bed upstairs, but there is always a room to receive someone else. And he says, implicitly perhaps, that that is as much a culture as the culture of the country house or of the bourgeois palace. These are people making a life, giving their life meaning. We studied endlessly in the historical and literary past, interpreting the products of various particular cultures. But this is the culture we never see, the culture we don't think of as cultivated.

He affirms that culture by describing it, using the tools of intuitive literary critical reading. He is not a sociologist and especially not drawn to quantitative methods. Indeed he has been formed in an English tradition which is deeply suspicious of quantification. Its orientation is expressed in a statement by Coleridge (1817, 109): "Men [by which I hope he meant men and women] . . . ought to be weighed, not counted." This was Coleridge's critique of utilitarianism and political economy, and of what early industrial capitalism had done to people; namely, Coleridge said, they talk about them as "industrial hands," as if there were a hand out there running the spinning machine, and it's just fortuitous that there are human beings attached to it! For it is this language that allows you to callously notice that a hundred thousand hands happen to be laid off this year! You can't count people, you have to weigh them. Hoggart inherits this tradition which has been inserted into the interstices of literary criticism. Rather than counting, he weighs, he describes. Although he is unfamiliar with anthropology, he is doing a kind of ethnography, treating his own life as if it were taking place in a village in the South Seas, looking at the strange things people do and say.

Indeed his methodology is exactly that of an ethnographer, listening first of all to the language, to the actual practical speech which people use, to the ways they sustain relationships through language, and to the ways they categorise things. For example, he is interested in how and why working-class people talk about Fate in particular ways, at particular times. Now "Fate," with a capital F, might be heard resounding down the corridors of gentry houses, but it's not really something which puts a stopper to life in the way which it does in the working class. Fate can deal you a very good hand, which means that it only deals it once, and that means you win the pools and you better do something with it 'cause it'll never come your way again. More often, Fate just deals you the old rough, raw deal you always knew was coming your way. And what happens? Fate. It's the language of a class without any command on history. It's the language of a class to which things happen, not of a class which makes things happen. And in that way Hoggart teases out the implications of the implicit value structure of a whole group in society, reading their physical bearing, the way they talk, the way they relate, the way they handle objects, the way they organise into patterns. He knew that these things had meaning, not by reading anthropology (he hadn't), but by reading literature.

He brings a kind of literary imagination to bear on the analysis of a culture. And if this locates him within the traditional literary cultural tradition, he is also outside of it, because that tradition had never taken the sorts of things he is writing about as worthy of any attention at all. If you began talking to Leavis about the front living room of a working-class house in Leeds, he wouldn't know what you were talking about! And what's more, he would not have thought that it was what "culture" was about. Hoggart, formed by that tradition, is trying to bring it to bear on the neglected, the excluded part of culture. So in that sense he was both inside and outside of the tradition which formed him. He was breaking from it, using it to deal with his own experience, and to generalise from it.

This is the extremely rich first half of the book and it was extremely important, and influential on emerging efforts to come to terms with "culture." The second half is Hoggart's attempt to read his own time—the 1950s—and that is, I'm afraid, a near disaster! His effort to understand the changes taking place in his own working-class culture is informed, not by a close critical reading, but by his assumptions about American mass culture and his adaptation of the American mass-culture tradition, about which I will have more to say shortly. He simply transposed the critique of mass culture straight to the United Kingdom. He looked around and saw—and he was certainly not alone in this (e.g., a book by a very distinguished social democrat, Anthony Crosland's [1956] *The Future of Socialism*)—in seeing America and its culture coming across the Atlantic and overwhelming them.

Still *The Uses of Literacy* is a landmark book because it fed directly into, first, a political debate and, then, an intellectual one. When I first read *The Uses of Literacy*, before I had met Hoggart, it was in the context of political discussions—trying to answer the problems outlined earlier—rather than in an academic setting, where Richard Hoggart was known as the author of a book on Auden (Hoggart 1951). In the political context, this was seen as an important book about how the world was going; in the academic context, I suppose it was thought to be one of those books that intellectuals write in their vacations, a sort of intuitive speculative reading about Britain, not to be taken seriously. Nevertheless, it was taken seriously as a response to, in answer to, significant questions we were trying to ask: Where is this society going? What is happening to culture?

Hoggart is also important in a second, institutional, sense because when he went to the University of Birmingham, he established the Centre for Contemporary Cultural Studies. Its brief was really twofold: first, to continue the work of *The Uses of Literacy*, to do more work like that, to do it in a more organised way, to get graduate students of different kinds to do that sort of work, to write in that kind of way about their own times, to find ways to train and refine sensibilities that were developed academically in relation to texts, and to extend them into the analysis of society. It was Hoggart who gave the project of Cultural Studies an institutional form. This is a crucial matter, for as Gramsci realised, no ideology or theory is worth its salt until it has found a party, that is to say, an organisational-institutional expression. Hoggart founded the institution, gave it the base, established a practice, brought people together, and made the project—which was in the air—real as an intellectual development.

Now I want to address the question of the kind of work that the early Centre, and others attempting to think about culture and cultural change, were drawing on. What was the field in which it operated? In particular, what was the field in which the term "culture" was located? What was the terrain in which this project was being offered? Where had the term "culture" been thought or elaborated? What was there for this new Centre, this new project, to draw on? What academic disciplines were feeding into it?

I have already identified the field of literary criticism as an important resource in the constitution of Cultural Studies and, in particular, the work of F. R. Leavis, perhaps the most perceptive and influential literary critic in England. (The closest equivalent American critic was Lionel Trilling; they influenced one another and both came to a kind of conservative liberalism—which is not the same as a liberal conservatism—in their response to the pressures, tensions, and differences within contemporary culture.) Leavis championed a methodology which insisted on what was called the practice of close reading. It says that one cannot make interpretations or judgments about texts in vague and imprecise ways. You have actually to show the meaning or the value in the language, the structure, or the thematic of the particular text. You have to be able to localise the qualities in the particular literary work as your critical judgment moves from one localised instance to another. It is exactly what I described as Hoggart's method; in that sense, Hoggart's work has always been informed by the practice of the close reading of texts. But, at another level, F. R. Leavis made an enormous claim for literary criticism and for English Studies in general. He was not in that sense a narrow academician. He believed that English Studies, with its mixture of close attention to the text and broad sensitivity to the ways language and feeling worked, was *the* central discipline of the humanities; it stood or ought to stand in the same place that philosophy used to stand. But Leavis was making an even bolder claim, for the status of English Studies extended beyond the academy. People trained in literature were in a better position than anybody else to make judgments about the culture as a whole, and not just about a particular text. Leavis was interested in the whole culture in which particular writers were located and in which particular texts were formed. Bringing this concern forward was, itself, an important contribution. He called upon people in literature to take on the much wider historic task of interpreting and judging the trends and movements in the culture itself. And indeed, his wife, Q. D. Leavis (1932), also a very distinguished literary critic, wrote one of the earliest books—*Fiction and the Reading Public*—which attempted to deal with popular rather than serious, "high-brow," literature. It was very informed by mass society and mass culture theory. That is to say, it took the position that most popular literature is emotionally debased. And those who read a great deal of it will be emotionally and intellectually debased in the process.

Still, Leavis's conception of the project as involving questions of culture as a whole rather than just about literature is one of the reasons why people who are formed in a close association with him, including Raymond Williams as well as Hoggart and others, are able to take a leading role in the effort to define this new kind of cultural criticism. But the problem was that the concept of culture embedded in Leavis's practice of criticism looks back essentially to the tradition of Matthew Arnold ([1869] 2014, viii): "The best that has been thought and said." That is what culture is. And there should be no doubt that the best that has been thought and said was not written in Richard Hoggart's front room. It was written somewhere else, by some other kinds of people. And it required elaborate training and sensitivity in the practice of literary criticism for people to be able to recognise it at all! You had to enter into the tradition and give yourself up to it in order to recognise what culture was. That is to say, it was predicated on the long work of historical selectivity and on the construction of a cultural tradition with all of its particular emphases and exclusions. The whole of popular literature was excluded on the grounds that it was not "refined," that our minds and sensibilities would not become refined and sophisticated in intercourse with it. It was the responsibility of the sensitive, trained literary critic to go through the tradition and discard the poor and the not so good and the flawed, and in that way, come out with the common literary tradition: a tiny selection, a handful of books. Actually, for Leavis, it was often not even whole books but bits of books that were deemed worthy: the middle of

Adam Bede (Eliot 1859), the first half of *The Mill on the Floss* (Eliot 1860), most but not all of *The Portrait of a Lady* (James 1881), and certainly not *The Ambassadors* (James 1903). Only a lower-middle-class puritan could have entered into a tradition which was not his own and become its gatekeeper, its refiner, its gardener, the way Leavis did.

He had the highest ambitions for this common tradition. If politicians read more literature, they wouldn't offer people the easy life of materialism which was going on in the fifties, what he called "jam today." If people read more literature they would understand the necessity for the infinite postponement of pleasure rather than the quick gratification. But how could culture survive in a context where people thought that life began and ended with new supermarkets? So, for Leavis, English Studies, both the literature and the critical practice, involved a rigorous use of the cultural tradition to keep the barbarians at bay. The "barbarians" was a complex enemy; it included the effete establishment critics of the *Times Literary Supplement* and the *New York Review of Books*, et cetera—what Leavis called the philistine wing of the cultural establishment. These critics weren't really engaged with literature, weren't really morally fighting it out. But it also included Hoggart's working-class people who wanted jam today.

Leavis's method did not allow one to "toss off" a little reflection on an author; it required a long apprenticeship. It required you to gather together a small group of people in a little room in Cambridge—because there weren't all that many people who could really aspire to do this job—and engage in a conversation, to engage in that difficult task of exploring the cultural values and meanings of the texts. One person might say, "I think this is pretty degenerate, don't you?" And another responds, "Not as degenerate as the text we read last time. Indeed, there's quite a good passage here," et cetera. The method of argument was always, "Is this so? This is so, is it not?" Anyone who did literary studies before and after the war was formed by Leavis, by this tradition, this practice, and these values. I was a student of literature at Oxford, where they hated Leavis—that "beetle-browed puritan"; the more seriously Leavis took literature in Cambridge, the more frivolously we at Oxford were to take it; the more closely Leavis read literature, the more we were to rely upon our intuitions and instincts. But even those of us formed in that dilettante tradition had to recognise the moral seriousness of Leavis. He really thought culture mattered; he knew it mattered. The conception was a highly elitist and refined one. It was not one adequate to engage the complexities of mass culture. It wasn't one which had as its object and subject the life patterns of the whole society. But nevertheless, he knew it was a serious matter requiring careful argument. It was the literary establishment that didn't give a damn about culture which prevailed, but it was Leavis who was right. And yet, though that Arnold-Leavis tradition was one of the few places in which "culture" continued to be studied and treated seriously, it could not provide an adequate basis for developing a science of culture.

One could, of course, also find the term "culture" in certain kinds of anthropology. And although anthropology was not very widely taught in British universities, there is an important thread in the notion of culture which comes out of the anthropological tradition: culture as a whole way of life or as the distinctive patterns with which people live their lives and relate to one another. This is a conception of culture which becomes central in the work of Raymond Williams. Unfortunately, the anthropological tradition in Britain was structural rather than cultural. It looked at social institutions (the family, religion, et cetera) rather than cultural practices. In both France and the United States, the anthropological tradition was more interested in cultural, linguistic, and symbolic questions. While there wasn't a great deal of cultural work and cultural analysis being done in British anthropology, there was enough of a serious tradition to have kept some important conceptions of culture alive. After all, an imperial country, which has destroyed hundreds of cultures around the world and negotiated its way in and through them, certainly knows what the concept is! It may have a slightly "up-country, bush helmet" sort of conception: "the native culture." But if you were a colonial administrator, you were perfectly well aware that something "cultural" was going on when, even in scorching heat, you nevertheless dressed for dinner. There is obviously something symbolic going on there! You can't explain it with Malinowskian functionalism because it's the opposite of functional. And you had to understand as well that there was a clash of cultures. After all, on the other side as it were, was some other culture which, somehow, you had managed to absorb or which you had to administer but which had its own way of life. You had to negotiate between two systems of law, between two ways of resolving disputes, between two kinds of marriage, et cetera. British anthropology is thoroughly marked, deeply inscribed, by its imperialist past. But it nevertheless, in the way in which these things happen, kept alive certain very important considerations about culture even though these were slightly displaced from the arguments that were going on in Cultural Studies and around the New Left.

A third source of theorising around the concept of culture was sociology. In the 1950s, sociology was American. British sociology has a long and distinguished past in social investigation (e.g., the work of Charles Booth and Henry Mayhew) and in the administration of social policy. But there has been no major contribution from British intellectual life to sociology as a developed theoretical field. There has been no Durkheim, no Weber; Marx came to us, we didn't produce him; there has not even been a Talcott Parsons. (You can have that one!) British sociology was always very empirical, very descriptive, very much on the side of social reform. Until very late in the nineteenth century, if you said you were a student of society, it meant that you looked at social conditions in order to ameliorate them. While some British sociologists did adopt the models of scientific inquiry earlier in the twentieth century, the real rise of sociology in Britain began in the fifties, by which time the particular theoretical models and research methodologies being adopted were very substantially American. While it is not necessary in the context of the formation of Cultural Studies at this stage to talk about American sociology in general, it is necessary to say something, albeit in an oversimplified way, about one part of the story: the debate about mass society and mass culture. It began in the 1930s with the work of the Frankfurt School and reached its height in the pluralist defenses of mass culture in the fifties.

During the thirties, Horkheimer, Adorno, and the other members of the Institute for Social Research saw in the rise of fascism important lessons about the nature of the organisation of consciousness, of social consciousness and culture. They argued that this social deformity—the possibility of which we had not dreamt in our normal understanding of the progress of the Enlightenment and rational thought—was enabled by the breakdown of the infrastructure of society. Consequently, we had to look at the unconscious forces and the deep authoritarian relationships which can be generated in a society that considers itself to be one of the most advanced and cultured societies in the world. When the members of the Frankfurt School went into exile to flee Hitler, many of them went to the United States. And they argued that some of the same signs of a breakdown into authoritarian patterns that they had recognised too late in Germany were visible there as well. In a sense, they challenged the defenders of American society and culture. The defenders took a surprisingly long time to formulate an answer; it was eventually delivered in the 1950s, when sociologists like Seymour Martin Lipset argued that authoritarian patterns were not replacing traditional social institutions like the family or religion, that the informal social structures were intact. In fact, they argued, capitalism is delivering on its promises; ideological differences are becoming less sharp; and America had successfully integrated all of the different immigrant populations, creating a new American identity. Pluralism works! It was a vindication, a positive affirmation that the society was tough enough, mass culture broad enough, to gradually incorporate all the subordinate and marginal cultures that entered into it. It was the great image of American society and culture as a "melting pot."

In the 1950s, as America's position of global imperial dominance grew, the forms of social and political analysis and understanding which had been engaged in that debate followed the trade. As the American flag went overseas, the modernising political scientists and sociologists who were going to create Middle America everywhere followed immediately in its wake. It is very strongly defined in a lot of writing during the decade. It is the Alliance for Progress in its very earliest stage. The particular type of pluralist and positivist social science, which became the dominant form through which America understands its society, its social structures, and its culture, is then generated and adopted everywhere. And if you look at the British sociological journals in the period, they read like footnotes, and footnotes to footnotes, in Merton and Parsons. Not only do they have no bearing on British life, but they have no sense of the distinctiveness of the life which is being considered. A methodological approach and its ideological presuppositions have been lifted out of one context and simply inserted into another.

In this mainstream sociological tradition, culture is the area of norms and values. It is the thing that coordinates the whole system actually. In Talcott Parsons's work, there is the biological system, the social system, and the cultural system. And he writes about the importance of the realm of the symbolic in the integration of different social groups and in establishing the lines of connection between one social group and another. But that is given very little concrete elaboration. In this theoretical position, culture is the realm of integration. But it doesn't tell you around which specific cultural values the integration is made. And it tells you even less about what alternative cultural values had to be marginalised or subordinated in order to achieve and maintain that degree of consensus which keeps the society stable. One of the strengths of this form of sociology is its awareness of the plurality of culture; that is not surprising considering that the site it was trying to describe is the United States. It does understand that there is a wide variety of different cultural patterns which are overlaid on one another. But what it is not able to talk about is the relationships between culture and power, the relations of dominance and subordination that may exist between these different cultures. And so, it cannot tell you how particular cultural patterns and values achieve their dominance, how dominant cultural patterns are formed. It cannot say anything about the power relations between the centralised and the marginalised cultural formations. Consider the essay by Edward Shils (1961) called "Centre and Periphery." It is a sort of log cabin–to–White House story of culture. It begins with the assumption that the culture of the masses (the American version of Hoggart's people) is pretty brutal and banal. But as the society continues to open up even more, gradually they too will be drawn into the center; the relations between the center and periphery will grow and multiply. Mass culture will diffuse cultural standards throughout the society and eventually we will all read Jane Austen *and* watch the television. The continued growth of this homogenised culture will secure pluralism. And in that way, though the periphery will never quite become the center (surprise!), the interrelations between periphery and center will keep the society culturally and socially stable. Pluralism works!

There is in this an important insight. However, the assumption that you could give a description of a complex society like America and account for its unity without reference to the relations of power between different cultures—as if cultural relations function outside of the impact of economic relations, of social structures, and especially power—produces a concept of culture which is evacuated. It tells a nice story, and it draws attention to certain important features, but at its center it is radically weak and limited.

There are other notions of culture present in other, alternative strands of the sociological tradition, often embodying a much richer sense of cultural meaning and a more insightful conception of the importance of symbolic and cultural relations to how groups interact with one another. One thinks of the structural tradition of Durkheim and Mauss, the phenomenological and interpretive traditions that arise from Weber, and symbolic interaction theory (with its various positions) built upon the work of the Chicago School of Social Thought. While each of these was to play some role in the development of Cultural Studies, they remained relatively unknown and unavailable during the period of its emergence and formation.

Consequently, during the fifties and early sixties, people setting out on the voyage to try to give the question of cultural relations a more central place in their understanding of the historical movement of a society found concepts of culture sustained in many places in their intellectual world—in the literary critical tradition, in some forms of sociology, in anthropological work—but in all these cases, the conception of culture remained in a sort of "half-life," untheorised and undeveloped, limited, and restricted. And that is why, in a sense, the first task that Cultural Studies had to do turns out to be the last task as well: to do some work in conceptualising culture more adequately than had been done in the traditions which were available.

Finally, I want to address the question of Marxism in relation to the early history of Cultural Studies. If the most powerful source for Cultural Studies was from literary criticism, especially in the tradition of Leavis, that tradition has itself to be located within a larger debate. One of Leavis's most important contributions was that he gave to the novel the kind of attention that other literary critics have traditionally given to poetry and drama. But for that very reason, he found himself writing alongside of, and in a kind of debate with, Marxist critics of the 1930s, when there was a good deal of Marxist writings around the Communist Party which attempted to bring Marxist theory to bear on the analysis of literature. There was in fact a whole school of writers and critics in the thirties— one thinks of Christopher Caudwell and Ralph Fox—who were using Marxist tools for analyses, specifically of the novel. Leavis was not only aware of their intellectual presence, but also that it was a challenge to his own project. And on several occasions he engages directly with it, and often incorporated some of the best of this work into his own journal, *Scrutiny*: e.g., the work of Edgell Rickword and L. C. Knights. Knights was one of the three major contributors to the journal but was extremely interested in the economic and social context of literature, especially Elizabethan and Jacobean drama. So Marxism was by no means absent from the writing that was going on around Leavis and his work. Still, when Raymond Williams (1958) reviews Leavis's work in the last part of *Culture and Society*, he locates his judgment in the context of this debate and concludes, quite straightforwardly and correctly I think, that Leavis won that engagement and deserved to. One has to remember what constituted, at the time, the mainstream, the main productions, of Marxist literary criticism: It is extremely bad and simplistic! It has not yet been influenced by what we would now call the Western Marxist tradition; it has not read the early works of Marx; it has not heard of Lukács, or Benjamin, or the Frankfurt School, or Gramsci. Its "Marxism" is a straightforward, mechanical application of the base-superstructure model to an analysis of the production of literature and of cultural artifacts in general. It is uninformed by the later critiques of reductionism and simple reflection theories of culture. (Caudwell is a different case because he had a rich and, by Marxist standards, highly unorthodox imagination. In order to try to develop a literary and cultural theory, he drew on a wide range of sources. As a result, he was regarded as an extremely bright, but rather fanciful child by the Communist Party itself.)

Against that background, Williams argues that anyone with an open mind—by which he means himself as we all do—anyone who has been formed by the literary critical tradition with its close attention to language and symbolic forms, even though they understand its social underpinnings and reject its intrinsic educational elitism, cannot be satisfied with a theoretical practice which simply brings a rather crude kind of machine to bear on every text, which does not offer any sort of sophisticated description of the complexities of the particular work being analysed. That is, Williams argued that Marxist criticism has to be better, not worse, than Leavis in critically reconstructing the complexities of the work, because understanding developed symbolic forms demands an account which acknowledges their complexity and then adds something more about its social and economic infrastructural relations. I think that is an important and essentially correct judgment.

Of course, when we deal with Cultural Studies and Marxism, we are talking about the postwar rather than the prewar period and, hence, about the Cold War. In the 1950s, talking about Marxist theory or Marxist criticism, even of the thirties, is not only not the thing to do, it is really a rather dangerous thing for intellectuals to be doing. Hence, if you find sections of Williams's early books—*Culture and Society* (1958) and *The Long Revolution* (1961)—somewhat obscure, that is partly the result of his having to find alternative terms for the Marxist terms, with which to talk about Marxist concepts. For example, in neither book does Williams use the term "mode of production." He talks about the system of economic life, the system of economic organisation, et cetera. While I am suggesting that these are code words for what are in fact Marxist concepts, I do not mean to suggest that Williams was simply evading the censor. He has acknowledged and accepted the inadequacies of the kinds of Marxist criticism which had been brought to bear on the cultural domain. And in the context of the Cold War, the embargo against Marxist concepts is so deep and profound that, in conjunction with its inadequacies, someone trying to break through that crust had to look for other terms elsewhere, terms which will not provoke so much hostility that they will prevent people from looking at the evidence and being informed by the analysis. Williams's refusal of the Marxist vocabulary signals a double operation: He needs richer concepts than the tradition can provide him with, but he needs as well to intellectually connect with people who often were quite unwilling or unable to think the problem in Marxist terms.

There is a complex relationship between the Marxist tradition and other traditions available to Cultural Studies in the period of its formation. I have already mentioned the overlap between the early stages of Cultural Studies and what I called the birth of the New Left. The early New Left really arose in 1956 as a political movement, and many of the people involved in it were engaged in a debate with Marxism about the inadequacies of certain Marxist positions. While this dialogue used Marxist language and Marxist concepts, the people in the New Left were distancing themselves from the Stalinist positions which had led, for example, to the invasion of Hungary in 1956, which is really the formative moment for the New Left. So there was an alternative kind of Marxism around in the early stages of Cultural Studies. It's not a very developed one. It is not informed by any of the major figures that one could cite today, writing from the 1920s onwards, who have contributed to the enrichment of Marxist cultural theory. Without that theoretical support, it was trying to wrestle against an extremely mechanical kind of Marxism in order to deal with and explain these complex problems, and not only in the sphere of culture. One of the things that people were trying to do in the 1950s was to understand the operations of class relations. It was quite true that class relations were changing in significant ways in the fifties and sixties. It was also quite true that capitalism had not disappeared, that the class formations had not disappeared nor been entirely incorporated. The question was how to analyse the class formations, the real dispositions of class relations; how to hold to the broad framework of class analysis, without being, as it were, tied up in knots by it. Many of the projects of the New Left in the period meant virtually trying to generate a new analytic language from scratch but which continued to operate within the broad framework or parameters of Marx's basic positions.

The New Left found the Marxism available during that period inadequate and it is perhaps worth quickly pointing to some of the reasons behind this rejection. Basically the Marxism of that period took a base-superstructure approach. It treated both politics and ideology as elements of the superstructure, the dimensions of which were given, fully and intimately determined, by the relations of the capitalist mode of production. This position obviously gives very little room to the efficacy of the superstructures themselves. Attempting to think that problem at the time demanded a kind of exegesis of Marx, and you could locate where people stood in relation to the Marxist project by the number of times they quoted from the Marx-Engels correspondence, for it is there that Engels begins to acknowledge that, in trying to overcome the long legacy of Hegelian idealism, they overemphasised the economic. There Engels challenged the notion that one can simply apply the same laws and models to every situation in just the same way, running every situation through the mode of production, as if it were a little meat grinder. He explicitly acknowledges that the superstructures have an effect on the base, so history is more complex than simple mechanical interpretations of Marxism were suggesting. That is to say, a kind of warrant was discovered within classical Marxism itself to bring to bear against the inadequacies of the traditional Marxist model as it had been inherited in the English tradition. Still, the initial debate with classical Marxism was carried out in a context of theoretical poverty. It was a few years later that the *Economic and Philosophical Manuscripts* (Marx 1961) were translated from the French, and reading groups formed around those texts. We had not heard that kind of Hegelian Marxism spoken before. It was a Marxism which gave a much wider reach to the elements of consciousness, to the question of human needs, et cetera. It opened up an important space within Marxist theory for the New Left to operate in, without the straitjacket of the base-superstructure machinery.

In fact, Cultural Studies has never found it possible to reabsorb the classical Marxist position on the superstructures—a simple base-determining-superstructure model—into its position. Early on, both Raymond Williams and Edward Thompson, each in their own different ways, assailed the simplicity of the base-superstructure model. Neither of them used it, preferring the Hegelian opposition between being and consciousness. Even the Althusserian structural Marxists, to whom both Williams and Thompson are opposed, have also undertaken a profound work of criticism and revision in relations to the base-superstructure problem as such, dismantling the centrality of the model itself. However, we must be clear about what it is that is being rejected in this criticism. After all, insofar as they want to continue to develop the analysis of culture within a Marxist framework, they must be attentive to the materialist presuppositions of Marxist theory. Marxist theory is historical, structural, materialist, and predicated against the sorts of idealist theories of culture that were to be found within the dominant literary critical and other cultural traditions. Therefore the distinctiveness of the Marxist version of Cultural Studies is surely that it finds a way of thinking the domain of cultural production, the domain of the symbolic, in relation to the material foundations. But isn't that precisely what the base-superstructure problematic was intended to generate? One can only answer that ambiguously: yes and no! It is intended to generate that but, especially in its early versions, it takes on and incorporates a particular notion of determination which has never been acceptable within Cultural Studies, a notion that essentially sees the lines of force, of influence, of structuration, working in predominantly one direction: from the base to the superstructure. On this view, determination means that economic relations (or the relations of the mode of production; the two are not the same) not only sets or establishes the terms and limits within which the superstructure operates, it actually serves to determine, in its detail, the content, mechanisms, and efficacy of superstructural forms and relations. That is, it is a *strong* determinist position. But the relationship between analyses of the modes of production and of the cultural superstructures does not readily support the notion of determination which runs essentially one way, nor does it easily support the notion of determination by which the economic is the content of the cultural in the last instance. It is on that problem, an assault on the problem of the inadequacy of the base-superstructure model understood as a strong theory of determination, that Cultural Studies engages Marxist theory. And the first main engagement is in Raymond Williams's (1961) *The Long Revolution*, which is the topic of the next lecture.

That is the state of Marxism in relation to Cultural Studies when the project is first formed. It is therefore not difficult to understand why, in the early stages of the Centre for Contemporary Cultural Studies, the major inspiration and methodologies are literary critical ones. Marxist questions are kept alive but very much in the periphery. It is in fact only with Hoggart's departure in 1969 (to join UNESCO) that the Marxist alternative becomes a significant reference point and resource for developing Cultural Studies.

Culturalism

The work of Raymond Williams has been one of the most important and powerful formative influences in Cultural Studies. This remains the case despite the fact that many of his conceptualisations are flawed, many of the turns he has taken and the positions he has advocated are inadequate, and he has been unable to follow through on many of the paths that he has opened—paths which could prove fruitful to the further development of the field. One must take his contributions into account in the spirit of critical respect, not for the truths they pronounce but as part of a serious intellectual project which offers us many useful ideas even if we reject the overall framework within which he frames them.

Raymond Williams is a very "English" figure, one of many marginal intellectuals from the provinces—in this case Wales—who have succeeded by their own combination of tough mindedness, dedication, chance, and luck. The war and the changes after the war helped a lot of those people to come into intellectual life; they are often referred to in England as "scholarship boys" [*sic*]. Williams is the son of a working-class family, raised in the Welsh border regions. His father was a railway signalman; his family has always had a strong labourist, trade union tradition. He was brought up as the bright young prodigy of the village, the first of his family to leave home to study, to attend university, and receive a higher education in the English context. This results in a huge cultural break in his life, one which many of the cultural theorists of this generation (including Richard Hoggart but not E. P. Thompson) have experienced. Williams is thus the product of a very important formation at a particular moment in British history. He grew up before the war as a bright young socialist. He attended Cambridge, the apogee of the higher education system, where the ruling class, if it exists, is manufactured. At the very least, attending Cambridge brought him into the highest places in economic, political, and cultural life. After Cambridge, he went to war.

The shock of moving from a Welsh border town or, in Hoggart's case, from a working-class neighborhood in a northern industrial city (Leeds) to the environs of Oxbridge could only have been experienced as a kind of subjective rupture. The contrast between these two cultural experiences and their inevitable impact on one another is not unlike the experience of migration—from one class to another, from one town to another, from the country to the city, or from the periphery to the center. It makes you instantly alive to the forms and patterns which have shaped you and which you have left behind, intellectually at the very least, for good. I say "intellectually at the very least" for it is almost as inevitable that you will try, symbolically at least, to return to it. Williams wrote a number of rather undisguised autobiographical novels about such efforts to return to his native Wales and to his family. And having retired from his chair at Cambridge, he has gone back to live in the border country in Wales. But that physical return cannot undo the process which took him from the Welsh borders to Cambridge. The process can only be thought about, reflected on. He does not have the capacity to remake a natural connection with his class roots. He can only reestablish the connection by doing something with the experience of having moved across a number of class frontiers in his own lifetime. And that is what his theorising about culture comes out of and attempts to reflect on.

When Williams arrived at Cambridge, he found that the culture which formed him, with which Williams has a deep and serious relationship, was simply unknown. Cambridge didn't know it existed and, if it had known, it wouldn't have known how to talk about it because it had no language for it. How could it? Cambridge is addicted to notions of culture which depend upon that which is written down in books, and the Welsh valleys have no books. They have an oral culture; they have a traditional culture; they have a political culture; but they don't write their culture in the sense of the canon of English culture. That personal experience not only shaped Williams's interests but also the ways in which he formulated the questions and approached their answers. But there is as well a second pattern common to this generation of cultural theorists which helped to shape their work: After the war, Thompson, Hoggart, and Williams were all involved, not in traditional university teaching jobs but in extramural teaching, in adult education. They are teaching classes with workers and nonacademics, classes for people who are not going for degrees. And as educators in the community, they are much more sensitive to those shifts and changes in postwar English social life which were taking place after the war. They experienced these extraordinarily compact and complex changes of society as they were trying to teach something—history or literature—to people who are also going through that experience, often to people from the same backgrounds that they themselves had left.

Williams's major books are *Culture and Society: 1780–1950* (1958) and *The Long Revolution* (1961). There is a whole range of literary studies—studies of drama, tragedy, novels, and novelists—but for Cultural Studies the most important text in that body of work is *The Country and the City* (Williams 1973b), which is about urban and pastoral traditions, and the social and historical basis of literary forms and genres. It is undoubtedly the most important of Williams's literary—as opposed to his cultural/theoretical—works. More recently, one has to take account of *Marxism and Literature* (Williams 1977), perhaps his most self-consciously theoretical and interdiscursive work, and *Politics and Letters* (1979), a long set of interviews with the editors of the *New Left Review*, which provides a very important commentary and retrospective on his own work. One can only admire the degree to which he is willing to take on board the criticisms which have been made of him and acknowledge the mistakes that he has made. It is a work where you can see a theorist going on thinking about the things that he has tried to formulate and trying to refine, improve, and qualify the formulations he has given.

Culture and Society attempts to reread the literary tradition from the late eighteenth through the early twentieth centuries, both in its liberal forms—which includes William Cobbett, John Stuart Mill, the Romantics, Charles Dickens, the social realist novelists, George Eliot, John Ruskin, William Morris, George Bernard Shaw, and George Orwell—and in its conservative forms—which includes Edmund Burke, Matthew

Arnold, Walter Pater, T. S. Eliot, and F. R. Leavis. It attempts to reread these traditions in a social and cultural context, and this defines Williams's engagement with and departure from the Leavis tradition, the tradition which formed him. This is the Leavis tradition, but reread in a broader cultural rather than a narrowly literary way.

Williams considers this body of diverse writing—which we have come too easily to think of as independent touchstones of literature separated from their historical context—and asks, What are these works about? What organises them? What are their preoccupations? What social experiences are these people arguing about? His response is that they are concerned with, and trying to find a vocabulary to talk about, the enormous historical changes which they were living through, changes which we retrospectively bring together in the phrase "the Industrial Revolution." The tradition Williams has constructed, in fact, covers precisely the span of the development of industrial capitalism, so it is reasonable for Williams to conclude that they were trying to describe how culture and society change in the course of industrial capitalism. Moreover, their efforts were organised, Williams argues, around certain key terms: industry, class, democracy, art, and culture. There are two questions that Williams wants to pose to this tradition and to the ways in which it mobilised the various key terms. First, how has the growth of industrial capitalism been understood, experienced, and defined? And second, what were the key positions taken up by the contributors to the "Culture and Society" tradition in relation to the different social struggles entailed by the development of industrial capitalism? For Williams, these concerns are summed up in the notion of culture, which consists of all those ways in which historical experiences are understood, experienced, defined, and judged.

It is of course not fortuitous that one of the key terms with which Williams reads the tradition is "art." Perhaps because he has been shaped by the study of literary criticism and literary history, he constantly privileges the artistic and the aesthetic. He is able to escape his training to some extent and to recognise that the problematic of culture requires him to explore how literary and artistic productions can be thought in social and cultural terms, rather than in the purely aesthetic and moral terms which Leavis and his followers appropriated. He remains a part of the tradition even as he struggles to escape it: His problematic is always framed in terms of understanding *literary* works as expressions of the culture which provide us with the terms in which we have understood and continue to understand the experience of industrial capitalism. The continuous focus of Williams's career has been on how we can understand the literary in relation to their historical, cultural, economic, and political context. That literary focus remains with him to the end, and I am always surprised to find that he is still as preoccupied with placing the literary text as he was in *Culture and Society*.

Culture and Society sets forth some of Williams's first conceptualisations of culture. The Culture and Society tradition is distinguished, he argues, because it stands at a distance from, and in a critical relation to, the dominant cultural traditions of its times. In particular, despite its diversity, this tradition stands against the ideologies which constituted the positive justification of the growth of industrial capitalism: political economy, utilitarianism, and possessive individualism. Political economy merely explains the laws of market society; utilitarianism, especially in its Benthamite form, provides a calculative ethic which enables people to decide what is good and bad in exactly the same way as they decide whether to pay the price of a particular commodity. Utilitarianism organises morality in the image of market exchange. Possessive individualism offers a conception of human nature that defends capitalism, not just as an economic system, but in terms of its correspondence to intrinsic human qualities and capabilities. It defines "Man" as intrinsically competitive and possessive. (Women were not included in the discourse, because it was thought that those who were carving out the world were men.) Hence, socialism and collectivism as well as the various organic conservatisms, all those rival ideologies, were doomed to fail, not just because they were not as modern and rationalist, but because they were not grounded in human nature. (That argument has not gone away!)

Williams presents the Culture and Society tradition as an alternative to these ideologies, although nowhere in *Culture and Society* is the dominant tradition actually defined. Because it begins with the alternative tradition, it is unable to give any sense of the cultural and social cost of the processes by which political economy, utilitarianism, and possessive individualism became the dominant ways in which people understood, respectively, the economy, morality, and the political process. Neither the particular ideologies nor their dominance emerged from nowhere or without struggles. Older forms of economy and society had to be destroyed in order for relationships and practices organised by political economy to become the dominant mode of production in agrarian and industrial capitalism. Without the identification of that dominant tradition as the foil against which the Culture and Society tradition formed and presented itself, *Culture and Society* reads like a play without the villain. And that gap is what separates Williams, from the beginning of his career, from sympathetic critics like E. P. Thompson who ask of him, Where is the struggle? Where are the opponents? Where is the fighting taking place? Or, using Morris's imagery—Thompson often quoted Morris—Where is the river of fire, the actual decision to go over to "the other side" that eventually divides the well-meaning, humanitarian bourgeois critic of capitalism (like Carlyle or Ruskin) from the socialist opponent of capitalism?

Culture and Society is an embattled book precisely because it leaves out any sense of domination and struggle, as it itself struggles to constitute a viable conception of oppositional culture. It is a vigorous critique of the imperatives of capitalist rationality. And it displays an admirable appreciation of the variety of different positions which can be advanced against such imperatives. Thus, Williams is able to draw upon critics of industrial capitalism from both the Left and the Right, from both the conservative positions of writers such as Coleridge, Burke, and Leavis, and the more radical progressive criticisms which people like Paine, Cobbett, and Morris advanced. He is in fact interested not so much in the political positions which individual figures advocate as he is in the nature of the critique which is brought to bear upon capitalism. But *Culture and Society* lacks the notion of cultural, ideological dominance and, consequently, cannot adequately conceptualise the notions of struggle and resistance. This becomes even more visible if we consider that the focus of the book therefore collapses, in a sense, into the center. Against the drive of industrial capitalism to refashion and remake the industrial and social world, the alternative tradition it offers is a liberal one; it remains incapable in the end of drawing out and evoking any more substantial, popular opposition to that tradition. Williams finds it impossible to go outside the tradition of great writers. He can only gesture towards a deeper democratic tradition, but he can never foreground it because, quite simply, it doesn't write. It cannot be located in the body of great books.

Since his perspective is literary, he goes to where the literary debate is: between the Right and the Left. Admittedly, he points beyond that to the large numbers of the silenced, who don't have a cultivated language, who don't have a literary productive apparatus available to them, but all he can say is that, while most people are swearing at them, particular writers—Paine, Cobbett, Mills at times, or Dickens—are speaking for them. But of course it is not in their accents, not with the same measure and impact of experience as in the language of those who speak for themselves. That is why it is important in reconstituting the formation of Cultural Studies at this moment to remember that at the same time, Williams is writing *Culture and Society* and E. P. Thompson (1963) is writing *The Making of the English Working Class*. And you only understand the forms that this problematic took on if you read the two books together. *The Making of the English Working Class* is about precisely the popular culture Williams can't find in the literary canon. Those are the voices which Thompson finds in the records, in the court documents, in the pamphlets, in the newspapers—the nonliterary history of a more radical and very complex culture. And it is a very complex formation, with its own social, cultural, political, and religious inheritance, but its complexity is unavailable to someone who only looks at the texts that have been produced by a selective literary tradition.

Thus, while Williams demonstrated that the existing literary canon can itself be reread in historical and cultural terms, he was unable to reflect on the degree of selectivity implicit within it, on the ways in which it is determined by the circumstances of its production, and on the ways it too easily ignores the languages and voices which have been excluded from the traditional culture. A dominant and traditional culture functions precisely by selecting particular voices and organising them into a tradition in order to exclude others. I don't attribute intentionality to that, but that is how tradition functions. What else is a tradition but a selection of some things and not others? And therefore one has to be aware of the limited nature of such literary evidence even while recognising its importance. A conception of culture and cultural evidence which works from the selective literary tradition alone cannot offer a strong sense of a dominant ideological tradition or of sharply polarised contestation and struggle, nor can it recuperate popular and democratic traditions of critique and opposition. Ironically, *Culture and Society* is the first and last of Raymond Williams's work in the Culture and Society tradition. The book simultaneously constituted the tradition (nobody had ever spoken of it as a tradition before), announced its existence, offered the last exemplification of it, and buried it. In *Culture and Society*, Williams positions himself as it were at the end of that tradition, as its inheritor, as the last person to approach history and culture with that kind of literary practice and sensibility.

Williams's next book, *The Long Revolution*, though drawing on *Culture and Society*, is a very different book indeed. The first part is Williams's attempt to integrate various ideas and influences and to generate at least an initial formulation of a cultural theory. I want to selectively discuss some of the concepts he presents, not so much as an attempt to explicate Williams's position per se but, rather, for their potential contribution to the elaboration of Cultural Studies and for their ability to position Cultural Studies in relation to other positions and traditions.

First, I want to take note of the close relation Williams posits between the concepts of culture, community, and communication. Williams identifies culture very closely with the way a sociohistorical experience is understood and defined. And the basis for a (cultural) community lies in the sharedness of those definitions of historical experiences. People locate themselves as belonging to a community because within it, some experiences are common and some of the ways in which they have been defined and understood are shared. How are they shared? Through the interactive communication between the members of that community. Consequently, all the means of communication—language and media in their broadest senses and not just the narrow sense of communication as the transmission of information (in which Williams is not interested)— provide the ways through which the individuals within a community, culture, or society exchange and refine their shared meanings and in which they collectively and socially define what it is they are going through.

Culture, for Williams, is inseparable from life as it is lived or experienced, and this is the second important emphasis in his work. The object of Cultural Studies, for Williams, is to bring forward the distinctive and unique, often peculiar, experience of a social group and to re-create and understand what it is that constitutes the identity of that experience. Cultural Studies attempts to find the common forms of experience and the shared definitions by which a community lives. Cultural Studies, therefore, is neither an objective description of how a group lives, nor an analysis or inventory of the ideas that a group has. Since culture is the interaction between the two, Cultural Studies seeks the life one is obliged to live because of the conditions into which one has been born, the circumstances which have been made meaningful and hence experienceable because certain frameworks of understanding have been brought to bear upon those conditions. Practices are not simply the result of an individual having been placed in a physical, economic, or material space, but of the attempt to live socially in ways which reflect how we understand and experience our circumstances. Those forms of experiencing have been built into the ways human beings live, into their practices. A practice is always cultured. It has been cultivated. It is impregnated with forms of interpretation. That is what culture is: experience lived, experience interpreted, experience defined. And that is what Williams calls experience. Notice how confusing Williams's language is here, for he talks about the experiences that people have by being placed objectively in certain conditions and he talks about the ways in which those experiences have been understood and defined. They vary between countries and between periods. Finally, he talks about how a society lives its distinctive ways of life, impregnated by its distinctive cultural forms of interpretation. Here we have the confusion between what Thompson, who does exactly the same thing, calls "experience 1" and "experience 2." You experience your conditions of existence, as Marx unfortunately said, whether you like it or not. That is your fate in life: to have been born at that time, in that place, in that class, et cetera. But *how* you live the conditions in which you are placed can vary, and that is where both Williams and Thompson locate the cultural.

While Williams considers and even embraces a number of definitions of culture in the first part of *The Long Revolution*, he emphasises a definition which he correctly describes as anthropological: culture as a whole way of life. In a sense, Williams wants to counterpose the notion of "a whole way of life" to that of culture as "the best that has been thought and said." The former offers a democratised version of the elite tradition in cultural theory. A whole is something distinctive, something which constitutes the particular pattern or configuration of shared definitions as different from another. What allows you to identify the distinctiveness of any culture is precisely that it forms a whole way of life. Consequently, cultural analysis must always seek to identify patterns if it is to discover shared ideas, ideals, and forms of communication. Of course, the real challenge is to discover those significant patterns which give you an understanding of how social interaction in that group works. It is the *significant* patterns that have to be identified. Such patterns are closely related to the important notion of the organisation of practices. Thus, while every society will have some of the same practices, they will be organised differently. Every society has forms of economic production, for example, but the structures in which those practices are organised vary. This helps us to understand what is distinctive, for example, about industrial capitalism as compared with agrarian capitalism.

The next notion of Williams's that we have to consider is more substantial and also more contentious: namely, that no one practice within a social formation has any primacy of determination over another, that no one practice shapes the active, shared culture. Williams wants to insist that practices interact with one another on a mutually determining basis. What is more, it is impossible to observe, identify, or abstract a practice out of its place within the whole set of relations. Consequently, cultural analysis cannot begin by first locating the forces and relations of production and then proceeding to identify the culture, because there is no way of describing the economic life without reference to the cultural forms in which it is organised. Culture is present in the economy as much as economic life has an impact on the formation and distribution of culture. So one has to think about the mutual interpenetration and interdetermination of one practice on another, rather than selecting out one practice and making it the primary determinant of the other forms of practices. This is obviously contesting the base-superstructure model in its simple forms.

How does cultural analysis proceed? According to Williams, it seeks to identify certain distinctive, underlying patterns or forms of organisation which are expressed in apparently very different practices. He argues that you can find something peculiar—a structure—within the English form of the organisation of industrial capitalism, a structure which, although it may not be instantly available on their surfaces, can be found as the structure of the way of life in the family, of what is being written about in the novel, and of the manner in which economic relations are conducted. That is to say, without quite knowing it (although he later acknowledges it when he considers the work of Lucien Goldmann), Williams is a genetic structuralist. Beneath the variety of surface practices is an underlying structure, a cultural matrix which expresses itself in different practices. And so cultural analysis not only identifies the underlying patterns, but discovers the similarities existing between the patterns of apparently different spheres of human activity. In other words, the patterns that are the object of cultural analysis exist not just in the ways people behave but within the underlying set of relations which constitute the social formation. The cultural analyst identifies the key ideas, the key words, the key definitions, which hold the whole culture together. But they also expect to find that matrix expressed in other, different practices. The work of analysis consists of looking for the similarities in the pattern, looking for the homologies. One finds, for example, a particular kind of individualism in Mill's philosophy, in George Eliot's novels, and in the relationships of the market; one finds that a particular kind of economic individualism is at the core of a whole number of different sets of practices and institutions. And you know it is a key configuration precisely because it is expressed in so many different places. Of course, there are always breaks, places where the homologies don't seem to exist, areas that quite simply "don't fit." These are the points in the social formation where new configurations of values, patterns of meaning, and understanding are emerging, being generated, and beginning to operate. Consequently, people's behavior in that area will deviate from the underlying structure; the patterns will not be homologous with those of other practices in the same social formation.

One may note that there is very little in this theory of culture that answers to, or takes into account, the theoretical and political positions of the Marxist tradition. It is in the second part of *The Long Revolution* that Williams confronts the question of class. He identifies class as one of the key terms and the formation of new classes in industrial capitalism as one of the most important aspects of the historical experience which people were trying to understand. He talks about that first of all in terms of the particular cultural values and meanings characteristic of each class taken on its own. There is, he says, an aristocratic culture, which holds a set of ideas, for instance, about poverty and the poor, which is very different from those of the emerging bourgeois culture. Therefore, you find resistance to the way the poor were treated by the ruling classes in nineteenth-century England, not only from the poor and the working classes, but also from within the dominant classes, between the aristocratic and the bourgeois fractions. The aristocracy, with its particular historical background, continued to believe that the wealthy had a paternalistic responsibility to the poor. Aristocratic culture had a different pattern of relations, one based more on face-to-face interactions and intimacy—even with highly unequal groups. Therefore it was impossible for it to abstract and impersonalise responsibilities as the bourgeoisie attempted in the Poor Laws. Political economists—bourgeois political economists, that is—offered nothing but functional justifications for poverty; they refused the notion that the ruling classes had an obligation, even an interpersonal one, to the working people. The Poor Laws were designed to get people back into the labour market. It is irrelevant that a particular worker has always lived on your estate, or how you feel about him, or that you know his family. If he is able bodied, he belongs at work. And if he cannot work, then one needs to know where he is, how he is doing, and when he will be able to reenter the labour force. That difference in class cultures is, for Williams, an expression of the difference between capitalist and precapitalist formations.

But the real object of Williams's cultural analysis is not the identification of particular class cultures, or the different value structures of different classes. Williams wants to raise the more dynamic question of what happens in the social formation as a whole, in which the different class cultures interact. He is interested in the pattern underlying the total society—the dominant value system—not just those differentiating among the classes within it. To continue the example, he wants to know what happens when the aristocratic view of poverty begins to converse or even quarrel with the bourgeois (political economic) view of poverty, which is at the same time embroiled in a rather serious quarrel with the people who have nothing to lose and who would like to be sustained during periods of industrial capitalist recession. What was the result of this social conversation between the classes, the "typically British" way of dealing with the poor, which incorporates some of the aristocratic view, some concessions to the working class, and some bourgeois political economy? What is the result of this interaction of different class cultures? It is something rather like the welfare state. What you give to the poor is defined as temporary: It is theirs but not by right and, therefore, can be taken back at any moment. It depends to a large extent upon the voluntary civil institutions of charity. Williams would say, correctly, that the British welfare state, which "boxes" state provisions for distribution, is a peculiarly English institution.

A distinctive culture emerges out of the interactions between different social groups or social classes: *That* is the object of Williams's analysis, what he calls "the structure of feeling." It is the description, even re-creation of how life is actually lived, of what it is like to think and act about a particular problem in a society. It seems to come naturally to people who are inside the society because they share the results of the historical experience which has produced this particular set of ideas about the family, culture, masculinity, the economy, et cetera. It is these structures of feeling that are reflected or expressed in the different social practices.

Obviously, then, the project and methodology of a cultural analysis of a given period of history is different from that of the economic historian, the sociologist, or the literary critic. Yet it is related to all of them; it must absorb some of their evidence because, if you are to understand the relationship between different practices, you have to know something about economics, social history, literature, and so on. This is a real problem in Cultural Studies: It does seem to define itself by claiming to know something about everything. Even those sympathetic to many of Williams's positions found this totalising identity rather problematic. Thompson, for example, asked where history was in Williams's scheme and claimed that what Williams had described was really the project of the historian, a project which Williams had apparently evacuated in his effort to make Cultural Studies the new queen of the sciences. It was not philosophy but Cultural Studies that would integrate all of the more local, regional knowledges of the other disciplines. Everybody else knows only about particular things, while Cultural Studies knows about the whole. And it is certainly true that *The Long Revolution* is not entirely free of that problem.

The final concept from *The Long Revolution* I want to discuss is that of the totality. The way in which totality is conceptualised in Williams's work, in fact, is characteristic of a larger position within Cultural Studies, which includes Hoggart and Thompson. The totality is conceived to address the problem that Williams started with: how to understand the relationship between cultural practices in the narrow sense and the rest of the social formation. How is "the whole" conceived? Williams's answer is, implicitly, posed against the traditional Marxist view, the view, for example, in the "Preface" from *A Contribution to the Critique of Political Economy*:

> In the social production of their existence, men inevitably enter into definite relations which are independent of their will, namely relations of production appropriate to a given stage of development of their material forces of production. The totality of these relations of production constitutes the economic structure of society, the real foundation, on which arises a legal and political superstructure and to which correspond definite forms of social consciousness. (Marx 1970, 20)

Here Marx talks about the importance of the formation of a mode of production (the forces and relations of production) as the real foundation upon which the legal and political superstructures arise and to which all forms of consciousness correspond. That passage is one of Marx's attempts, not only to display the levels of the social formation, but to define the determining relationships between them. Without directly confronting that position—for the reasons I discussed in the previous lecture—Williams offers an account of the totality which recognises the validity of much of the Marxist position. His position is responsive to the exploitative nature of industrial capitalism, to the nature of class formations and of struggles between classes, and to the reality of class domination. But Williams wants to give a greater measure of determinacy and effectivity to culture. Indeed, as I suggested when talking about the two kinds of experience, he wants to integrate the cultural into what a Marxist would call "the material social practices" and to assert that there is nothing outside of those material social practices. That is what constitutes a social formation. His position, therefore, denies the primacy of determination by the economic level. There is no simple correspondence of the kind suggested by the notion of reflection implicit in the base-superstructure model. One has to think of the interpenetration of all the mutually determined levels.

What is at the center of the totality of practices is not economic determination but human energy, human practice, the material activity of human beings: the construction of their own lives, the reproduction of their own species, the forms of social organisation and government, the forms of the family and social relations, et cetera. In other terms, at the center of Williams's conception of totality is an essentially philosophic anthropological conception of Man. It is the conception of Man in Marx's (1961) *Economic and Philosophic Manuscripts of 1844*, a Hegelian conception: Promethean Man, Man the creator, Man who does not exist apart from the activity. It is *Man*, not merely because that was the available generic term, but also because it reflected the sexual division of labour at the time. It was taken for granted that those who were remaking the world were gendered, though this issue is certainly never consciously addressed either in Marxism or in Williams's work. It is Man the producer, Man as the active practitioner—human practice rather than the economy—that stands as the determining center. The social formation is nothing but the various particular and definite forms which Man's activity has taken. In this place, under those conditions, men (and women) have actively produced that form of the family, organised the economy in that way, et cetera.

It is this philosophical position which Althusser correctly defines as the humanist problematic, humanist not in a moral or political (e.g., liberal) sense but in the philosophical sense: at the center of such a position is undifferentiated Man, living in historical formations which are simply the organisation of men's cultural, social, economic, et cetera practices. It is a widely held position, a general position in cultural theory and certainly not exclusive to the English tradition. Nor is it, I should add, the position that Williams ends up with later in his career, though it is quite close to it.

But the "culturalism" I have been describing was not entirely homogeneous; there were significant differences among various authors who agreed on the general position. Shortly after *The Long Revolution* was released, Thompson (1961) published a major review of it in two parts in *New Left Review*.[1] He raises a number of important criticisms, many of which eventually had their impact on Williams's own development. First, he argues that Williams's notion of culture is too organic, too evolutionary, and lacks any sense of contestation within the cultural realm. It seems to suggest that the different classes have a rather polite English conversation with one another about what to do, for example, with the poor. Thompson argues that this does not correspond to the history of the Poor Laws. A more adequate account of culture would talk about "whole ways of struggle" (see part 1, 33) rather than a whole way of life. It would recognise, within a particular social formation, the contestation among different groups and classes, each with its own distinctive cultural values operating on a different cultural matrix. And the result is the effect of the unequal struggles conducted between them and not of a polite conversational compromise.

Therefore, Thompson rejects the image of a unified struggle—the long revolution—which is so powerful in Williams's work. Why, after all, is the long revolution so long? Why aren't there any momentary shocks or, for that matter, any sustained bursts of disruptive activity in this "long revolution"? Because the whole process is conceived in enormously gentle and humane terms, society and its social processes are assumed to be basically good. Yes, the workers have been bandied around but they have been drawn into a structure of feeling which is not so bad. We are on the route to democratisation and though it may take two centuries, in the end we will be more civilised because the structure of feeling will have been even further modified. Everybody has had and will continue to have an influence on what the cultural pattern is.

Thompson argues that you cannot conceptualise culture in this way, as if it were a single thing, because if you follow that line of reasoning to the end, you arrive at T. S. Eliot's (1949) position in *Notes towards the Definition of Culture*: We are all one culture. Yes, there are differences—

1. I'm responsible for having made up the issue without a crucial page. There is a page which is missing out of the middle of it, which is where Thompson's twelfth issue was supposed to appear. That is a typographical error which is likely to live with me for the rest of my life. And that is why you will find that Thompson's review of *The Long Revolution* was never reprinted.

we are rich, you are poor; we eat roast beef, you eat beef pies; we have art, literature, and the Oxford Boat Race, you have television and the Cup Final. But it is really all one culture, one way of life, within which everybody can talk to one another, even like one another, *as long as they stay in their own place*. If you push Williams's position, you end up in the conservative position. If we are to avoid this, we have to see the break— this is characteristic of Thompson's Marxism—we have to draw the line of fire within the culture. Then we can look at cultures, not as the evolution of a way of life but as the continuous struggle between contesting cultures. So Thompson redefines the process of cultural change, not through modification, adaptation, and negotiation, but through contestation and struggle.

The second major critique Thompson raises against Williams is also typical of his position and concerns the place and status of history in Cultural Studies. While I have already pointed to the truth embedded within this question, one needs to recognise its limits as well. For if Thompson is correct that Williams too easily privileges Cultural Studies, the same is true of Thompson and history. For Thompson, being a historian is rather like a sacred talisman. No matter how significant the differences between him and another historian (e.g., Gareth Stedman Jones, who advanced an extremely rigorous and systematic form of structuralist history against Thompson), the terms of the dispute are secondary to the shared commitment to the discipline of history, to the recognition that this is where such work ought to be and indeed *was already* located. Because in addition to affirming history, Thompson was also producing his own account of British history in terms of ways of struggle: in particular, the struggle between the radical culture of the popular democratic forces and the industrial capitalists in the 1790s and 1800s, through Chartism. Thompson opposes his historical account with Williams's cultural account, which seems to leave out history. Certainly, if you stand far enough removed from history and content yourself with reading books of the period, you might reasonably conclude that the Poor Laws were really the result of a conversation between different dominant class characters. But if you get into the history and discover what was actually happening on the ground as it were, if you know the degree to which the Poor Laws were fought by men and women, especially in the provinces (and no one ever writes books from or about the provinces), then you know that an account of the history of the Poor Laws cannot ignore the notion of cultural contestation and struggle.

So Thompson's affirmation of history is not just an ideological one; it offers important insights which underpinned the interruption he made into Williams's notion of culture by interposing the notions of history and historical process, and of contestation, struggle, and change as central to the way in which we define how cultures change and develop. These interruptions profoundly modified Williams's definition of culture in *The Long Revolution* and the analysis Williams goes on to offer. After Thompson's review, Williams begins by thinking about the problems of struggle and domination rather than the definition of common, shared cultures.

But Williams is influenced, not only by the explicit critique, but by the actual work Thompson has undertaken. *The Making of the English Working Class* is a book that belongs to this problematic in Cultural Studies, although it is a historical work and Thompson would never think of it in those terms. Perhaps of even greater importance to Cultural Studies is Thompson's (1975) work on the eighteenth century—work which results only partly in *Whigs and Hunters*—including such essays as "Time, Work-Discipline and Industrial Capitalism" and "Patrician and Plebeian Society," because in those essays he demonstrates an even deeper sense of popular struggle than he has of class struggle. He demonstrates a real affinity for those popular struggles in which the people are opposed to those in power. His understanding not only of cultural struggle but of preindustrial struggles is illustrated in his analyses of how an agrarian population was cultivated to the habits of industrial capitalism: how people whose day was structured by diurnal rhythms, by physical and geographical things, by the temple of the seasons, et cetera, had to learn new practices of timekeeping, and how it was not just a matter of being compelled by the industrial labour discipline, but rather, that they had to internalise new meanings of a work week and a workday which were given in confined conditions, which were adapted to the rhythms of the machine, of accumulation and productivity. That, he says, is a deeply cultural experience. We have too often given accounts of such changes in the Industrial Revolution as if they were only a consequence of economic or technical developments, as if they were the product of the reorganisation of factory labour. But there is no historic change like that which does not also involve the production of new meanings and the transformation of people's social practices according to different definitions and rhythms. That is what the real transformation is. The economic history of the Industrial Revolution doesn't tell you how a peasant population—a farming population—becomes a factory population, an urban population. It doesn't tell you why it is that nobody came to work on a Monday. It is no wonder that industrial entrepreneurs could not understand this Monday holiday which lasted for thirty or forty years into the Industrial Revolution, this traditionally marked folk practice which large numbers of people brought into the cities, the small factories and workshops, and lived by. The economic and technical accounts don't explain the process by which rural recreation had to be reconstructed, partly by religious influences, partly by the compulsion of the State, and partly by the influence of dominant local figures, into a rationalised recreation—a recreation which could be bounded in a manner quite different from a seventeenth- or eighteenth-century cricket or football match. The boundary of a seventeenth- or eighteenth-century match was the beginning and end of the village. It went as far as the player could run. Modern sports have emerged only in conjunction with and as a consequence of the destruction of an earlier culture, partly by imposition, partly unconsciously, within the larger process of the adaptation to industrial work and urban life. Football becomes something that happens on the day you don't go to work. And you have to go to a particular place, a small place by comparison. It must be bounded because you live and work just outside of it. It constitutes the cultural boundaries of work and nonwork, time spent serving others and time for yourself, work and play, confinement and freedom. It constitutes the cultural categories of living in an industrial society. Thompson helps us understand how those internal systems of meaning have been interjected, how they have been lived subjectively, how they have structured our passage through time. Thompson's historical research demonstrates, as well as any explicit Cultural Studies work, that we can only understand what we are like, how we live, how we pass the time, by understanding the categories in which we frame or live our experience.

There is, however, at least one other significant reason for the oft-noted shift in Williams's work into a direct dialog with the Marxist tradition. Between *The Long Revolution* and *Marxism and Literature*, there was an enormous change in the intellectual climate and culture in England, due in part of course to the development of the political movement of the 1960s and seventies. This not only meant that one could more easily talk about and within the Marxist problematic, it also enabled publishers, especially *New Left Review*, to bring into England translations of many of the important works of so-called Western Marxism. This had a profound impact on many British cultural theorists, including Williams. It opened up a much more active dialog and debate in English intellectual life generally and meant that Williams could stop referring to Marxism indirectly, covertly, in a displaced form and could actually confront the fact that he had really been arguing about the inadequacies of Marxist cultural theory all along, something that he could never recognise in *Culture and Society*. There he took on the Marxist tradition but never identified it as the object of his concern. But *Marxism and Literature* is his coming out; there he acknowledges his place within and his indebtedness to that tradition; there he acknowledges that its history is his history.

That coming out actually began a bit earlier, in a wonderful essay, "Literature and Sociology: In Memory of Lucien Goldmann" (Williams 1971). In it, Williams connects his own project and theory in *Culture and Society* and *The Long Revolution* with Goldmann's (1964) *The Hidden God*. He draws a close parallel between his own notion of the structure of feeling and Goldmann's sense of genetic structuralism; in fact, he says, they have been talking about the same thing. But Goldmann has been working within a Marxist tradition, albeit a very different one from that which he fought against in *Culture and Society*. At about this time, Williams goes to Italy where there is a long-standing and thriving Center for Cultural Studies in Naples. There he is confronted with the work of Gramsci. The Italians want to know how Gramsci fits into Williams's theory. Where is the notion of hegemony? Where is the notion of domination? Where is the notion of struggle? Where is the notion of contestation? And Williams writes the essay, "Base and Superstructure in Marxist Cultural Theory," which is published in *New Left Review* (1973a) and revised for *Marxism and Literature* (1977). In the essay, Williams not only introduces the notion of dominant, residual, and emergent cultures, he also actively engages with the critique from a Gramscian position, reformulating and transforming his own definitions and conceptual paradigm.

Marxism and Literature is not what it seems. It is more directly about Marxism than any of Williams's other works but it is only incidentally about literature. Actually the first section—titled "Basic Concepts"—deals with culture, language, literature, and ideology. The second section is on cultural theory and deals largely with reformulating his earlier work in the context of an active engagement with contemporary Marxist theory. It isn't until the third section that he remembers that "literature" is in the title and that's what Oxford asked him to write about. Nevertheless, the book is the best available statement of his current position: neat, concise, clear, and effective.

However, the early parts of *Marxism and Literature* continue, in a rather odd way, the strategy of *Culture and Society*. He replaces the covert engagement with Marxism with a covert engagement with structuralism. If Marxism can now be named, Saussure, Althusser, and other semioticians can only be hinted at. The first chapter on language is obviously crucial because language is the medium in which the definitions and interpretations Williams is interested in are formulated. If thinking about language has been transformed in the interim by the impact of semiotics and the structuralist view of language, Williams conducts a displaced dialogue with it at best in which he argues, with Thompson hovering like an avenging angel over his left shoulder, that cultural analysis must choose historical process over system and structure. Thompson has taught him that cultural change has to be thought historically. He rejects Lévi-Strauss's efforts to freeze the historical process and conceptually categorise its component elements. That is, he cannot understand the argument that an account of historical change has to stop the historical process in order to grasp it analytically. And against the Saussurian view of language, he advances Volosinov's (1973) theory in *Marxism and the Philosophy of Language*. It is important in terms of his revised definition of culture that one understands what it is that Williams uses Volosinov to do. He uses Volosinov to acknowledge the structuralist claims that language is not simply a transparent reflection of reality and that the relationship between signifier and signified is not fixed. But he argues that Volosinov arrives at a conception of the sign—of the vehicle of symbolic constructions and productions—which acknowledges the discontinuity between form and meaning in the sign without requiring him to abstractly and absolutely divorce them (which Williams is suggesting structuralist approaches require him to do).

It is in the second part, on cultural theory, that some of the new positions begin to emerge. As I have said, Williams opposes the base-superstructure metaphor and not merely on the grounds that the relationships are really more complex than the model can ever grasp. His is a more theoretical opposition: that the model constitutes a false abstraction. The Marxist notion of the base refers to the mode of production—the relationship between productive forces and social relations of production—but Williams argues that it is impossible to identify in Marx the difference between productive forces and social relations. Moreover, it is impossible to give an account of the mode of production without taking cultural definitions into account. Consequently, we are confronted with a relationship in which "the base" refers to something highly abstract. And one has to make yet another abstraction, at an even higher level, in order to win the superstructures from that abstract base. In the end, that last abstraction is both inadequate and unnecessary to arrive at the superstructures which are, after all, composed of nothing but concrete human practices.

Thompson has taken this argument even further by arguing that all the practices in real life are interwoven with one another. Therefore, nothing can be punctuated by the notions of base and superstructure. Thompson's example is the question of the law in the eighteenth century. Does it belong to the superstructures? Yes, it is obviously part of the whole ideological machinery of the eighteenth century. It is a highly elabourated area in intellectual life, especially in complex texts like Blackstone's (1766) *Commentaries on the Laws of England*. And yet, the old economic relations are being destroyed because of the intrusion of forms of economic contract and of market exchange which could not have functioned without being legally defined, without the legal apparatus. Can one claim that "the law" is in the courts and in the law books but not in the contractual bargaining of the marketplace? The law is everywhere. Of what possible use is an abstraction which assigns a special place of primacy to one level of the social formation when, historically, we need to study it as an interactive totality?

The view that all of history is human practices, without any primacy assigned to any determining level, is built upon a conception of totality (in Williams it is a cultural totality; in Thompson, a historical totality) grounded in what I have described as a philosophical humanism. It also rests upon a particular notion of theory, one strictly opposed to abstractions. Theory is only the generalisations which emerge from working with some of these concepts on a particular sociohistorical corpus. It is not the formation of necessary abstractions, operating independently of any account of the texture of lived experience, which can be used as analytic frameworks (which is not to deny that conceptual frameworks have to be used) to cut into the undifferentiated appearances which real experience presents us with. Thompson's (1978) opposition to abstraction is, once again, so all-encompassing that in *The Poverty of Theory*, he claims that Marx's (1977) *Capital* fails because it is still replete with (Hegelian forms of) abstractions, because he uses abstractions like the mode of production even though he knows that you cannot simply enter a particular formation or field and find it. Precisely because it is an abstraction, it must remain unseen. In fact, all modes of production always appear only inside definite social formations, in concrete human practices. So it is impossible to describe economic relationships except analytically.

Both Williams and Thompson argue that the work of abstraction diminishes the human lives you are trying to give an account of. If the purpose of cultural theory and analysis is to reconstitute the thick texture, or structures of feeling, of lived experiences which constitute the distinctiveness of different groups or classes or communities or societies, how can that be accomplished with a pair of abstractions like base and superstructure which are so rarefied, so far away from the descriptive thickness with which one has to deal? And that is at the center of the problem which both Williams and Thompson have, not only with the notion of base and superstructure, but with any abstract conceptualisation and with certain kinds of theorising. It is a humanist objection which holds that the people cannot, should not, be thought of in such thin terms, especially since it is the purpose of cultural analysis to reaffirm their experiences, to bring them forward again in their richness and complexity, in a sense, to do something to pay them back for having been left out of the great tradition. What does *The Making of the English Working Class* do? It speaks. This is what it says in its preface:

I am seeking to rescue the poor-stockinger, the Luddite cropper, the "obsolete" hand-loom weaver, the "utopian" artisan, and even the deluded follower of Joanna Southcott, from the enormous condescension of posterity. Their crafts and traditions may have been dying. Their hostility to the new industrialism may have been backward-looking. Their communitarian ideals may have been fantasies. Their insurrectionary conspiracies may have been foolhardy. But they lived through these times of acute social disturbance, and we did not. Their aspirations were valid in terms of their own experience; and, if they were casualties of history, they remain, condemned in their own lives, as casualties. (Thompson 1963, 12–13)

Thompson claims to be speaking for and recovering the lost voices that have never been heard in history: the voice of the poor artisan; the voice of the poor stockinger; the voice of a leveler. Of what use to somebody who wants to honor the experiences of the excluded cultures of a society are a pair of conceptual scissors which can only cut things into bits? Why divide things which ought to be thought together? Why see as differentiated things which need to be seen as a whole?

I do not want to leave this critique of abstraction entirely unanswered here, although I shall return to it in later lectures. It is true as you look around in any society that it is extremely difficult to see the dividing line between the base and the superstructure in people's concrete practices, just as it is difficult to neatly divide social practices into pregiven categories and assign them necessary relations of determination. That is how history presents itself—as an undifferentiated set of interwoven practices. The question that remains unanswered in Williams's and Thompson's views is whether thinking about history is the same as living in history. It is also true that, from within history, from a certain position in the social formation, particular strategies and actions may seem valid and reasonable; but again, that leaves open the question of whether it is the analyst's task merely to recuperate and celebrate such responses, or whether we are not to judge them and, if necessary, account for their weaknesses and failures. This is the point at which the structuralist paradigm parts company with the humanistic paradigm.

Nor do I want to leave the description of Williams's position in *Marxism and Literature* at this point, for he makes some important contributions to cultural theory in the second section, and it is worth referring to them, if only briefly, in order to remind you that Williams goes on producing in spite of the flawed problematic on which he has been working. After all, one can produce important insights on a flawed theoretical ground. Thus, despite the problems with his position, Williams (1973a) has elaborated the very rich distinction between dominant, residual, and emergent culture in "Base and Superstructure in Marxist Cultural Theory." This is a very important way of thinking about cultural change. One needs to look at the emergent elements in a cultural situation, those which are just coming through, which are not yet in a position to define the whole society, which are obviously in the process of making new definitions and new ways of experiencing social life. And one needs to look at the residual elements in a cultural situation. This is especially important because, I think, in general, leftist cultural analysts are especially bad at looking at that which has been apparently discarded, at the irrational and outmoded forms of culture and consciousness on which people can and often do draw in order to construct new understandings. For example, religion is the great lost subject in Marxist scholarship all because of a rather casual observation by Marx that it is the opiate of the people. We seem to have thought that that wrapped it up. But the reality of it is that throughout the world, both in the secular and the nonsecular world, structures of religious consciousness, forms of religious practice, and religious institutions are constantly being appropriated and reappropriated into the modern formation. Their power lives on and they have a real impact on how the modern is constructed—in the Islamic world, for example. Their languages live on. They can be taken to another culture where they suddenly allow people to resist dominant structures in ways that the religious forms never conceived initially, as, for example, Rastafarianism has done.

An adequate account of the whole culture of the modern world cannot be given without reference to the traces of residual ideas and practices which are appropriated into an enormous variety of social struggles. It is philistinism on the part of Marxist scholars to dismiss the social effects of residual cultures in contemporary culture and society. Why is it that the critique of capitalism has always drawn on the supposed remembrances of precapitalist cultural forms as well as on the explicit dreams of postcapitalist forms? We all know the power and the appeal of such residual ideas as we are about to rush off to the countryside, a countryside that doesn't exist, a mythical countryside. It was constructed in newspapers, literature, and music, most of it generated and produced in the towns. The point is that these images from the past are recuperated into the present, where they work again. We work on and with them; we even build on bits of them in order to envisage what we cannot know, what we have no image for. When you try to imagine what tomorrow is going to be like, you can only draw on the legacy of the past.

This is not to say that Williams's theorisation of these notions is adequate. He fails to recognise, for example, that residual cultures, when brought into the present, often continue to have their irrational effects which constitute constraints and limits on how you can think about the future. They are not simply positive terms. But both residual and emergent cultural forms are important, not only in constituting moments of contestation with and resistance to the dominant cultural forms, but also in constituting the ongoing process by which the dominant cultural forms are able to change and adapt to new circumstances precisely by incorporating such residual and emergent forms (e.g., think of the first time the hippies appear on the cover of *Time* magazine). Then it is clear that the dominant culture is working effectively, and in a hegemonic way. Hegemony here is evidenced by the fact that the dominant culture need not destroy the apparent resistance. It simply needs to include it within its own spaces, along with all the other alternatives and possibilities. In fact, the more of them that are allowed in, and the more diverse they are, the more they contribute to the sense of the rich open-ended variety of life, of mutual tolerance and respect, and of apparent freedom. The notion of incorporation points to the extremely important idea that the dominant ideology often responds to opposition, not by attempting to stamp it out, but rather by allowing it to exist within the places that it assigns, by slowly allowing it to be recognised, but only within the terms of a process which deprives it of any real or effective oppositional force.

Those are extremely rich concepts for thinking about the nature of cultural change, but they are inadequate by themselves without a way of conceptualising both the cultural and the social formation as a whole, and of conceptualising as well the proper place of the former within the latter. Those are, after all, the questions that Williams wanted to address. It is here that one might expect Williams to return to the notion of the structure of feeling, and at the end of the section on cultural theory there is a rather weak and inadequate defense of the structure of feeling, which I think is a lost concept. Williams's (1979) defense, reiterated in *Politics and Letters*, is that the term itself is valuable because "structure" suggests the definitive power of culture but "feeling" denies its systematisation.

But there is another conception of the cultural which he introduces in *Marxism and Literature*, a conception which obliges us to recognise that social practices do not exist outside of the meanings we negotiate for them, the meanings with and through which we live them. Alongside this view of the cultural, Williams proposes a conception of the totality which recognises that there is no simple set of correspondences, no straightforward transmission belt, no way in which changes in the economic base—even allowing for a bit of cultural lag and the occasional nonfit—will result in corresponding changes in the sphere of culture and consciousness. One needs more adequate concepts for thinking the relationship between economic practices and cultural practices. One needs a more complex account of the nature of cultural change, which does not oblige it to rest on the determining primacy of the economic relation. Williams reminds us that much of the damage accomplished by the discussion of base and superstructure is the result of conceptualising the base as the economic in any simple sense. It is not the base as economists write about it that does something. Indeed, you might say that it is everything but that which economists write about. The real question of the base is how the relationship between material production and the organisation of life is itself organised. It concerns the way in which social groups are organised or organise their lives in order to appropriate the material world. And what Marx said about it is very simple: that the organisation is quite different from one period to another. And it is a significant change when a society stops organising its material life within feudal social relations and starts organising it within capitalist social relations. It is likely to have significant consequences, and other things are likely to change as well. However, Williams argues that once we understand the base in this broader way, we must stop thinking about its consequences in this simple manner as well and recognise that there is no single set of relations or practices which gives a determining structural configuration to the social formation as a whole. Rather, the question of determination is simply that of the interplay of one practice on another. Such a model, he argues, allows us to grasp—both conceptually and analytically—the lived experiences of a culture, the way the practices of a particular social group, and the meanings which are attached to them, are organised.

Here we can see the culturalist project of generating a new conception of totality, which has a particular philosophical position, a particular way of conceiving of how practices are related to one another, a particular conception of determination, and a particular definition of culture associated with it. I have traced this position largely but not exclusively to Williams's work, because that is the most sustained site of theoretical work that has been done in the English tradition from this direction. The culturalist position wants to incorporate both sides of the idealist and materialist debate. Williams is enough of a Marxist to recognise that people are placed in social and economic relationships of which they are not in control. On the other hand, he is sufficiently revisionist or distanced from the classical Marxist tradition to want to give a much greater effectivity to the level of culture and consciousness. It is this level he is trying to analyse and which has never been sufficiently acknowledged in the Marxist tradition. But the way in which he accomplishes this synthesis relies on the confusion between the two senses of experience. What the theory actually seeks is a fusion of the two, which is why he holds on so strongly to the concept of the structure of feeling.

Although we can now see all kinds of weaknesses and errors in Williams's work, it is a sufficiently substantial approach to the questions of cultural theory and Cultural Studies to merit serious study. It has important ideas and has been quite influential. It makes a particular kind of break with the mechanistic definition of base and superstructure without which Cultural Studies would never have taken off. It introduces key notions like the importance of experience, and the fact that culture must be seen as the frameworks of interpretation and experiencing. It produces the notion of community, of shared definitions between groups as constituting the basis of a cultural life, and so on. It brings a very rich repertoire of concepts into the field, and I think one ought to try to differentiate the concepts and their uses—and perhaps their connections with other trains of thought—from the particular way in which Williams packages them together. One is not required to take the packaging of a serious theory but one is required to approach it critically and analytically. One is also obliged to acknowledge the genuine production of theory which I think went on in a totally inhospitable climate. It embodies a very courageous theoretical project, and one has to acknowledge that. Criticising serious theories is often done in too narrow and schematic and knowing a way. We are the beneficiaries of people who have struggled with thinking difficult things for the first time on ground which is unprepared for that kind of thought. We're the inheritor of Leavis's particularism and Mill's individualism and Williams's culturalism. To begin to generate notions of culture which are democratic, notions of culture which are popular, notions of culture which are materialist, is a real labour, and one wants to acknowledge the work and learn from it without swallowing the whole pill.

Structuralism

Some of the most important theoretical advances in cultural theory, even in Marxist cultural theory, have been accomplished only by engaging with theoretical positions and discourses from a different tradition. Just as Marx's work advanced by a continuous engagement with Smith and Ricardo, so Marxist Cultural Studies has found its own internal intellectual resources inadequate. It has had to go outside of its own domain in order to engage other ideas and modes of thinking which do not begin from Marxist presuppositions. Of course, it has had to transform and adapt them as it draws them into a Marxist discourse, but this does not prevent such borrowings from having continuing effects within Marxism.

I do not intend in this lecture to follow the convoluted history of structuralism through its most current developments. Structuralism is one of the major paradigms which intervened into the whole field of cultural theory, not merely nor even primarily as a particular set of theories or theoretical propositions, but as a mode of thought, a distinctive cast of mind which offers quite a different angle of vision from that of Williams and Thompson. I will focus on the non-Marxist sources of structuralist thinking, concentrating on the seminal work of Émile Durkheim and Claude Lévi-Strauss. There are a number of reasons for this admittedly rather odd choice. First, I want to talk about the early sources of structuralism because of structuralism's complex and indeed ambiguous relationship to classical Marxism. From the viewpoint of classical Marxism, these sources are already contaminated: sociological rather than materialist. Second, I am opposed to an intellectual and social amnesia which forgets the origins of things; it is important to remember that structuralism was well established, especially in French intellectual circles around the early work of Lévi-Strauss, before it appears in its Althusserian form. In fact, we need to recognise that there are different times, places, and ways in which structuralism has been imported into Marxism.

I begin with Émile Durkheim, the founder of modern sociology but also, in a very particular way, of modern structuralism. Moreover, the legacy of Durkheim is interesting because it also marks the relationship between cultural theory and sociology itself. There are after all many ways of reading him and many different theories and disciplines which have located his work as an important source. Thus, there are not one but (at least) three Durkheims, and Cultural Studies has had some exchange with all of them. First, there is the Durkheim who has always been the main source and intellectual inspiration for British, and to some extent American, structural anthropology. The key texts are *Suicide* (Durkheim 1951) and *The Rules of Sociological Method* (Durkheim 1982). This is the Durkheim who taught social scientists not to look at the surface flow of social relations as their principal subject matter, but to dig deeper into the institutional structures and processes of a society. There is a touch of the structural about that precisely because of the displacement of interest from the phenomenal forms of social relations to the structural institutions which define and characterise one society and differentiate it from others.

Second, there is the Durkheim which Talcott Parsons ([1937] 1967) constructed by slicing his work in half. In this elegant exercise, Parsons maintains that we need *The Rules of Sociological Method* to found a positive science. We need *Suicide* as an exemplary application of positive science. The fact that there is no such complete positivist methodology in *Suicide* does not matter; great sciences have been founded on and advanced by mistake. What is relevant is that Parsons took Durkheim's concern with rates of things rather than just with their numbers to point towards a statistically based science, a quantitative sociology. But equally important in Parsons's construction of Durkheim is that some of Durkheim's writing had to be left out entirely: what Parsons called the idealist texts, including *The Elementary Forms of Religious Life* (Durkheim 1947) and *Primitive Classification* (Durkheim and Mauss 1963). It is precisely from that excluded part of Durkheim that a third Durkheim is constructed, a Durkheim which leads directly to Lévi-Strauss and structuralism.

These works by Durkheim, which contributed to the formation of the structuralist paradigm, are largely those written with or influenced by his close relative and intellectual collaborator, Marcel Mauss. The early French structuralists also drew on a larger field of work, especially the large and crucially important work published in *L'Année Sociologique*, the "house journal" for a dispersed group of researchers led by Durkheim which included Mauss, Granet, and more distantly, Saussure. This body of work was a major intellectual source of French sociology, although it is all but invisible in Britain and the United States. It was also the source and inspiration for Lévi-Strauss, who not coincidentally holds a chair named for Mauss. In fact, in his inaugural lecture, Lévi-Strauss defined his project as attempting to complete the program that Mauss and Durkheim inaugurated. (Lévi-Strauss has never been given to profound modesty.)

I want to focus my comments on some of the ways in which Durkheim contributed to the formation of structuralism and ignore for the most part the ideas and arguments which have been influential in defining the dominant sociological tradition. In *The Rules of Sociological Method*, Durkheim says the first task to be faced in founding a science of society is determining what it is that it is supposed to study. If we want to construct a positive science, we have to study the *facts* of social life instead of the ideas we have about those facts, which are all that has been studied. We have confused the representations of social life in our minds with the facts of social life themselves. A central concern of *The Rules of Sociological Method* was how to convert those representations into real facts, whether by making social representations *the facts* or by treating them as if they were facts. It is of course this project which defines the anti-idealist, positivist Durkheim.

The later works, like *The Elementary Forms of Religious Life* and *Primitive Classification*, return to these representations and begin with the observation that all societies form ideas about the relationships and social contexts in which they live. These ideas form what he called "the collective representations of a society." Understanding the mental life of a particular society involves constructing an inventory of the collective representations which the different social groups in the society, as well as the society as a whole, have held over a long period of time. Moreover, these collective representations have a social function: They help us to regulate our behavior towards and relationships with one other. They are what allow us to integrate or adapt our behavior to the common structures and needs of the society. Further, they take on a facticity of their own, for these systems of collective representations get codified in language and books, institutionalised in different apparatuses and systems. That is, for example, what the law is: the set of collective representations which people have as to what ought to be legally binding in their society. In this codified, institutionalised form, they have the very important social function of constraining and limiting our behavior. They prevent us from behaving in ways which fall outside of the range of the acceptable or conventional, that is, outside of the collective representations in a society.

Closely related to the system of collective representations by which people represent their society to themselves, every society develops its own distinctive collection of norms which have a powerful structuring effect on our behavior. These norms, as collective representations, are collective and not individual productions. There is no way an individual could generate a system of collective representations about law. Not only are they collective, they constrain our behavior from outside. They do not operate on our behavior like an internal system of values but as an external system of limits or constraints. They prevent us from doing particular things or they generate, for example, feelings of the sacred in relation to particular powerful and important collective representations. Because collective representations cannot be reduced to a set of individual psychological processes and because they constrain behavior from the outside, they have the "facticity" which Durkheim thought was required to make sense of sociology as the science of society. They are irreducible to the individual atoms which compose a society. That was what Durkheim referred to as society sui generis or the social element.

It is perhaps worth elaborating on the sociological notion of norms, because Cultural Studies has borrowed from this particular adaption of Durkheim's work. The operation of norms obviously implies the existence of those who do not keep the norms. It divides society into those who are within the framework of the normative structure of the society and those who are outside. Those within are people whose behavior is rule governed, i.e., governed by those rules or norms sanctioned by the society. Those who are outside, whose behavior is not governed by those rules, have been given different names in different contexts: deviants, exceptions, and the excluded. In this conception, a society has at its core a set of collective ideas and norms which hold the whole thing together; and if a society is to reproduce itself, it must also reproduce those collective representations and normative structures. That is the nature and the source of social order, which is only maintained insofar as the normative structure of a society controls or defines the limits of acceptable behavior within the society. Consequently, social order is dependent on constraint. Those who are not within the normative order are subject to control, preferably being induced back into the structure. It is within this conception of social order that Durkheim talks about crime as more than an infringement of the social or normative order, for it takes on a symbolic importance within every society by creating the opportunity for the ritual act of punishing those who are the exception to the rule. Only through punishment does a society reaffirm its normative integration and the power of its normative structure. The very process of violating the norms helps to integrate the social order.

Obviously, there are close ties between this Durkheimian tradition and certain variations of Marxism organised around simple theories of domination and control. One could articulate Durkheim's theory of collective norms into a theory of ideology. Perhaps this is why the whole framework of deviance and the sociology of crime have, on occasion, been simply, if somewhat surreptitiously, transferred out of mainstream sociological theory and into forms of theorising in cultural theory. For example, the development of an interest in and a theory of subcultures rests upon a clear transposition from deviance theory, although its questions are often presented in a more social interactionist framework: What is the definition of the situation of a particular group? How does it differ from the dominant definitions? How are those whose definitions differ brought, invited, urged, or constrained back into the mainstream? What is the process by which the deviant is labeled? What is the importance of the excluded for the maintenance of the dominant collective representations? Thus, despite their perfectly straightforward lineage from mainstream sociological theory, all of these ideas have proved themselves capable of being fruitfully adapted into some areas of Cultural Studies.

It was Durkheim's interest in collective representations which attracted people like Lévi-Strauss. After all, when Durkheim talks about religion, he is interested in how and which people's ideas about society get expressed in religious or symbolic form. When Durkheim looked at primitive religious systems, he was interested in the ways these systems expressed some of the complexities of social relations in a complicated system of symbolic signs. In totemic systems, for example, the relationships between different social groups are expressed in a symbolic system which represents them in the relationships between animals or things in nature. The relationship between natural and human relations in forms of symbolic organisation is the subject matter of Lévi-Strauss's (1969b) first book within an explicit structuralist paradigm, *Totemism*. In the light of his later work, *Totemism* can be seen as an attempt to understand the relationship between classification systems which are given in symbolic form and the ways in which society has organised and classified the relationships among different social groups.

Lévi-Strauss is a distinguished French ethnologist and anthropologist whose fieldwork was done among various primitive Indian tribes in both North and South America. He began his Indian career as a follower of Franz Boas and the American tradition of cultural anthropology, and it is here that we can locate the beginnings of his interest in language. Boas has always insisted that if you were going to study a particular people, the first thing you had to learn was the language. This is not only a matter of survival, of whether you can speak to the people and inquire into the mundane necessities of one's own life, it is also a matter of understanding what the people are about. You have to understand their language because their language is the primary symbolic system they use to give their social reality an intelligible form. Therefore, the categories and forms of language are themselves the most significant clues available to their symbolic universe, to the cosmology of the worlds within which people live. Language, in this sense, is the imposition of intelligibility on a world. The world has to be made meaningful, and this can only be accomplished by breaking it up, giving names to the various bits, and establishing relationships among them. It is in the structure and categories of the language itself that one can find clues to all of this. Therefore, in cultural anthropology, language was not just a vehicle of communication but an object of study in its own right, an object which gave a clue to the internal collective symbolic systems which were being studied.

It is from this perspective that Lévi-Strauss criticises the dominant tradition of functional anthropology, which has tried to decipher the symbolic systems of primitive peoples principally in terms of their material (not in a Marxist sense but, following Malinowski, in biological terms) function. He poses his objections by demonstrating the absurdity of the Malinowskian notion that the way to study symbolic systems is to dissolve them into their concrete satisfaction of social needs. Lévi-Strauss asks if these complicated symbolic systems are really good to eat. Do people who identify themselves with sweet potatoes really do so because they have a particular kind of sweet tooth? And are the others therefore the sour sort? In contradistinction to that functionalist tradition, Lévi-Strauss argues that the signs are not for eating, they are for thinking with. They are forms of symbolic organisation which need to be understood in terms of their own complex internal organisation. One can then ask how these systems of symbolic classification and organisation relate to the social relations and material environment within which the people live.

The first obstacle to this project that Lévi-Strauss has to face is the product of a certain kind of hubris which is associated with Western rationalist science, which maintains that there is only one viable logic: its own dominant rationalist logic. Against this ethnocentrism, Lévi-Strauss identifies what he calls analogical modes of thinking, which he argues characterise the kinds of logic one finds in the symbolic systems of primitive peoples. Lévi-Strauss wants to say that there are many logics which work in different ways, but they all allow us to understand and simplify the complexity of the world. In this way, he affirms the status of analogical logics and modes of thinking in the worlds of myth, totemic systems, and other primitive forms of classification, which he describes as the ways these people think about themselves and their societies. And they need such systems just as much as Western society needs its systems based in rationalist logic. Moreover, if you try to superimpose rationalist logic on the logic of these more primitive systems, you may think that you are helping to enlighten them. But of course, having not understood the relationship between these forms of classification and people's lives, you will have robbed them of the logic that they need to understand what they are doing. How will you be able to explain to them whom they can marry and whom they cannot? And if you deprive them of the ana-logic logic with which they make sense of their kinship system, you will deprive them of the basic language with which they organise large parts of their lives. In such societies, although they are complex in their own ways, they may have no visible relations of production as we know them. What they have are relations of kinship, which then serve to define other relations as well—relations of power, relations to the spiritual world, and relations of economic production. And they need the analogic logic of their own way of thinking, a logic which is intelligible to them. Thus one of the first and most important arguments Lévi-Strauss makes in his at-tention to the world of symbolic classification and signification is the plurality of cultural logics.

Moreover, trained as he is at the summit of French intellectual civi-lisation, he is not satisfied with merely recognising that language is the clue to understanding the culture of a society. He is committed as well to finding a way of giving this project the imprimatur of science and avoiding a method which appears to be little more than the presentation of a series of intuitive hunches: "This seems so, does it not? Don't you feel it on your pulses?" Lévi-Strauss is the first major cultural theorist who finds the promise of scientificity in that discourse of the humanities which appears to have the rigor, the precision, and the law-like struc-ture of science: the methodologies which linguistics bring to the study of language. After all, linguistics, and especially phonology, can tell you how it is that people produce a certain range of sounds; it can tell you why the range of sounds in one language is different from that of an-other; it has a material, biological base, because it must always begin with the physiology of the human body. But rather than the historical linguistics which was still dominant, he turns to the structural linguis-tics of the phonologists (who in examining the actual sounds of different languages were the first people to identify the elements of a language and the rules of selection and combination as the basic grid which allowed the production of intelligible linguistic sets) and, especially, of Saussure.

And it is here that we can locate the inspiration for his important, even groundbreaking, early studies: *Totemism* and *Structural Anthropology* (Lévi-Strauss 1972).

In order to establish the possibility of a scientific cultural anthropology, Lévi-Strauss begins with the Saussurian distinction between *langue* and *parole*. In the simplest terms, parole is the multiplicity of actual speech acts which all of us perform in the everyday use of language. Langue, on the other hand, consists of the elements and the rules which make it possible for us to speak at all. The important feature of the relationship between parole and langue is that we can perform the first without knowing the second. We may not know a single rule about the phonetic, grammatical, and semantic relations of language—rules which allow us to produce intelligible speech—but we do still produce such intelligible speech all the time. Equally important, we know when somebody is not doing it correctly; that is, we know when someone has broken a rule even though we may not know the rule. These rules are, at least for the majority of us, internalised at an unconscious level. This linguistic unconscious is not to be confused with the unconscious in the Freudian sense, for there is no active or necessary repression in the former case. Linguistic rules are, after all, open to inspection and rigorous description. That is precisely the task of the various forms of structural linguistics. But the fact remains that somehow, unconsciously, every speaker of a language has had to acquire the appropriate rules.

The relationship between parole and langue is particularly significant, however, because the former is potentially infinite while the latter is necessarily finite. The set of rules must be fixed and closed; one cannot have the freedom to decide to speak English in a different way, based on a different set of rules. Yet it is possible to say whatever you like, including that which has never been said before, out of the fixity and the limits of the rules. Thus what the distinction between langue and parole offers is the possibility of a scientific approach to something whose essential feature is its creativity. Why do we study culture if not to locate the most original moments, those things that have never been thought or said before, and the source of their possibility? And in language, the most common of our symbolic activities, we are in fact original most of the time. We say things which we feel we are the authors of. But what do we use to say them but the same rules of language which everybody else uses? Lévi-Strauss argues that while you can go on studying the infinity of cultural speech acts which have been produced throughout the world, the scientific analysis of language has to study the langue. You cannot build a science by observing an infinite set of things which can go on forever. But the finite set of rules which allows this infinite production can be the object of a scientific inquiry. Thus structural linguistics attempts to show how an infinite set of actual speech or cultural acts can be performed out of a limited matrix of rules or, in more contemporary terms, on the basis of a series of deep structures.

Langue as the object of scientific inquiry is a collective, unconscious matrix, which raises the question of how that matrix is to be described. According to Saussure, the matrix of a language consists of a limited set of elements, which might be as arbitrary as the different phonemic bits of which a language is made up or with which a computer works, and the rules which tell you how to select certain bits and how to combine them with others in order to produce well-formed chains in order to say things intelligibly and correctly. This is an elegantly simple model consisting of elements and rules of selection and combination. The production of signs, messages, and utterances involves selecting certain elements from the field (the selection operates according to principles, some of which are not a part of langue itself), and combining them with other elements that have been selected according to the rules of combination. But while every sentence or speech act has a sequence and can be described in such terms, this is true only of parole. Parole has sequence; langue has no sequence. Langue is, after all, a way of expressing how sequence is produced; it can only be described as sets of elements and the rules of combination among them. Langue is a static, frozen system, while parole is always changing and in motion. Langue is synchronic deep structure: "deep" because it is not necessarily conscious; "structure" because it expresses the processual and dynamic sequencing of linguistic performance as a static system of rules.

Now I want to briefly look at how Lévi-Strauss uses this model from structural linguistics to study myths. There are four steps:

1. Identify the constituent elements of the myth; such elements are never isolated terms but, rather, relations between a subject and a function at a particular moment.

2. Construct a table of all possible ways in which the constituent elements can be combined.

3. Take this table as the object of the analysis. Each actual instance of combination is just one possible realisation or manifestation of the possibilities included in the table. The table is a kind of inventory of all the possible myths you could ever make.

4. Describe the law or structure of this table: That is the meaning of the myth.

Take, for example, the three constituent elements: Tiger jumps over the stream; tiger drowns in the stream; mythmaker shoots the tiger. Given a rule of combination, the mythmaker can construct numerous different myths by drawing on these three elements. The tiger jumps over the stream and attacks the mythmaker. In the struggle the mythmaker shoots the tiger. The tiger stumbles off, falls into the stream, and drowns. Alternatively, the mythmaker might shoot the tiger but only graze it. The tiger runs off, jumping over the stream to escape the pursuit of the mythmaker. The mythmaker stalks the tiger for many days, until one day they meet accidentally in a stream where both are bathing. In the ensuing struggle, the mythmaker strangles the tiger, who drowns in the stream. And surely there are others that you can construct. In analysing this myth, you are not trying to understand the richness of any particular version, wonderfully embellished as it might be with beautiful language: how beautifully striped the tiger was, how brave the mythmaker was, how the mythmaker lurked in the bushes, and so on. What you want to know is what are all the possible myths that you could construct and tell out of just those elements and those rules of combination. One of the things you are trying to explain is why over there in the next classroom, where they are supposed to be doing physics, somebody else got hold of the tiger and the stream and the shots of the mythmaker and is telling a beautifully worked myth in a very different way: The tiger drowned in the stream and returned as a ghost. One day the mythmaker saw it jump over the stream to attack him. The mythmaker shot the tiger, but since it was a ghost and could not be harmed by any mortal, it continued its charge. The mythmaker died of fright and has returned as a ghost to tell the tale.

These variants have apparently totally different meanings but they are constructed out of exactly the same elements and the same simple rules of combination. Indeed, to become a mythmaker, one need not memorise every single myth that has been told but simply remember the elements and rules of combination. Then you can go on forever simply by building on and rearranging and building the basic sets of elements. This approach allowed Lévi-Strauss to address a central anthropological issue, which is why people seem to tell basically the same kind of myths in a thousand different societies and cultures that have never had any contact with one another. Historicists offer what one might call the *Kon-Tiki* solution: that somebody must have carried the myths to these different lands and peoples. Apart from whether such an account is very likely, it in fact does not explain the actual results, since it is not the case that different peoples all have identical versions of the same myth. Lévi-Strauss argues that what is common across the different myths of these diverse cultures is that they all have identical structures. Suppose instead of the stream, it was the sky; instead of a tiger, it was a bird. We can now construct new myths. Now the mythmaker shoots the bird or the bird scares the mythmaker to death. It is really just another version of the same myth. The meaning of the myth is not in its particular contents, but in the logic of the arrangement of its forms.

Such structural analyses often demonstrate an elegant simplicity usually associated with mathematical explanation. Lévi-Strauss, then, takes the structural method and, by analogy, he transfers it from phonology to language in general, from language in general to primitive systems of classification and social organisation, from systems of classification to the analysis of how myths work, and from myths to the analysis of how kinship systems work. And that extension of the linguistic paradigm by analogy has been going on ever since, attempting to apply the insights drawn from structural linguistics to any social domain. This is the beginning of structuralism per se. So, for Althusser and Balibar, the mode of production also functions like a language. For Lacan, the unconscious is structured like a language. The danger in this analogical extension is that sometimes, in a significant but unnoticed slippage, the "like" disappears. So instead of being structured "like" a language, we just say they are languages. Kinship is a language. The unconscious is a language. Mode of production could become a language. Take two units: forces of production and relations of production. Combine them. Combine them in such a way as to give freedom to both elements: the capitalist mode. Put one inside the other: the slave mode. It's quite simple: It is a kind of formal diagrammatic expression of what Marx said took centuries of life and blood and history and exploitation and so on to realise.

At this point, it may be useful to try to identify some of the important characteristics and implications of a structural approach to symbolic systems and cultural forms. First, meaning does not arise in the world; it is not there waiting to be discovered. Meaning is not something which is out there in the world apart from language which language, acting simply like a mirror, reflects. The world is what it is, and societies use the instrumentality of symbolism to make certain relations in the world intelligible to them. They have to impose a system of meaning on the world. The system of meaning is derived from the categories into which they break up the world, and from the rules of combining and recombining those meanings which they have identified for themselves. Meaning and intelligibility are articulated onto the world. It is not given or already present in the world and then simply expressed or reproduced through language.

Second, there is no one-to-one relationship or correlation between the forms and symbols which are being used and the things to which they refer. There is at best an indirect relationship between the form of symbolic expression (and its meaningfulness or intelligibility) and the social relationships and institutions of a particular society. Indeed, the relations are never fixed. If you start with the fact that a limited set generates an infinite variety of actual forms, you can only be interested in how the relations vary. The denial of any one-to-one, predictive relationship between the symbolic form and the external reality leaves open the question of whether there are any referents as such in the real world at all. Further, this is often taken to mean that structural analyses cannot deal with such relations, that they are only concerned with the internal dynamics of symbolic systems. The slide from the denial of any simple relation to the absence of any relationship whatsoever is an important one, one which can be located in how Lévi-Strauss himself makes the connection between symbols and reality.

In an early work analysing the Asdiwal myth, in which people sometimes go upriver and sometimes go downriver, Lévi-Strauss (2004) is interested both in the symbolic organisation of this set of stories and in the fact that, in certain climatic conditions, the people actually do go downstream sometimes and upstream at other times. Clearly there is some relationship between what actually happens in terms of the organisation of the tribe and the kinds of stories they tell themselves. This is when Lévi-Strauss comes closest to something like a Marxist position. He talks about myths as offering an apparently logical solution to a social contradiction. In other words, there are certain problems that concern the survival of the group: for example, problems about where they go in different circumstances to ensure their continuation. And they tell stories which relate to that, stories which both demonstrate that they do, and guide them to, make the right decisions at the right times. It is the kind of difficulty in life which can be overcome in symbolic form. But this does not mean that one looks at the structure of the myth as a reflection of the economic organisation of the tribe. The myth is only analogically and indirectly related; at best, it can be understood as refracting the social and economic relations to which it refers. But when Lévi-Strauss says that myths are about contradictions, he is principally concerned with the contradiction between nature and culture rather than with the contradictions that concerned Marx. The contradictions which Marx identifies, and which he sometimes talks about ideology helping to overcome, are the contradictions of social, economic, and political organisation. Lévi-Strauss is rarely concerned with these kinds of contradictions. He is more often interested in the way in which primitive people resolve social relations by appealing to their direct and unmediated relationship to nature. Nevertheless, at this stage, Lévi-Strauss is still interested in both symbolic forms and social structures, and in the relationships between them. But as his work developed, he became much more devoted to an analysis of the internal relations—the structures and forms of the myths and symbolic systems—and less interested in the relationships between those symbolic structures and societal contradictions existing outside of them. By he time he writes *Mythologiques* (four volumes: Lévi-Strauss 1969a, 1974, 1978, 1981), he treats myth entirely as a self-sufficient system of logic rather than as an attempted intellectual solution to real contradictions. The important point is that that movement is characteristic of structuralism. It is a movement away from the interface between the symbolic and the social and into the internal organisation of the symbolic forms themselves. As it continues to develop, structuralism becomes progressively less concerned with the relationship between symbolic systems and social structures.

Third, the most important question to ask about any symbolic form is not what caused it but how it is organised. Lévi-Strauss is not interested in the causal questions typical of Western rationalist logic but in questions of arrangement. There is thus a displacement in structuralism from content to form, from the *what* of a culture to the *how* of a culture. It is the pattern or structure and its transformations, not the contents which these forms might be said to contain, which give you the clues to a culture. Structuralists classify, arrange, and identify the operative logic; they are not concerned with why this classification is operating nor with what outside of the system of classification may have led to this particular symbolic organisation. Consequently, the way in which structuralism expresses change is in terms of a movement from before to after or from one system (variant) to another. If you want to describe the differences between two stages in a society, you simply construct a comparative classificatory system. In each of two columns, you list the things that differentially characterise the two stages. It is, of course, a common enough practice which we all do, for example, in representing the stages of industrialisation. We represent change as difference; change is reduced to a structural system of classifications. This is obviously a much more limited, less historical, and less dynamic way of dealing with change than is customary in the Marxist thought that I identified in the work of Williams and Thompson.

This way of talking about change—as structural transformation—has important implications across a number of topics including the question of creativity and originality. For example, the ideas of progress, individuality, and originality in Western rational logic dictate that the only valuable cultural productions are the ones that nobody has ever produced before and, in fact, the more unlike previous productions they are, the more they are to be valued. On the other hand, the mythmaker is not concerned with whether the story he or she is telling is rather like a story you have heard before. The mythmaker understands that you always have to give people something of what they know already—that old tiger and the stream—in order for the audience to recognise the starting point: "Ah ha! Here we go again!" The change, the innovation, is defined precisely within that already recognisable structure, just enough difference to keep them interested. It has to remain familiar enough so that people know that you are working on the same ground. And therein arises the pleasure of a great deal of culture: getting back to where you came from. Freud and many modern cultural theories recognise the pleasure of, and the inseparability of, repetition and innovation. No cultural statement entirely sweeps away the past to create a tabula rasa, upon which it can suddenly make an absolutely unique statement, unrelated to any statement ever made before. Change and innovation come about through transformation, through transforming what is already given, producing the new out of it, leaving some of the old elements out, bringing new elements in, making a new rule of combination, and so on. Thus, structuralism proposes a new and important conception of change.

Fourth, structural analysis is formal. As compared with Williams's work, it is not only the attention to form that is significant but that the methodology is itself formalist. It tries to formalise as far as possible, indeed even when there are intuitions. It is important to acknowledge that structuralism does not do away with intuitions in its interpretations of particular cultural forms. For example, Lévi-Strauss's analyses are often so brilliant that one may momentarily fail to question the legitimacy of his categories or to ask how they were derived. Consider his famous analysis of the myth of Oedipus (Lévi-Strauss 1955). Is it self-evident that all of the variants he brings together are in fact transformations of the same basic Oedipal myth? Are the categories into which he breaks down the myth self-evident? Are we sure that every other interpreter, or even any other, would arrive at similar categories? In fact, the entire formal apparatus often works on top of the most brilliant intuition. Structuralist methodology is not scientific in the sense that it eliminates all but the most rigorous procedures. The method is more intuitive than it pretends. Though it is based on a familiarity with how symbolic systems function, it is not outside of the moment of intuitive guesswork, and sometimes Lévi-Strauss can guess very wrongly indeed. But after the initial guesses, it brings its machinery of formal analysis into place. Such formalisation does help to objectify the evidence that justifies one's intuitions and procedures. At the very least it allows a more rational kind of dialog with the other person than is allowed with the purely intuitive assertion that you can feel it on your pulses.

Fifth, a structural approach is concerned with rules and the rule-governed nature of human activities. Whether talking about language, symbolic systems, social organisations, political systems, or kinship systems, all are organised around and by systems of rules whose formation cannot be ascribed to the creativity of the human subject. Structuralist man and woman are not the Promethean, creative figures celebrated by Williams and Thompson, capable as it were of making the world anew, or at least of constituting its meaningfulness anew. Innovation arises only from the observance of social rules and regulations. Of course, sometimes it is the break with the rules that is most significant, but such breaks are themselves understandable as transformations. Thus, although Joyce ([1934] 1990) broke the rules of normal spoken English, the culture did not reject *Ulysses*; instead, people learned the rules of how to read it. Innovation may depend upon breaking and transforming rules, but it always constitutes another set of rules. This conception of culture is antiromantic. The notion that culture is the expression of our ultimate ability to grasp our world and give symbolic form to our awareness is reconstructed in structuralist discourse in terms of our ability to innovate within necessary constraints, to use rules in order to transform our situations.

Sixth, structuralism is concerned with the plurality of logics. That is, it argues that cultures may be distinguished, not as Durkheim would have it, by their collective representations or the content of their ideas, but by the particular logics with which they organise and arrange their world, logics which will be related to each other in different ways. This notion provides an opening to reconnect Lévi-Strauss to Marxism because one can reformulate the Marxist project in terms of discovering the distinctive social logics of different social formations and, indeed, of particular classes and social groups. But Lévi-Strauss clearly refuses this way of reading cultural logics. Rather than situating different logics in their historical specificity, he argues that they arise out of the infinite potential logics of the human mind. They are cultural universals in a sense, features of our common human nature. We all have the potential to tell stories in the different modes of various logics. It is in that sense that Ricoeur (1968) describes Lévi-Strauss as a Kantian, because he is interested in the transcendental categories of the mind, albeit without the transcendental subject.

Finally, let me try to relate some of the structuralist commitments to the questions which Cultural Studies, as discussed in the previous two lectures, puts on the agenda. The importance of the so-called unconscious level at which the structure operates, while not unconscious in the fully Freudian sense and not the result of a specific psychoanalytical process, represents a significant break from the humanist tradition of Williams and Thompson. This becomes even clearer if we see this as a specific instance of the more general topography of structural analysis. The characteristic analytical move of structuralism is from the level of phenomenal relations to the determining structure below. It is the "scientific" break from where things appear, where people speak and live, where they tell a hundred stories. It is the rejection of E. P. Thompson's efforts to recover the consciousness of real people and Raymond Williams's attempt to recover the structure of feeling of life as it was lived in particular periods. Structuralism turns its attention from consciousness and experience in favor of the structure which is determining everything else. While Lévi-Strauss may occasionally use this topography to claim that he is trying to illuminate the relationship between the infrastructure and the superstructure, it is clear that his infrastructure is not the same as Marx's. On the other hand, one might also use this topography to claim that Marx is a structuralist because he also is moving away from phenomenal relations to a determining structure. Surely the whole point of *Capital* (Marx 1977) is to begin to analyse the structure. It is true that Marx's structure is not a formal system, comparable to the rules of combination and the elements out of which you produce transformations, but it is something which can be analysed in that way, as Althusser will attempt. You could, given a certain understanding of the constituent elements of the capitalist mode of production and some rules of combination, generate the variety of its surface forms, including early industrialism, late industrialism, imperialism, and postcapitalism. You can in fact use the approach as an analytic scheme to produce different historical periods. Nevertheless, the basic drive in the structuralist problematic is to displace the diachronic (history, process, change) into the synchronic (system, structure) where only the latter has the possibility of being scientifically defined.

I have tried to describe the basic assumptions and implications of the structuralist paradigm as one finds it in Lévi-Strauss and early semiotics (e.g., Roland Barthes), prior to Althusser's effort to reread its relationship to Marx and Marxism. The use of linguistics as a rich generative metaphor enables semioticians to analyse the whole inventory of modern cultural production in the way Lévi-Strauss suggests analysing the inventory of any particular culture, including the systems of different cars, of fashion, and of news photographs. Barthes himself contrasts his work with sociology, describing his own project as the analysis of the sociologics of different social and cultural formations, that is, the use of structuralist or linguistic methods to analyse the inventories of the different cultural signifying systems, systems of meaning and intelligibility, in different societies.

I want to conclude by briefly summarising the differences between structuralism and the more humanistic orientation of culturalism as a series of displacements: first, the displacement from a Promethean to regulative notion of human life; second, the displacement from the domain of agency and consciousness to that of the unconsciousness; third, the displacement from notions of history and process of those of systems and structures; and finally, the displacement from a concern with cause and causal explanations to a logic of classification and arrangement. But there is another displacement that has to be recognised: the displacement of the speaking subject. Lévi-Strauss's mythmaker, the one who produces language, tells stories, and gives meaning to a culture, is not someone who is called upon to produce and share the fruits of inspiration. The mythmaker is spoken by the structure at his or her disposal. The mythmaker uses the cultural machinery which is available. The telling of myths, then, is less a question of the subject than of a process without a subject. It is through these anonymous processes that systems of intelligibility and meaning are produced. There is also a displacement from operating on the relation between the cultural and the material (at least in the classical Marxist sense) worlds into a preoccupation with the internal relations within a symbolic system which allow it to produce meaning and intelligibility. In a weaker sense, there is a displacement from a notion of language as expressing or reflecting the meaning of the world into a notion of language as producing meaning, as enabling human societies to signify. Finally, there is a displacement from the language of practice to the language of discourse. In fact, the heart of the structuralist revolution, by which the paradigm is extended to all social life in semiotics, is the assumption that all social practices are made meaningful in just this way, and hence are semiotic. They do not exist outside of the meanings which different societies give to them. They can be described only in terms of their intelligibility, of their capacity to signify.

Rethinking the Base and Superstructure

This lecture focuses on the central metaphor in Marx's work which has defined and framed the concerns of Cultural Studies, the base and superstructure. It is the way Marx often inflected problems of cultural theory and the terms within which ideology is often presented. Yet it has given people working on a Marxist terrain with these questions more problems than almost any other concept in Marx, not least of which is its precise status as a metaphor or model. Here I can only offer a brief commentary on some of the major formulations in Marx's oeuvre, for it is in Marx's work itself that we see the ambiguities and uncertainties of the metaphor and, eventually, its limitations. In fact, there are a number of theoretical questions collapsed into the base-superstructure metaphor. First, it is one of the central ways in classical Marxism of expressing the nature of the determination of material circumstances (or of economic forces or of class relations) over the areas of the superstructure and the ideologies. Second, it is used in Marx to designate the nature of the relationships existing between different practices of levels within the social formation. And finally, it offers direction in thinking about the nature of the complex whole of totality that one refers to when one speaks of a society or social formation. Inquiring into the relationship between the material base and the superstructure is obviously central to any attempt to understand the more specific relationship between economic relations and ideological forms. It points to the problematic task of trying to connect, locate, or situate practices that we would normally refer to as cultural or ideological practices within the framework of a classical Marxist schema.

The base-superstructure metaphor has defined a series of problems for people in Cultural Studies who want to go on working within something like a Marxist problematic. It also provides the point at which those dissatisfied with the framework of Marxist discourse have attempted to make important revisions. Of course, some of the problems are there, at least tendentially, in Marx's texts, while other problems result from the ways in which others have taken those texts, the tendencies they have followed, the interpretations they have institutionalised. For example, a particular notion of the determination of social formations, present in some of Marx's texts, has come to constitute the classical Marxist position, with its very particular way of privileging the categories of economic and class contradictions. Hence, the metaphor is one of the main points at which the question of the relationship of other social contradictions (such as gender or race) to Marxism has to be posed.

The metaphor of base-superstructure usually occurs in Marx's work in relation to his account of a general historical materialist method. That is how it appears in *The German Ideology* (Marx and Engels 1970), in the "Preface" to *A Contribution to the Critique of Political Economy* (Marx 1970), and in the "Introduction" to the *Grundrisse* (Marx 1973). The metaphor opens up to a general materialist method because it says that where you begin is important, just as it is important how you then move on to explain the other parts, that is, how you see the determining relationships between your starting point and the other parts. That is to say, base-superstructure is often formulated within Marx's struggle against idealism; it is part of the so-called inversion of Hegelianism. It attempts to display how historical development can be explained, not from the ideas we have of it, but from the actual material practices and circumstances. The metaphor, then, occurs in the context of, and is inseparable from, the three main premises which distinguish Marx's method. The first is the historical premise: that there are no universal or eternal historical forms. All historical forms, epochs, and modes of production are historically specific and are subject to the specificity of historical determination. The second is the structural (which is not necessarily the same as structuralist) premise: that the principal objects of analysis are the laws, tendencies, and structures of a particular mode of production. Specifically, materialist analysis directs attention to the systemic properties of capitalist social formations. The third premise, which is most directly related to the question of base-superstructure, is the materialist (understood in a very particular way) premise: that human societies can only be understood as the result of the combination of social organisation and its dependency on the modes by which it extracts the means of its survival from nature.

There are a number of different but related questions involved in the metaphor of base and superstructure: a definition of the object of the analysis; a description of the relation between subjects and history, and of the structure of the social formation; and a theory of change (it is here that charges of reductionism are relevant) and determination. This complexity is made all the more problematic by the fact that Marx offered numerous formulations of the metaphor as a response to these various questions in different works, including *The German Ideology*, *The Critique of Political Economy*, the "Introduction" to the *Grundrisse* and *The Eighteenth Brumaire of Louis Bonaparte* (Marx 1978b). While I want to focus on *The Critique of Political Economy* and *The Eighteenth Brumaire*, let me begin with some brief comments on *The German Ideology*.

Marx says that he starts with the material production of life and the form of social intercourse which is connected with and created by it. That is civil society—social relations and productive forces—the basis of all history. But Marx quickly adds, also its action as the State. (This is a typical rhetorical strategy in Marx—to add a phrase which seems to raise once again all sorts of complexity since it is unclear how we are to interpret it.) Marx thus starts with the framework of relations and forces and how it finds itself represented or expressed as that thing which we call the State. The method, then, explains the different theoretical productions (forms of consciousness, religion, philosophy, ethics, and so on) as having their origins in and as growing from that base. In that way the whole social formation can be displayed or articulated.

The formulation in the "Preface" from *The Critique of Political Economy* begins at a rather different point, for there the objects of Marx's attention are relations, not individuals, classes, or society. Rather, the beginning is defined by the fact that in the social production of life, men and women enter into definite relations that are independent of their will. This is a conception of the social formation in which the individual subject or agent has been radically displaced or decentered into the relations they are obliged to enter whether they will it or not. They find that their position in the world is already predetermined by the relations into which they are born and by which, inevitably, they are framed and shaped. These relations open up spaces which are, so to speak, waiting for us. Whether or not they are already named, they already carry with them a whole range of things—meanings, practices, identities—about which we can do little.

The problem of the social formation is then momentarily displaced, as Marx begins with a particular formulation of the relationship between history and subjects. This is clearly different from the formulation offered in *The German Ideology*, the text from which Thompson and Williams attempt to derive their models, where Marx's emphasis is quite different, claiming to begin with Man the maker of things, with history as nothing but the activity of men and women. On this model, what is really at the center of the analysis is human praxis. But this is still a different emphasis from what we find in *The Eighteenth Brumaire*, where there is a double-sidedness between practice and structure. There Marx says that men and women make their own history, but in circumstances which are not of their own choosing.

But it is worth considering the more objectivist position of the *Critique of Political Economy* in more detail. Without *The Eighteenth Brumaire*'s double relation between practice and structure, the *Critique* simply states that there are relations which exist in a social formation between different kinds of practices. That is how the society is formed and shaped. That is how it produces itself again and again through time. Individuals are the agents or bearers of those relations; they are placed and positioned in them. Their activity and agency is, so to speak, given by the lines of relationships which already exist. Moreover, these relations are definite; this is not merely the traditional sociological (i.e., the Durkheimian) proposition that men and women belong in society. It is a Marxist proposition that men and women belong within a historically specific structure of social relations.

More concretely, the relations which concerned Marx were relations of production, the social relations connected with the social production of life. Thus, the structure to be analysed consists of relations of production that correspond to a definite stage of the development of the productive forces. However, we must tread cautiously, for this is one of the slipperiest formulations in Marx. Precisely where is it that the social relations end and the productive forces begin, especially since Marx and Engels say that social relations can sometimes themselves become a productive force? The articulation of both social relations and productive forces into the productive forces (the base) was necessary to prevent us from translating productive forces as simply technology. They may not have always succeeded but they made a very good attempt at reminding us that even the question of the forces available to a social formation at any one time are not the consequence of machinery, or whatever technology it might be, and that the particular level of technology is itself the result of social relations interacting with other kinds of productive forces. Thus, despite the continuing tendency among some Marxists to read technological determinism into Marx's texts, it does not seem to be what Marx's formulations intended. Rather, it is the sum total of the social relations and the forces of production which defines the base or what is elsewhere called "the structure." It is this which Marx (I hope to his endless dismay) called the "economic," for some of the most gigantic category mistakes ever performed on a particular body of theory result from that conflation of labels. It is clear that this sense of the economic would not be recognisable to any self-respecting economic faculty in the Western world. Marx's use of "economic" does not correspond to the narrower, technical, and disciplinary sense of the term; that is not what it is. The two registers of the term do not include the same things, although we have to recognise that the confusion can be found in Marx's own formulation. Thus, however one ultimately responds to the base-superstructure model, it is crucially important to distinguish the materialist basis of human societies from what we contemporarily understand by the economic.

It is perhaps worth noting at this point, even if somewhat tangentially, the way in which this formulation begins to open itself up to structuralist readings. On this model, different social formations can be identified in terms of the ways in which forms of social organisation are generated which allow men and women to intervene in nature so as to socially reproduce their life. You can then differentiate formations by taking the social relations of production as a set of elements which, in different combinations, generate the different formations, exactly like a language. That is what Balibar calls a "combinatory" and Althusser, perhaps with his nerves failing a little bit, simply calls a "combination." In this simple but elegant way, it is possible to reduce the great complexity of different historical formations and epochs by identifying how the social relations are organised among themselves, how the forces of production are organised among themselves, and how those two elements are combined. It is of course at a very high level of abstraction or a very low level of reduction (depending on whether you are feeling kind or not). Nevertheless, it is a way of describing what Marx would consider the essential structure of great historical epochs.

Returning to the *Critique*, Marx argues that it is to the structure of the base that the legal and political superstructures and definite forms of social consciousness correspond. It is important to recognise here that in this topography, the superstructure has two floors: the first floor consists of political and legal structures and institutions; the second consists of the ideological forms of social consciousness. This distinction is often collapsed, even occasionally by Marx himself, into the ideological forms. But, once again, we must recognise a common rhetorical strategy in Marx's texts: He often elaborates complex ideas and then condenses the whole thing into a single sentence or image. This condensation does not deny the complexity of the idea. For example, he encapsulates the entire description of the base and superstructure given here into the statement that "being determines consciousness," not "consciousness determines being." So there is little ground for Williams and Thompson to appeal to this language in their attempts to rescue consciousness and a larger conception of being by reading this language as if it existed outside of the whole base-superstructure topography. It is a summary of base-superstructure. They like the weaker expression precisely because it appears to be more open ended, less structured than the detailed description of the multileveled social formation. But the two statements are not different formulations; they are part of the same formulation.

But the major problems and questions concerning base and superstructure arise when Marx attempts to describe and explain historical change, especially how change proceeds from one form of organisation to another. Marx says that there is a close correspondence between the superstructures and the base, since the former is "raised on" the latter.

Consequently, they move in tandem, and the superstructures will change when the base changes. But Marx clearly saw problems with this view of the relationship, and he quickly added the caveat that, of course, you can understand shifts in the base much more precisely—he uses the metaphor "with the precision of a natural science"—than you can changes in the superstructure. You can begin to ask how far the objective relations of production in this period really outrun private possession. You can begin to assess the ludicrousness of this enormously socialised form of production still existing under the sign of private ownership. You can analyse such things much more precisely than the speed at which legal, political, philosophic, aesthetic, and other forms of ideological production and consciousness will fall into line. But he does expect them to fall into line. This is, therefore, a particular form of determinacy in which primacy, even in the arena of the superstructures, is given to the dynamics of the base.

While this model of the relationship between the base and superstructure has the appearance of complexity because it differentiates the levels of the social formation—base, political and legal forms, forms of ideological consciousness—it actually fails to acknowledge the real complexity of determination, since the upper stories of the apartment house arise, not only on the foundations of the base, but in such a way as to necessarily correspond to it. Consequently, when the base changes, the superstructures will come into line as well. The model has the appearance of complexity—without complexity. It looks as if it is differentiated, but when you ask how it moves, it moves as one. There may be a bit of a time lag between the movements of material relations and the movements of cultural and ideological relations, but there is little interference between them. The possibility that the two could be moving, for any sustained period of time, in different directions, or that there could be a disjunction between the two, is not allowed. To put it in another way, it looks in the end as if Marx's notion of the social formation as a totality here is an expressive one. The relations occurring in the base express themselves at every level, without the need to attend to the unevenness between them, or the systematic differences between them, or even the forms of mediation between them.

The first crack in this model came from those building historical models. Even if we allow that it works on capitalist social formations, one might reasonably ask about feudal societies where people were tremendously influenced by, for example, religion. In response to that question, Marx advances a different model of determinacy in which the mode of production—the mode in which people extract their livelihood from nature—explains why it is that in different societies different forms play the central role in holding the society together. Marx is not denying that the principal determinacy rests with the base, but he is acknowledging that sometimes the way in which the base determines the other levels is to assign one of them the dominant position: here politics, there religion, et cetera.

This is a very different notion of determinacy from that in which politics or religion comes into line with and expresses or reflects changes in the base. It is where Althusser gets the notion that the way in which the base determines the superstructure is not by defining its content but by assigning dominance to one instance. From this perspective, you would be perfectly correct to note the importance of the place and role of religion in feudal society. That does not mean that religion has become the determining factor. Rather, the determining factor has given religion dominance in the feudal formation. A similar, albeit not identical, argument is made in the 1857 "Introduction" to the *Grundrisse*, where Marx says that in all forms of society there is one specific kind of production which predominates over the rest, and this mode assigns rank and influence to the others. Althusser appears to be legitimated. But a little further on in the same paragraph, Marx argues that it is always a particular "other" which determines the specific gravity of every other relation which has materialised in relation to it. This seems to generalise determinacy across the face of the social formation as a whole, a more culturalist view of determinacy. It gives me some pleasure that one paragraph can generate such diverse models of determinacy: that determinacy doesn't rest with the economic base but is suffused throughout the social formation as a whole, or that it operates in a precise structural manner, not by appearing, as Althusser (1970, 113) would say, as "His Majesty the Economy" taking a stride out of everything else to determine what will actually happen, but by determining which instance will take the lead today.

There is yet another source of problems and controversy in Marx's writings on determinacy, because there are at least two ways Marx formulates the principal (i.e., determining) contradiction in capitalist social formations. In one formulation, the principal contradiction is between social relations and productive forces. Put simply, he foresees a growing gap between the continuous development of the modern productive forces of capitalist society and the social relations required to operate them, including the relations of possession, control, and expropriation (i.e., private ownership) in which those productive forces are located. It is the gap between those forces and relations which constitutes the contradiction, which is in turn responsible for the constantly shifting nature of the relations between them.

But of course elsewhere, especially in *The Communist Manifesto* (Marx and Engels 1964), Marx's attention is not on a structural analysis of the capitalist social formation but on the nature of the struggle and contradiction between the social classes. There the principal contradiction is located in the contradiction between capital and labour. While there is obviously some relationship between these two contradictions, they are not the same. Therefore, depending on which of Marx's works you are reading, there is a significant difference in whether shifts in the superstructures are principally related to a contradiction of the structure or a contradiction of different social formations and practices. This means that we need to distinguish between two different objections which have been brought to bear against the base-superstructure model: economic reductionism and class reductionism.

Economic reductionism charges that, in spite of all the caveats and qualifications added to the model, the base is really the content of the other levels. The others are, in a sense, only the forms of the appearance of something other than what they are. That is why I alluded earlier to the complexity of the social relations of production, productive forces, and *their appearance as the State*. It is as if the State really is simply an instance of economic relationships. We erroneously think that the State is constituted on the domain of the political and, therefore, spend considerable time thinking about political institutions, processes, and so on. But really, in this model, the State is nothing but the expression at the political level of relations which are essentially part of the structure. The model not only asserts that the base generates the other levels but that their essential content is to be found in the base as well. Consequently, the model seems to strongly suggest the reduction of all the levels in the social formation to the base. While it does not require such a move, it quite clearly does not allow for the other levels to have their own real determinate effects. They have effects in this model only in realising what the base directs them to do.

The second charge brought against this model, class reductionism, draws on *The German Ideology* and *The Communist Manifesto*. In the former, one finds a much clearer relationship between the superstructures and the classes, expressed most succinctly in the notions of the ruling class and ruling ideas. In *The German Ideology*, Marx seems to acknowledge that ideas have a constitutive role in effecting social domination and maintaining rule. But the problem is that he goes on to equate certain dominant ideologies with certain classes. In other terms, the problem is the ascription of whole ideologies to whole classes. The question of the determinate effects of particular ideological forms is answered by appealing to a necessary and intrinsic relation between ideas and classes. The objective position of a class in the social relations of production assigns it a particular view of the world and particular material interests. Those who are in the capitalist class have a set of material interests which are in an antagonistic relation to the class which is exploited and has only its labour to sell. Outlooks, worldviews, or ideologies tend to follow and cluster around the social interests of these two antagonistic groups. Those who do not live and experience the struggle between the classes as it is defined at the structural level, who don't live it out exactly as determined by their position within the class relations, are living in false consciousness. That is to say, there is an objective ideology or set of ideological positions which you would expect classes (and individuals) to have as a consequence of their class positioning. When they don't have it, it must be because they don't recognise their true interests.

There are many objections to notions of false consciousness, but perhaps the most telling is not theoretical but political. I wonder how it is that all the people I know are absolutely convinced that they are not in false consciousness, but can tell at the drop of a hat that everybody else is. I have never understood how anyone can advance in the field of political organisation and struggle by ascribing an absolute distinction between those who can see through transparent surfaces, through the complexity of social relations, to the base (and who consequently act according to the real structure) and the vast numbers of people throughout the history of the world who are imprisoned, who are judgmental dopes, and who just can't tell what things are. They live their lives from day to day; they get their wages and salaries; they buy things; they eat; they raise families; they travel about; and in all this they just can't see reality, their own interests, or what they ought to think and do. Indeed, I have always undertaken to move from the opposite position, assuming that all ideologies which have ever organised men and women organically have something true about them. They have truth that people recognise; they really allow us to grasp and define what our experience is. Of course they may not tell us the full truth: They may accentuate certain things at the expense of others; they may be partial in the understanding which they give. But they are not false in the sense of being simply lies, misrepresentations, or misrecognitions. Consequently, false consciousness is not an adequate theorisation of the problem of class positioning and class ideologies.

These are only some of the statements of, and problems with, the classical Marxist position. But I do not want to leave the position yet, not only because significant work was done on the positions, work that is often ignored by those who have mobilised effective critical analyses of the position, but also because we have to acknowledge that Marx's accentuation of the materialist over the idealist elements was in part a polemical strategy. We cannot read all of his texts as if they were written in the British Museum. Some were written in sharp contestation with other philosophical and political forces. Marx was, after all, battling against the young Hegelians, who thought that history marched from idea to idea. Somehow, he had to interrupt that. Thus, *The German Ideology* is a vulgar text in a sense. It says quite crude things, like remember your stomachs or think about housing before you think about the Idea. It asks, "Whoever lived by Catholicism alone?" and "Who could swallow politics?" It asserts that you need the material world and you need to understand how people organise to reproduce their material existence. Marx is a young *enragé*. He is formed, after all, by Hegelianism, so he is not just contesting some enemy out there that he doesn't care about. He is wrestling with bits and habits of thought in his own work, with the high point of idealist philosophy, with an idealist philosopher who understood history, not someone who forgot it, with somebody who had read political economy, not somebody who pretended that the Idea could generate everything. In order to deal with Western idealist philosophy at its most advanced point, he had to "bend the twig" very far, as Althusser later says of his own structuralist encounters. He doesn't want it to break, but he does want it to move hard to that side that everyone else has abandoned. Indeed, Marx felt about nineteenth-century thought as one is sometimes moved to feel about twentieth-century thought: If you let a materialist idea alone for just a moment, you find that it has slid over to idealism. There is still a real pull into idealism built into academic life and into the structure of Western thought. It is partly implanted in the philosophical distinction between Idea and Being. Once you begin with that double-sided framework and try to get them together, you find that idealism is the most powerfully available language for talking about complexity.

We can see in Engels this effort both to recognise the polemical importance of Marx's emphases and to rescue Marxism from the epigones who go on repeating as scientific truth what had been a sort of vulgar joke in a political pamphlet. Engels implores Marxist scholars to study history afresh (that should be printed on the brow of every Marxist scholar) and to avoid using Marx's materialism as a level for the mechanical construction of history, à la Hegel. After all, Marx was struggling against Hegel, and Hegel thought that history was really a huge construction, and once you got it, you could just set the Idea in motion and watch all of history simply unfold, as the sort of meandering of the Idea towards the recuperation of itself at some high synthetic point. But it was precisely that kind of idealist construction that Marx and Engels were trying to dislodge.

Engels then argued that when you actually study a particular historical period, you see that all the sites interact with one another. Politics affects the economic, the economic affects the family, and so on. And so, like Williams (before Williams it's true, but the owl of Minerva flies at different times), he begins to ask about the reciprocal effects of the structure and the superstructure on one another. The more detailed your analysis, the more your list of apparently accidental things grows. One need not apply the determinacy of the base to everything that has ever happened in history. The important task is to trace out the main tendencies, the more prominent lines of connection. Rather than a simple base-superstructure determinacy, Engels posits an infinite series of parallelograms of forces which overlap one another and give rise to a single result. This anticipates Althusser's notion of overdetermination in which an event is determined by a number of different forces.

In his letters, written towards the end of his life and after Marx's death, Engels (Marx and Engels 1934) continued to wrestle with the legacy of a model which had become fetishised, which was no longer a useful tool for thinking. He attempted a number of other formulations and solutions. While none were adequate, they mark the existence of a real theoretical problem in Marx: The relationship between the material and ideological relations was inadequately theorised by Marx.

I say that because, in my own reading, Marx understood that himself and started to do something about it. While not subscribing fully to the Althusserian notion that there is an early, Hegelian, false, prescientific Marx and a late, true, structuralist, scientific Marx, nor to the claim that there is an absolute theoretical break or rupture between the two, I am certain that Althusser is correct to say that Marx's work is not a homogenous unity, that it is not a coherent whole, and that much of the later work, especially *Capital* and the political work written towards the end of his life, is based on presuppositions regarding the question of determinacy that are different from those of the base-superstructure model. There is a break of sorts which occurs at two sites. It occurs first of all politically, in the aftermath of the defeats and disappointments of the revolutions of 1848. It arises specifically with the collapse of the Communist League, with Marx's own recognition that the ways in which he had formulated the rhythm of the break in the contradictions between classes or between capital and labour in such texts as *The Communist Manifesto* did not provide an adequate rendering of the history that he had just lived through.

Let us take a moment to consider *The Communist Manifesto*, a wonderful book, which is like a work of music before it is a work of historical prophesy. It is a magnificent rhythmic invocation of the rhythms of a class struggle and of the possibilities for sharpening and deepening it. It offers a vision of a kind of continuous splitting of the Red Sea. However complex class structure is, the class struggle continuously divides it until in the end one is left with the confrontation of class against class. The interests which are built into those contradictions in the structure will eventually manifest themselves in the huge division of the world between these two classes, and then the epochal struggle will begin, and out of that struggle, socialism may arise. But as an actual prediction of what happened in Europe in the midpart of the nineteenth century, it was incorrect. Not only was it incorrect, it was incorrect in a disastrous manner. If it had been allowed to stand (as the predictions and prophecies of later Marxists have been allowed to stand), the political and historical cost would have been enormous. As Engels later said, they mistook the birth pangs of capitalism for its death throes. It has been the unfortunate inheritance of much of Marxism to continue living in the wake of that misunderstanding. Occasionally, some Marxist will, in the name of scientificity, predict yet another death throe that does not occur. One was predicted in the wake of World War I, and it has had disastrous effects on the understanding of how socialism could emerge and survive in Europe. There have been too many last stages, too many death throes. And the prediction of impending death was really a profound error of historical judgment. It really defeats Marxism to take Marx as a prophet, and his writing as the equivalent of *Capitalism's Almanac* where you can look up what will happen tomorrow. If you invest the last vestige of your faith in Marx, and he makes a wrong prophecy, that can only destroy Marxism for you; you have made a commitment that Marx did not invite. He was a very great thinker who, like all great thinkers, made mistakes. He had to go back over *The Communist Manifesto*, not to refute it but to analyse the actual turn of events that he had come so very close to predicting. After all, Marx was not wrong to say that in the 1840s there was going to be a major historical rupture in the developing capitalist societies. He was not wrong about that any more than Lenin and others were wrong about predicting that there would be a series of revolutions in Europe around 1917–1921. There were. They were not wrong in that sense. What they were wrong about was the range of what could actually occur. But that is not just a historical judgment; it is also a judgment on the analytic tools which were being used. *The Eighteenth Brumaire of Louis Bonaparte* offers Marx's rethinking of those actual events. It explains how that punctuating revolution that Marx predicted for 1848 ended up with a man on horseback with a three-cornered hat, how it happened that the gigantic revolutions for liberty at the center of Europe in the middle of the nineteenth century ended up, paradoxically, advancing and developing the capitalist mode of production.

However, before discussing *The Eighteenth Brumaire*, I want to talk about the second site of a break within Marx's career. This theoretical break occurred at the same moment, but in the context of his preparing work for *Capital*. It is the moment of the *Grundrisse* notebooks (Marx 1973); it is the moment of his withdrawal into intellectual labour, when the revolution is going to be worked on inside the British Museum. It seems to me that there is a break in this period with many of the presuppositions of the base-superstructure model, visible both in the work which precedes *Capital*—specifically in the 1857 "Introduction" to and the *Grundrisse* notebooks—and in *Capital* itself.

The 1857 "Introduction" is Marx's most elaborated statement on method, and it is worth considering it briefly. While Marx still conceives of the base as the relations between social relations of production and productive forces, he is now interested in analysing the different constitutive relationships. After all, the material reproduction of life does not only consist of production; it also includes consumption and exchange. So Marx begins to unpack this base, which before had been taken together as a simple, single combinatory. Now it consists of relations which are not only not the same but importantly different. If the relations of exchange, of production, and of consumption are not the same, and yet they function together as a whole, it cannot be a simple formation in which each relation corresponds to the other. Consequently, we require a different way of conceptualising how this combination works. Since the relations are different, the approach must look not so much at correspondences but at differences. It must then ask how and under what circumstances different relations constitute a whole functioning system.

Relations of identity do exist, but increasingly for Marx they have much less explanatory power than the relations of difference, which give you an awareness of the different tempos and conditions of existence of the various relations which make up the economic. That is to say, if the base consists of relations of production, consumption, and exchange, each has its own conditions of existence. There can be crucial breaks in any one of them and each can lead to a breakdown in the functioning of the capitalist system. For example, conditions in which labour refuses to work or erects barriers to the exploitation of its labour power rupture the productive system. But when demand falls below the level at which people are able to take up what has been produced, there is a crisis of consumption or low demand, not a crisis of overproduction. Consequently, you can differentiate these relations from one another. When you look at capitalism, all these different processes are functioning together, not because they are the same, but because they are different and because they are articulated together. This suggests a radically different conception of how things fit together into a unified structure from the notion of an expressive totality found in Marx's earlier formulations. This is a structural totality in which the different bits are unevenly, even contradictorily, related to one another. It is a totality in which each of the different practices has its own given level of determinateness. Thus, Marx has to think their unity or totality in terms of how one relation is articulated to another.

Marx observes that theory is not simply given in the nature of the facts at which you are looking. Theory is an operation on the facts, on the evidence. By necessity, one has to break into the evidence through the formation of concepts. Observation, theorising, and abstraction are inseparable. Similarly, theory is never totally devoid of reference to the real world. Far from it. In my opinion, Marx does not support the Althusserian notion of a theoretical practice which depends only on the logical coherence of its own internal formulations and which bears no relation to its power in explaining particular historical developments. But neither does Marx support the notion that theory is simply an act of generalising out of evidence that you already know. What he says is that, in the first instance, any set of historical events presents itself to us as a mask of complex, unordered, and contradictory phenomenal forms or events. One has to break into them with the necessary abstractions. One has to cut into the thick texture of social life and historical experience with clearly formulated concepts and abstractions. The end result is what he calls the production of "the concrete in thought" (Marx 1973, 101). That is to say, the ability to grasp the real relations in concrete historical instances depends upon the production and mediation of theory. Historical understanding always involves a detour through theory; it involves moving from the empirical to the abstraction and then returning to the concrete. The closer you come to reproducing the concreteness of an historical epoch the more levels of determination you have to take into account.

Let me give an example. No statement functions at a higher level of abstraction than that which equates the mode of production with the relations between the social relations of production and the forces of production. But depending on the question you are asking, it may be an absolutely necessary level of abstraction. If you are inquiring into the difference between the feudal epoch and the capitalist epoch, it offers a useful level of abstraction; it says something important about what distinguishes them. Are they the only terms which are relevant to the analysis of particular feudal societies? Of course not. There is much more that you need to know before you can talk about any feudal society or before you can talk about phases in feudalism. That is to say, this level of abstraction has a time dimension. So also the capitalist mode of production, as a level of abstraction, relates to a particular time—from the appearance of early capitalist agrarian relations right up to the present. If you want to know about the capitalist epoch, the mode of production is the first common abstraction which will tell you something of that epoch and the way in which labour and capital are related in the appropriation of nature throughout the whole of that period. If you want to know something about the capitalist mode of production in agrarian society in Britain in the seventeenth and eighteenth centuries, you have to add other levels of determination. In part, you have to add more levels of determination simply at the organisation of the economic. But of course there is no economic mode of production that exists outside of political, ideological, and legal relations, and until you have added those levels of determinacy to your analysis, you are unable to talk about any particular society at any particular moment.

Some of the greatest problems in Marxist analysis have resulted from misunderstanding the level at which the abstractions are working. If you want to explain why there was an economic recession the day before yesterday, there is no point in trying to read it off an abstraction that tells you something about the capitalist mode of production from its first appearance to its last. It is simply an abstraction operating at too high a level. It does not have a sufficient level of determinacy in it to generate explanatory propositions about particular societies. Indeed it can't tell you anything at all about particular social formations. In fact, however, much of Marx's work is precisely trying to analyse the capitalist mode of production. He understands that the task requires him to abstract that particular concept from all the others. He has to virtually ignore everything else, all the other real determinations, while he is unpacking that particular abstraction. *Capital* actually contains a number of different discourses operating at different levels of abstraction. The highest level of abstraction, which is simply that of the commodity form, occurs in the first chapters of volume 1 (Marx 1977). Who has ever seen a commodity form running around doing something to an economy? It describes what Marx calls the "cell form of the economy." Compare that level of abstraction with the analysis at the end of *Capital* in which Marx talks about the Factory Acts of the 1840s. The latter is not at the same level of abstraction; you simply cannot make the same kinds of statements about both. Similarly, the discussion in volume 2 (Marx 1978a), which describes capitalism in terms of the abstract relations of production, consumption, and exchange in different economic forms, is operating at a very different level than the more historical and therefore more determinate discourses of Marx when he's talking about particular societies at particular periods.

The fact that these levels of abstraction are not clearly marked off from one another in Marx's own work does not absolve us of the responsibility of recognising them. If we fail to recognise them, we create almost insurmountable problems for Marxism, both theoretically and politically. It is here that we would locate questions of the complex organisation of power and determination in the social formation. If you want to define the capitalist mode of production, you describe the relationship between capital and labour, and you describe what capital does: It possesses the means of production; it locates labour in the free market; and it exploits labour power. That is all; there is nothing else. Whether the capitalist is tall or short, brown or white, Chinese or American, is of no consequence whatsoever. However, the moment you want to talk about the formation of the particular capitalist class in Britain and the particular ways in which that class has evolved historically, then you have to say something about its emergence out of other social and class formations. You have to talk about its history, about how it separated and identified itself. You have to ask how the early forms of market exchange began, and so on. As you lower the level of abstraction, you come closer to the details of particular concrete historical formations, and you have to bring other determinations into your discourse in order to make sense of what you are talking about. Consequently, when Marx says that the wage is paid back to the labourer for the reproduction of labour power at the culturally defined, customary level, he is operating at the highest level of abstraction and he is not concerned with analysing what the customary level is. But if you ask yourself about the nature of the social reproduction of labour power in any particular historical formation, how could you describe it without analysing the question of the family? For after all, the family has long been precisely the site at which relations of production are culturally and socially reproduced. Similarly, if you are talking about labour at the level of the capitalist mode of production, it does not matter whether labour is black, brown, yellow, red, or white, or whether it is highly advanced or not. You are simply asking about the absolutely basic functions which labour performs inside the capitalist mode. But the moment you ask what is the difference between the way in which a particular labour force is constituted in the United Kingdom and in South Africa, how can you describe that without talking about forced and unforced labour, or about the way in which the exploitation of labour depends on the differences marked by race and ethnicity within the different sections of the labour force? You can't do it. This suggests that at least some of the so-called silences in Marx's discourse are the result of the relevant level of abstraction rather than from the fact that he thinks these other determinations are insignificant. What I am saying is that it is important to remember that Marx's object of analysis is capitalism as a mode of production at a very high level of abstraction. It is not the only level at which he talks about it, but it is overwhelmingly the level at which his abstractions operate. At that level, he is constantly tempted to bracket other kinds of determinations, which are crucially important to understanding actual societies in real historical periods.

I do not mean to suggest that all of the problems with Marx's theorisations of capitalism result from misunderstanding the relevant level of abstraction. For it is the case that the model is largely predicated on one route by which capitalism has emerged and developed—that of the United Kingdom. Consequently, it does not take any account of the very different ways in which capitalism has been introduced, for example, by conquest and colonisation. If you understand labour only in the forms in which free labour was gradually generated in the British context, you do not understand the different forms in which the nets of capitalist relationships were expanded and extended on a global scale. In these latter contexts, it is often not the case that capitalism has tended to erode what Marx calls the particular local differences within labour. Far from it. The tendency in those social formations has been to use, develop, and build on those precapitalist differences and to maintain them as the way in which capitalism has actually exploited indigenous labour, indigenous social formations, and their material resources.

Capital is not a historical work; it is an analytic work. There isn't a history to match it, but if there were, Marx would write more like he writes in those sections which describe particular events. That is why he says that one must take care not to think that the relations he has been describing simply appear in a lucid way, one form dissolving into another, like a marvelously self-sustaining system. Instead he acknowledges that the relations he has described have been written in the actual history of real social formations, of actual people, in letters of blood and fire. Marx understood that, understood that capitalism actually emerged in Britain as the result of gigantic historical upheaval and exploitation. But it is also possible, and perhaps even necessary analytically, to describe that development at a high level of abstraction in very simple terms, in terms which do not richly capture the exploitative relations which capitalism eventually or inevitably involves. This does not mean that as we push Marx's concepts more and more towards concrete social formations, all we need to do is incorporate the determinations he has left out, such as race, ethnicity, and gender, leaving the concept of the mode of production untouched. Nor did Marx intend to leave the analysis of real social formations to somebody else. In fact, one of the best examples of how that kind of analysis would be done is precisely *The Eighteenth Brumaire*.

The Eighteenth Brumaire is an analysis of what happened between 1848 and 1851 in France. The moment Marx starts to operate on the terrain of such concrete events, he uses a different terminology from that of either *Capital* or *The German Ideology*. At the two different levels of abstraction, there are two quite different languages about class and politics. At the level of the specific conjuncture, all kinds of social and political forces come into play that could not conceivably appear at the level of the mode of production, and which have no precise class location: the army, priests, officials, lawyers, writers, and journalists. Newspapers in *The Eighteenth Brumaire* are almost hypostatised as real people, as political forces. But even the classes themselves are fragmented and mobile terms. Where are the two fundamental classes—capital and labour—in *The Eighteenth Brumaire*? Marx hardly talks about them. Instead, he talks about the great landowners, the industrial bourgeoisie, the financial bourgeoisie, the industrial proletariat, the peasantry, and the lumpen proletariat.

These are the real fractions, divisions, and subdivisions of classes which actually matter in a political analysis of a specific conjuncture. The capitalist class does not rule in *The Eighteenth Brumaire*. What rules is a political bloc, which consists of a fraction of the capitalist class and fractions of other classes organised under it. The language of politics in *The Eighteenth Brumaire* is never a language of whole classes ruling over other whole classes.

Unlike the vision of *The Communist Manifesto*, *The Eighteenth Brumaire* is a story of the defeat and increasing marginalisation of the proletariat. But the relationships between classes and political parties are no longer simple. There are diverse political parties and positions—the Constituent National Assembly, the Legislative Assembly, moves towards popular democracy, towards republicanism, and towards monarchy— and each has its own complex relations to the different class fractions. The bourgeoisie is crucially divided between one fraction that thinks it can rule most effectively through monarchy and another that favors republicanism. And the proletariat never appears on its own politically in *The Eighteenth Brumaire*. It never totally abandons its reformism, its links with other classes. It never takes its place as *the* historical class. It is constantly making alliances with fractions of the bourgeoisie—first with the financial bourgeoisie who at least believe in elections, and then with the other side. Finally, the proletariat is the only thing which ends the warfare between the different fractions of the bourgeoisie and unites them. It is against the proletariat that the bourgeoisie forms a party of order built around a language of family, law, order, and property. And it is the proletariat that gets constructed as the other, as a party of anarchy, of socialism, communism, republicanism, and democracy. Here is the construction of a political terrain, built upon particular ideologies and forms of symbolism. Thus the relationship between classes and political organisations cannot be described at the level of the determinacy of the mode of production; it requires a quite different kind of analysis. You have to analyse the meaning of Monarchy and of the Republic in France. You have to describe the traditions that sustained the different political regimes. You have to understand how different political parties constructed different ideologies and different sets of slogans. You simply cannot analyse a concrete historical conjuncture—which is what most of us are trying to do most of the time—at that level of political complexity without addressing all of these questions and more.

Nevertheless, one can still ask how the mode of production can be reinserted into this history since that is what gives determinacy to everything; that is what moves the superstructures. Let me try to schematise how it is Marx reintroduces the mode of production into *The Eighteenth Brumaire*. The first thing to note is that there was no single mode of production in France; rather, the mode of production was a combination of two modes of production: one, capitalism, becoming dominant; the other, a peasant economy, declining. Does this mode of production tell you the form in which the politics of the bourgeoisie will appear? No, it cannot specify the political, and Marx doesn't try to make it do so. The determination is extremely weak, extremely distant. We can only say it establishes certain limits within which the political relates to the economic, that it sets limits and opens possibilities, possible forms, including some that were not tried during that time. Other than that, the determinacy cannot be cashed in at this level.

But if we turn to the question of how the struggle for power during this period was resolved, we can see even more clearly the distance between abstract notions of the mode of production and concrete historical analysis. Marx argues that with the failure of all the classes (fractions and alliances) to achieve stable rule, the French capitalist mode of production is represented politically by Napoleon. This is obviously a different and rather scandalous view of determination and representation. The classes, the great historical forces, have been replaced by a single figure: Napoleon Bonaparte. Perhaps he represents capitalism indirectly, because he represents the bourgeoisie; perhaps he was born there or holds their ideas or shares their interests. But Marx asserts that such questions have nothing to do with it and cannot answer the question of what class forces Napoleon represents. Instead, he represents the peasantry because it was there he found a political base after the bourgeoisie continued to oppose his seizing universal political power. Although the peasantry in France belong to an old mode of production and can't advance into the nineteenth century on the basis of the peasant mode of production, they are willing to support Napoleon because they "like Napoleon's ideas." But how does he represent capitalism without bringing the bourgeoisie into play? He develops the State, which is nothing but a refraction of the relations of production. Yet the State is independent of the different classes. It is the State itself which advances the development of the capitalist mode of production, not by representing the interests of any single class but precisely by functioning in an openly independent way. It is during this period that the French State gains a kind of power with which it has continued to operate; it is here that the legacy of French State capitalist planning begins, and this legacy has meant that French capitalism operates differently, with modes and mechanisms different than those that describe capitalism elsewhere.

There is a relationship here between base and superstructure, between classes and the emergence of new structures of political power, but the analysis is radically different from an attempt to apply the classical base-superstructure model in a straightforward way. The model that Marx actually employs does have a place for social contradictions other than those which arise from the contradiction between capital and labour. The analysis is built, centrally, upon references to social movements, social groupings, alliances, and blocs which do not have a clear class character, although it is clear that the intrinsic language of the analysis remains decidedly materialist. *The Eighteenth Brumaire*, then, offers an alternative to the classical base-superstructure metaphor without giving up the ground that the metaphor has won.

Marxist Structuralism

In this lecture I want to consider Marxist structuralism, or more specifically, the Althusserian break. It is such an important moment in the development of theorising in Cultural Studies that we have to recover it and reflect on it in some detail. It represents a very substantial break in the paradigms which are being used, though its consequences are more contradictory than that might suggest. My intention is not to provide a complete reading of Althusser's work but to relate some of his more important positions to the line of continuous theorising which I have been sketching out here. Thus, the reading of Althusser will be defined by my own preoccupations and biases.

I want to begin by suggesting something about his general project in relation to the paradigms and problematics of Cultural Studies which I've already talked about. Althusser's status as an important theorist emerges at the point at which non-Marxist structuralism begins to intersect and overlap, not only with classical Marxist propositions, but with some of the problems I have alluded to in classical Marxist theorising. From my point of view, Althusser picks up on a whole range of structuralist theorising outside of Marxism and uses many of its advances, conceptualisations, and formulations to rethink a number of problems within the Marxist tradition: the effectivity of the superstructures, the problems with the base-superstructure metaphor, and the problems of economic and class reductionism. He brings these two different strands of thinking into a generative but unstable synthesis.

He accomplishes this, in part, by attempting to show that Marx himself was a structuralist and this is one of the places which I would certainly part company from Althusser. It is certainly true, as I suggested earlier, that much of what Althusser attributes to Marx's work and style of thinking is indeed structuralist in the sense in which Althusser wants to call them that. However, it seems to me a result, not necessarily of theoretical advances alone, but of political advances as well, that Marx's thinking begins to develop in ways that push him in the direction of the structuralist problematic. It is also true, as I said in the discussion of *The Eighteenth Brumaire* (Marx 1978b), that many of those advances are in no sense fully clarified or theorised. Therefore, it seems to me that there is something questionable about Althusser's insistence on reconstructing so thoroughly the selective tradition of Marxism and giving the Marxist imprimatur only to a part of the Marxist corpus, that part which, with substantial argument, can be shown to have similarities with the tradition of non-Marxist structuralism. I refer to this because it defines the fervor with which Althusser goes about punctuating Marx's work into two periods. The theory of the epistemological break is required to enable Althusser to separate those parts of Marx's work that are truly structuralist from those parts that are not. In the arguments which distinguish between a Hegelian and a post-Hegelian, or a humanist and an antihumanist Marx, what is really at stake is Althusser's distinction between a prestructuralist and a structuralist Marx.

My reading of Althusser will then focus on some of the major points that he advances in order to assess whether and in what sense it can be grounded in Marx's work, and to what extent it involves the introduction of new modes of thinking which ought to be recognised as such. This is not an exercise in defending the purism of Marxism but of attempting to clearly identify where the theoretical strands and influences in Cultural Studies are coming from. As I have already argued, the classical Marxist formulations of base and superstructure have failed to provide convincing and adequate theorisations and, consequently, people have had to go outside of the Marxist problematic in order to develop alternative concepts. Whether or not they then chose to return to Marxist ground is neither here nor there. The fact that they have gone outside is important. That theoretical conflation of different traditions has real and continuing theoretical effects which you can feel in the discourses that follow. We also have to recognise there are lines of thinking which reflect the continuity and persistence of non-Marxist structuralism as an intellectual tradition in its own right. I think it is quite wrong, for example, to see Foucault's work as having been generated principally out of an argument with Marxism. Although he does carry on such an argument, his own line of thinking has very clear roots in forms of French intellectual theorising and in actual research projects on, for example, the history of science, that have their own lines of continuity.

The importance of these reflections is that they transpose the form of the argument with structural Marxism so that it is no longer a question of whether a particular text is "the true Marx" and can thus be allowed into the canon. Such attempts to retrospectively seal the tradition and to stitch particular texts and positions into it often put the writer in particularly awkward positions. Poulantzas (1973), for example, in *Political Power and Social Classes*, seeks to advance the most heretical of propositions in the most orthodox of modes, appealing to a nonexistent agreement about "what the Marxist tradition says." I do not think it helps to cover the tracks of what is actually going on intellectually by saying that it is all already there in Marx and disguising real theoretical work as explication de texte. I think this is how Althusser began to use Marx in *Reading Capital* (Althusser and Balibar 1970), which is not my favorite work of his, and how Poulantzas and many others have used Marx since. Rather, we need to see their work as an effort at theoretical and conceptual clarification.

The purpose of Althusser's project is, in part, to use the concepts of pre-Marxist structuralism to retheorise the practical structuralism of Marx. There is a further extension of that project which becomes evident only in his reading of *Capital* (Marx 1977), namely, to produce the structuralist Marx. It is this additional move, which takes the "structuralising" of Marx beyond anything in Marx, which I will call the "hardening up" of the structuralism of Marx. I have already discussed some of the ways in which structuralist conceptualisations and terminology are used by Althusser to clarify what he thinks is the implicit structuralism of Marx, which operates, as he says, at the practical but not the theoretical level. One is the project of thinking the difference between modes of production by conceptualising each mode as a structuralist combinatory. That is to say, you have the elements of a mode of production and the different rules of combination through which the forces and relations of production are combined, for example, either in feudalism or capitalism. With this notion, you get a kind of useful, though highly reductive, abstract formula which allows you to begin to think theoretically the difference between one mode of production and another. I want to examine some of the fruitful sites of Althusser's rethinking of Marx, but also, to point out where he goes too far and, in his fervor, eliminates many of Marx's important and complex insights. I will focus my comments on three broad areas: the problem of the subject, the nature of the social formation, and the theory of determination. I will postpone a discussion of Althusser's theory of ideology until the next lecture.

One of the most controversial, but also one of the most important, and I think justified, concepts with which Althusser rereads Marx is the "decentering of the subject." As I have argued above, Marx offered many formulations of the relationship between subjects and history in his efforts to arrive at the notion that, although it may be said that men and women make history, they do not do so under conditions of their own choosing. They are always placed and located in social relations whether they will it or not. Thus, from a very early stage in his writings, Marx insists on the decentering of the subject. Whether his polemic is aimed at philosophical or anthropological humanism, the move away from notions of a fully transitive historical agent is central to Marx in any period. The position that "men and women make history" or "men and women make the world through their practice" is foregrounded in particular texts—for example, in *The German Ideology* (Marx and Engels 1970)—but that emphasis is always secondary to the larger project of displacing the subject. And that way of thinking bears striking similarities to, and has some of the same effects as, some structuralist concepts and modes of thinking. It parallels Lévi-Strauss's dethronement of "men" and makes the principal objects of Marx's analysis relations and structures rather than the agents or subjects of them. That is to say, one of the achievements of *Reading Capital* is to have recognised that one can think of the social relations and modes of production as processes without a subject (a scandalous proposition if you think about it for a moment), and this is grounded, not only in non-Marxist structuralism, but also in Marx's own work. Althusser generates the concepts necessary to formulate the argument with terms drawn from the structuralist vocabulary. Thus, when Althusser speaks of classes as agents which are nothing but the bearers and supports of social relations, it is substantially no different than Marx's claim that classes are positioned by the relations of production in which they are located. Althusser has theorised, through a series of homologies with structuralist positions, the relationship between agency and structure. Marx's practical decentering of the subject is presented as analogous to the linguistic proposition that the speaker is positioned by the rules of language, or Lévi-Strauss's claim that the mythmaker is located by the discourses of the myth.

It is certainly true that that is the most common way that *Capital* speaks about the relationships between capital and labour, or between the capitalist class and the working class. *Capital* could not have been written as it was without that insistence on the determinant nature of human praxis. Although human practices may sustain the social structures, they are situated and constrained by them and, moreover, the relations at the structural level can themselves become the object of scientific analysis. However, it is also true, as I have suggested, that one has to understand the analysis in *Capital* as an abstraction at a particular, very high level of abstraction. One of the effects of Althusser's use of structuralist concepts, not only to rethink formulations in Marx and then to distinguish between the structuralist and nonstructuralist elements, is that it privileges that level of abstraction, which is more easily conflated with the level at which non-Marxist structuralism works.

Let me remind you of an example I have already used to point to the problems that arise if one fails to recognise the different levels of abstraction in *Capital*. As a theoretical contribution, *Capital* works most of the time by the analysis of what Marx calls the laws and tendencies of the structures of the capitalist mode, rather than in terms of the identification of particular classes. When Marx is talking at this level of abstraction, he identifies the contradiction of the mode of production with the objective contradiction between the forces and relations of production. But when he talks about the contradiction of class, he concretises it in terms of the contradiction between capital and labour. Those two contradictions are not superimposable. The contradiction between the forces and rela-tions of production, which has to do with the objective possibilities of a particular mode of production for being organised socially in different ways, has, of course, class connotations. But it cannot be reduced into the contradictions between capital and labour; least of all can it be re-duced simply to the politics of the struggle between the capitalist class and the working class. Those are in fact three different levels of abstrac-tion within which Marx describes the contradiction of a social forma-tion. They have a relationship to one another; they are as it were grafted on and over one another. But they are not reducible to one another; they cannot be equated in any simple way. You might say that the political and economic conflicts between different classes are the ways the contradic-tion between the forces and relations of production is enacted and finally resolved.

One of the consequences of the particular way in which Althusser at-tempts to structuralise Marx is to give an absolute privilege to that highest level of abstraction. That is the level which most corresponds to the level of abstraction at which structuralism is able to reduce the diachronic complexities of a particular cultural and social formation to a simple combinatory or an expression of a deep structure. But abstraction at that level is not adequate to analyse either complex social formations of a specific kind or particular political or historical epochs and moments, for now we are dealing with levels that have not been entirely generated by the relationship between the forces and relations of production. Even in *Capital* itself, when the dominant discourse—operating at the high-est level of abstraction—focuses on a more specific historical account, it moves to other levels of abstraction. You find reference, not only to classes, but to class fractions. You find a different kind of account of how modes of production are generated and transformed in which a greater weight is given to elements which had been bracketed out at the level of modes of production.

For instance, Marx gives two accounts of exactly the same thing, though at different levels of abstraction. In one account, he writes about the shift in the capitalist mode of production from absolute to relative surplus value; in a second account, he writes about the Factory Acts as an example of an historical moment which began to set limits on the extent to which labour could be exploited. The Factory Acts represent a double achievement: On the one hand, by putting a limit on certain tendencies of capitalism, they constituted a real gain for men and women in the labour movement; on the other hand, paradoxically, they generated the necessity for capital to move from absolute surplus value and find alternative sources of relative surplus value. While the first account, operating at the highest level of abstraction, requires a formal bifurcation within the rules of how capital creates surplus value, and hence in the very form of surplus value itself, the second account, at a much lower level of abstraction, requires an analysis of the historical process by which the transition between the two forms of surplus value actually come to pass in the British social formation. This account of exactly the same process requires references to levels of determination, political organisation, and groups that cut across class lines (e.g., the fact that the factory proletariat is supported by elements of the bourgeoisie and, indeed, elements of the paternalistic aristocracy), and so on.

If we return now to the question of the subject, we can see how some of the apparent ambiguities in Marx's position, what Althusser would like to reject as the prestructuralist elements in Marx, are the result of different accounts operating at different levels of abstraction. Clearly, at the higher levels, Marx is working more with the notion of men and women as bearers of relations; but at the lower, more concrete levels, he works more with the notion of men and women as making their own history. But this second notion does not return us to the humanist subject, for in no sense does this second notion conceive of human beings as agents who can see through to the end of their practices. Remember that the successes of the labour movement in constraining the absolute exploitation of labour time also had the unintended consequence of shifting capitalism into another phase built upon strategies of the relative appropriation of surplus value. That cannot be what factory reform intended. So at no level in Marx is there a notion of human agency which is indeterminate, in which people are the authors of the results and effects of their own practices. But there is in Marx's discourse a great deal of difference—depending on the level of abstraction at which it operates—as to whether the notion of the subject as the bearer of relations, in the fully structuralist sense, is appropriate.

The second major area in which Althusser has significantly rethought Marx's conceptual framework is the question of the nature of the social formation, both temporally and spatially. I will begin by discussing Althusser's antihistoricism, which raises important and long-standing questions about evolutionary modes of thinking in Marx, about the historicist Marx, and about the question of the influence of Hegelianism on Marx's early, middle, and later thought. Certainly Althusser is quite correct to point to the essentially synchronic—rather than diachronic or processual—mode of analysis and emphasis in Marx's more mature work and especially in *Capital* (although again, I would point out that it is not the only discourse in *Capital*). *Capital* is not concerned with the long genetic sequences of history but with how one may conceptually interrupt or punctuate those long evolutionary trails and identify particular phases or conjunctures. No matter what the level of abstraction in Marx, there is always that interest in the discontinuities, or what Althusser calls "the breaks." Althusser correctly sees this emphasis in opposition to a particular way of conceptualising the social totality. In objecting to the notion of an expressive totality which can be found in both E. P. Thompson and Raymond Williams, Althusser offers a conception of the totality as a necessarily and irreducibly complex structure. Rather than a formation composed of identities and correspondences, Althusser argues that Marx is always concerned to bring forward the differences and specificities that fracture any attempt to make totality into a simple coherent whole. Rather than the reductive historicist totality, which begins with either the philosophical abstraction "Man" or the historicist affirmation of men and women in their practice, we have instead a sense of the social totality as an inevitably and complexly structured whole, irreducible to either humanism or historicism.

While I think that Althusser is correct, his emphasis is, once again, too single-minded and one-sided. Although Marx insists that he is writing about the laws and tendencies of a capitalist mode of production, that does not relieve Marxists of the responsibility to recognise that capitalism is not an internal organisation of economic life, that it is constantly subject to change, and that particular modes of production depend on their specific historical conditions. By attending only to the emphasis in *Capital*, and remaining always at the highest level of abstraction, Althusser— and even more forcefully, many of his followers—convert a legitimate antihistoricism in Marx's work into an antihistorical position, as if one could proceed without the notion of histories at all. But this certainly cannot be reconciled with Marx's problematic.

A second structuralist idea which Althusser uses to rethink Marx's notion of the social formation is that of "levels," which attempts to displace relationships experienced historically and processually into a spatial model. Thus language itself is understandable only if we think of it operating simultaneously at two levels: the level of phenomenal appearances, or the actual speech acts which people produce; and the level of the formal structure from which the infinite variety of possible speech acts is generated. Althusser takes the model even further by elaborating a number of levels within the social formation: the economic, the political, the ideological, and the theoretical. Again, I want to begin by pointing to the value of this way of theorising what I take to be the untheorised assumptions of Marx's analyses. One can separate the particular way Althusser uses the notion of levels and the particular levels he identifies from the important project of trying to differentiate different forms of practices by identifying their objects. For example, we can observe that the specificity of political practices depends on the fact that its object is principally the condensation of power into the State. Although it doesn't follow that political practices are totally different from all other practices, their specific object does differentiate them from ideological practices— whose objects are clearly systems of representation. It is of course true that there are no political practices which are outside of the ideological, just as there are no ideological practices which are outside of the political (and the economic for that matter). Similarly, we can say that economic practices have to do with the transformation of material things, with the operation of labour on material objects, which might themselves be the products of material labour. This does not mean that such a description exhausts what we can say about the economic, because, as I have said before, production is by no means the only category necessary for analysing economic relations. At the very least, production leaves out the relations of consumption and exchange, but now we can also add that economic practices do not exist outside of the political and the ideological. This complexity of relations does not obviate the necessity to distinguish analytically between practices which foreground and attempt to transform different objects in specific ways.

There has been a real advance accomplished by differentiating the specificity of different types of practices based on Althusser's borrowing the notion of levels from structuralist thinking and applying it, correctly I think, to Marx's work. On this basis, we can describe *The Eighteenth Brumaire* as an account of a particular set of historical events, which while recognising their economic and ideological determinations, is principally focused on the political. That is why the discourse inserts the mode of production in the way that I suggested earlier. Of course, the analysis could have been written differently. You could give an account which foregrounds an analysis of the capitalist mode of production in France, which would not be particularly concerned with Napoleon's ideas, although it would obviously understand that those were one of the conditions of existence of the mode of production at that particular moment. Nor would it be concerned with the variety of political regimes which appeared during that period in France, although again it would understand that these too were one of its conditions of existence. Each of the conditions has its own specific effect, but in a more general sense than is suggested by Althusser's notion of levels. Different discourses would foreground the political, the economical, the ideological, or the mode of production—which I want to distinguish from the economic. Thus, the notion of levels is useful to understand the way different texts and discourses are located or directed. I would add, however, that I don't support the actual lines of division Althusser draws. I think that there are complex differences within and between the levels of practices that cannot be squeezed into Althusser's four levels.

The final major site at which Althusser significantly contributes to retheorising Marxism is the problem of determination and, in particular, the attempt to develop nonreductionist ways of thinking about determinacy. The problem has been widely recognised, as I have suggested before. There is here a real inadequacy in the inheritance of Marxist theorising, and in Marx himself. This does not diminish his importance as a theorist, which does not depend on whether he is right at every point. Engels's letters (Marx and Engels 1934) point to and acknowledge this as a genuine site of difficulty in Marx's work, although as Althusser correctly suggests, he does not succeed in finding an alternative way, one which does not fall back into forms of economic reductionism in theorising the relations between the base and the superstructure, or the relations between different practices within the social formation. Althusser's work on this problem not only demonstrates inadequacies of the formulations we have in the tradition, but actually offers new ways of thinking embodied within the concepts of "overdetermination" and "relative autonomy." The first of these concepts is overdetermination, which appears in both *For Marx* (Althusser 1970) and in *Reading Capital*, although it appears in a much more systematic way in "Ideology and Ideological State Apparatuses" (Althusser 1971b) and in "Freud and Lacan" (Althusser 1971a). It is borrowed from Freud as well as from linguists such as Jakobsen, who had already appropriated the Freudian notion into the analysis of language. The concept of overdetermination operates within a set of concepts, including condensation and displacement, which figure prominently in Freud's (1938) *Interpretation of Dreams*. There Freud argued that an idea, a symptom, or a dream symbol can itself be the condensation of a set of different chains of meaning, which are not manifest in the way in which the symbol is given. It can be the displaced representation of a set of forces which is invested in the symbol in a way which is different from their investment within the discourses to which it apparently refers. Therefore, if one finds a recurrent symbol in a dream, the analyst cannot look for a single unconscious formation or process as the meaning or referent of the symbol. One has to conceive of it as overdetermined; that is, the same symbol can be determined at different levels, by different kinds of discourses.

Of course, given Althusser's need to define the true Marx as the structuralist Marx, he has to locate these ideas in the Marxist corpus; he has to suture or stitch the concept into the tradition. So he points to Lenin's account of the 1917 Revolution, which denies that it is nothing but the pure expression of a contradiction of the mode of production. It was also determined by the fact that the troops at the front couldn't get any shoes and that the whole structure of Russian society was collapsing. Thus, the revolution occurred partly as the result of the deepest structural movement and partly as a result of apparently contingent factors. In fact, Lenin concludes, great historical ruptures are usually the condensation of those two levels of determination. Althusser also finds legitimacy in Mao's distinction between the principal contradiction and secondary contradictions, which makes particular historical events the condensation of different contradictions. Finally, Althusser appeals to a long series of arguments in both Marx and Lenin about the relationships between the political and the economic. This is the argument which Mao resurrects when he talks about the ways in which, in a particular social formation, at a particular political or historical phase, practices other than those directly attributable to the mode of production can take command. This allows him to argue that the transformation of Chinese society may take place precisely through politics rather than economics taking command. This is the concept that Althusser claims to be recasting into structuralist terms such as displacement: the insight that the economic might work through and be represented in events which assume a political or ideological manifestation.

The second concept, closely related to overdetermination, which Althusser introduces is the relative autonomy of different practices, which has proven to be the site of major debates and contestation. The obvious critique of relative autonomy is that, in the end, it is so vague about the relations between different practices as to offer little theoretical assistance. But if one considers it carefully, it is actually addressing the question of the specificity of particular practices, events, or contradictions. It says, first, that the real content of a practice is not given by some economic realm outside of the practice. The practice is not simply an empty form whose truth is guaranteed by the appearance or representation of a content which is really elsewhere, in the economic. That is the force of *autonomy*. But why *relative*? Why not simply *autonomous*? The force of *relative* is to deny that such practices could be analysed as if they were outside the structuring effect of the social relations of production. They are not outside the structure and effect of social relations, although each practice has its own specificity. Of what does that specificity consist? In part, it consists of the fact that every practice has its own specific forms and its own relations to other practices and to institutional sites which appertain to it. But more important, its specificity is defined by the fact that it has real effects on the reproduction or the nonreproduction of a particular mode of production. Those effects are neither given nor guaranteed by its reduction to the mode of production. Thus, the specificity of any practice, its specific effectivity, is not outside the way in which the social formation implicates and is organised by its economic life; but the contents, the temporalities, the transformations, and, indeed, the very existence of the practice cannot be read off of or simply derived from the economic. In this form, the concept of relative autonomy is an attempt to break with the notion of reductivism without denying the structuring effect of overdetermination. On the one hand, it affirms real specificity. It uses the term "autonomy" because it wants to say that the practices or events one is analysing have real effects, which cannot be reduced to the effects ascribed to them by the mode of production. On the other hand, it is a way of thinking about the relationship between specific practices and the reproduction of the mode of production.

Unfortunately, Althusser's elaboration of this concept and, specifically, his conceptualisation of the last question hardens the structuralist lines once again, for he affirms that, in the end, the content of all practices, events, and contradictions guarantees their functional correspondence to the mode of production. Ultimately, everything that happens is not only an expression at some other level of the forces and relations of production, but it corresponds to it in the sense that it will, by definition, guarantee its effective reproduction. Thus, in "Ideology and Ideological State Apparatuses," while he denies that ideology is a simple reflection of the mode of production, he ascribes to it a particular function for the mode of production, namely to reproduce the social relations of production. Then, since he wants to think the process in terms of "determination in the last instance by the (economic)" (Althusser 1970, 111), ideology, after a sort of period of free relative autonomy wandering about, must be stitched, or recuperated, back in the last instance to the mode of production. Thus, in the end, his account of ideology is functionalist. He simply gives the different levels of practice and different kinds of contradictions the ability to exist independently of the base and to have their effects, while asserting that, in the end, all they can do is to guarantee that the capitalist mode of production effectively reproduces itself.

I have never understood why that second move into functionalism is inevitable or why it is intrinsic to the concept of relative autonomy. One can think of the resolution of particular contradictions, at whatever level, the results of which cannot be predicated to and derived from the mode of production but are rather well outside of it. They may have conditions of existence that cannot be made to correspond in any direct way to the mode of production. Political resolutions, for example, might set limits on the mode of production. Marx's analysis of the Factory

Acts is precisely an example of such an historical event, an event where classes—and in this case not the dominant one—use ideas and practices of reform to impose limits on a particular tendency in the mode of production. Those limits, it is worth pointing out, worked against the ways in which capital and capitalists ideologically understood their interests. Consequently, they resisted it, often to the death. The fact that the limit had the structural effect of displacing the mode of production from one set of processes to another—outside the activity and intelligibility of the actors in the situation—was itself an effect of the way in which that political struggle was resolved. But it was not a matter of agency or even of intelligibility. It was an effect of the structure which had the consequence of shifting the rhythms and changing the mechanisms of a capitalist mode of production. And there are other instances available in Marxism: for instance, in Engels's discussion of the importance of the different systems of law and their articulation to capitalist modes of production. He contrasts cases like France, where a particular kind of legal system was effective for the ongoing reproduction and development of a mode of production, with cases like Germany, where it was not.

Consequently, I do not believe that relative autonomy needs to be recuperated back to determination in the last instance by the economy, either in some directly transitive sense—in the way in which the economy finally is the only principle of articulation and resolution—or in the more general sense that all practices always, inevitably, and positively function in relation to the capacity of a mode of production to reproduce itself. I prefer to hold on to the notion of relative autonomy as an important if not secure theoretical advance in Althusser's work, an extremely weak but useful conceptualisation. At the moment I'm not disposed to give it up, though I know the logical and theoretical critique to which it has been exposed. The problems which Althusser encounters in "Ideology and Ideological State Apparatuses" are a result of this unquestioned functionalism, where ideology is always effective for and recuperated to the dominance of the mode of production, for there is no place in which to insert contradiction—and hence its very possibility—not to mention the concrete reality of struggle, which is absent. It was in response to real protests by people who thought that they were operating at sites of contradictions, with their own ideological positions, assuming that they could have real effects, that Althusser adds a footnote on the possibility of struggle to the essays. That the notions of struggle and contradiction are absent in the original essay is one of the dangers of the term "reproduction." Whether thought in a Marxist framework or not, "reproduction" leads back to the notion of the unproblematic and uncontradictory ways in which, over time, social formations produce themselves in their basic structure and organisation again and again.

In *Reading Capital*, Althusser offers a different solution to the problem of nonreductive determinism, one which, while more theoretically cogent and internally coherent, is, I am convinced, less effective. The theory of structural causality involves the same sort of structuralist hardening up that we have seen before, only, this time, of the notion of overdetermination. The different kinds of contradictions and practices which are displayed in a rather open way in the notion of overdetermination are suddenly ascribed to their fixed levels, and those levels are given an enormous degree of absolute rather than relative autonomy. Athough they have different temporalities, different contradictions at their source, and different processes, the relationship between those practices and contradictions and the determination in the last instance by the economic is defined by the fact that the economy makes one of the levels dominant. The economic determines only by determining which of the other levels of practice shall be dominant in terms of its effectivity. Althusser has thus transposed the displacement of effects, as it is described in the notion of overdetermination—for example, from the economic to the political or the ideological—into a structural model of the hierarchical relations between different practices, following Lévi-Strauss. Determination by the economic is now only a formal operation of determining the order of the hierarchy. Yet each of the three levels—the ideological, the political, and the economic (it remains unclear whether the mode of production is inside the combinatory)—remains rather free floating, and whichever of the levels is dominant has an even greater independence, generating its own mechanisms of action and effect.

Structural causality is, admittedly, more coherent than relative autonomy. It has the elegance and simplicity of the best of structuralist explanations. But it cannot explain how the economic operates, how it manages to assign dominance to, for example, religion, or later to put religion aside and place something else in the leading position. The problems of understanding specific historical events or periods have been absorbed into the model itself. Determinacy here is purely formal—a determinacy of the model. Although again, the model makes important advances in thinking about the question of determination, it seems, by hardening its structuralist lines, to replace the problems of concrete analysis with the formal autonomy of the theoretical model. And this leads us to the question of Althusser's notion of theoretical practice.

Althusser's understanding of theory starts with the distinction between science and ideology. This distinction, which is crucial for Althusser, is generated partly in the attempt to defend the existence of a "scientific" Marx and to discover where it begins, but also partly in the attempt to clarify and oppose those modes of theorising which have produced, on the one hand, real problems in Marxism and, on the other hand, versions of Marxism which seem inadequate to Althusser. That is, theoretical practice is articulated against nonstructuralist modes of theorising. It is opposed to empiricist positions, which suggest that theory is constructed by generalising from empirically observed instances and examples; and it is opposed to historicist positions, which suggest that theory is the result of the development of the real relations of the social formation, so that different social formations produce different sets of theoretical categories. In its fully articulated form in *Reading Capital*, the distinction gives rise to the idea that there exists a specific theoretical practice, which is for all practical purposes completely autonomous.

Althusser grounds his notion of theoretical practice in Marx's methodological text, the 1857 "Introduction" to the *Grundrisse* (Marx 1973). But again, as he has done with other texts and ideas of Marx, Althusser hardens up and structuralises the model of theory which Marx offers. In the 1857 "Introduction," there is a clear outline of the importance that Marx gives to theory and, in particular, to nonempiricist modes of theorising. He refuses the notion that one can simply begin with a set of phenomena in the real world and, by observing them and distributing them into their manifest groupings, generate the theoretical categories with which to think about them. In contrast, Marx argues that if you take a slice of empirical historical reality, the different phenomena you are trying to explain represent themselves in thought in the first instance as an unholy mess. They are replete with different interpretations, definitions, historical temporalities, and so on. Althusser suggests, and I think he is correct, that Marx insists that one can only begin to theorise phenomena by breaking into this apparently seamless phenomenological web (the point from which Thompson and Williams want to take off) with concepts which are clearly formulated and which belong to a theoretical paradigm. One has to take responsibility for the concepts one is generating in relation to that empirical material. Only in that way can one break down the material into forms amenable to proper conceptualisation and theorisation. This is the notion of necessary abstraction which is, as Marx says, the only way in which the mind can operate. How else does the mind work except by developing, using, and refining concepts which are able to break into the thick empirical texture of historical reality and produce what Marx calls "the concrete in thought" (1973, 101). The concrete in thought is now not the empirical material with which you started. It is that material clarified conceptually, through the addition of more levels of determination as you become more concrete, at whatever level your discourse attempts to operate. In this admittedly crude way, Marx is trying to think the importance of theory as it is articulated onto social relations, as opposed to Hegelian modes of thought in which it is assumed that it is the conceptual categories which produce the social relations in the first place.

Althusser's notion of theoretical practice is properly attentive to the moment of theorisation and the necessity of the break from the empirical social relations which concepts generate. But the autonomy of theoretical practice means that it slides back into a position where it is the theoretical categories which generate the social relations. The question of the relationship between the conceptual system and the ongoing social realities which it sets out to explain in the first place is largely bracketed in favor of the relations among the theory's concepts. There is a sense in which the movement into the epistemological forms through which conceptualisation and theory take place takes a privileged position over their capacity to tell us anything about the social world. At that point I think it is not unfair to say that Althusser's conception of theory, like so many of his other concepts, picks up important things in Marx in the course of structurally clarifying his work, things which we did not see before, but then, by hardening up the structural conceptualisations, moves into an essentially idealist position.

This move is especially true for many of those who have used Althusser. While Althusser has significantly advanced the critique of certain common forms of theorising which fail to recognise the specificity and importance of the moment of theorisation, many have moved the argument to the point where it is the theory or the discourse which produces the real. Theories may differ as to what the mechanisms of this production are, but the point remains that it is the conceptual, theoretical, and discursive categories which produce the real; and the gap between those categories (and what they in fact produce) and actual historical existence cannot be closed. This is the epistemological position taken up by contemporary discourse theory, and I think it produces a conception of theory that is, in important ways, non-Marxist. I shall return to this in the next lecture. Of course, I am not arguing anything so absurd as that the 1857 "Introduction" gives an adequate account of the relationship between theory and the real; there are still many gaps and problems that remain untheorised within its theory of theorisation. But I am arguing that the account of theoretical practice as autonomous which is offered in *Reading Capital* has slipped the problematic of Marxism. Those advanced, new notions of theory with which Marxism certainly will have to reckon at some point may be more effective and more adequate epistemologically than anything to be found in Marx. Nevertheless, those accounts are different from what is found in Marx—both in the accounts which Marx gives of conceptualisation and in the applications of theory he undertakes.

Whatever one's relation to Marxism, it is impossible to think about culture or the debates in cultural theory outside the continuing effect of the Althusserian intervention. In that sense, most people working in the field are post-Althusserians, having had to take account of the break in the theoretical problematic which has been made. Althusser's work has changed the discourses, shifted the terminology, broken up the conceptualisations, and discovered secrets hidden away in Marxist discourse in places where people had not looked. The by now taken-for-granted objections to Hegelianism, to historicism, to empiricism, and to essentialism were first formulated by him. Regardless of whether it was truly a work of excavation and piety, of trying to find the "real" Marx, it is a genuine work of transformation. Althusser rightly argued that the historicist and humanist definitions of Marx had been a profound misrepresentation and foreshortening of Marx. He uses a range of concepts, many of them not generated within the Marxist problematic itself, to clarify certain formulations in Marx, to differentiate certain parts of Marx's discourse from others, and to transform into a more theoretically rigorous set of statements positions which may or may not have been marked, but which are certainly there in a very ambiguous, confused, and untheorised form. That is, in anybody's account, a major theoretical contribution. The concepts are often resonant and allow us to go on thinking even though we know their logical impurity. It is a break, not a break from ideology to science, but a break from "not so good thinking" to "rather better thinking."

There are, however, consequences of the Althusserian break that have been almost as negative as the above have been positive. Without denying the generative ways Althusser goes outside the Marxist problematic, takes up concepts that have been developed in another discourse, begins to apply them to the Marxist problematic and Marx's discourse, tries to understand Marx's discourse in the light of that new conceptualisation, and produces extremely positive reformulations of problematic points of Marx's work, one has to acknowledge the fact that he continuously constructs a structuralist Marx which is largely of his own production. I have repeatedly called attention to the hardening up of the structuralism which Althusser finds in a practical state in Marx. I think that is going on manifestly as one moves from the essays in *For Marx* through *Reading Capital*. Moreover, Althusser's argument works largely by creating a kind of Marxist talisman, within which theoretical disputes could be resolved by locating a position within either the "true" or the "false" Marx. It operates by the punctuation of the epistemological rupture, that is to say, by the division of Marx's work into the Hegelian and the non-Hegelian, the prestructuralist and the structuralist. More than simply being an inadequate way of reading texts, in terms of the purity of its epistemological problematics, it is an absolutely inadequate notion of theorising which denies the difficult but necessary struggle of trying to work your way between "good and bad ideas" or, more usually, between "not so good" and "rather better" and "pretty inadequate" and "sort of hopeless" ideas. By reducing theory to a question of internal conceptual coherence and textual privilege, Althusser opened the door to theoreticism which privileges a logical and epistemological rigor at the expense of the extremely difficult question of how thought is articulated to social relations. Althusserianism produced a discourse which was rigorously theoretical at the expense of almost anything else. It produced a conception of intellectual work built upon an absolute either/or. If you weren't operating with the properly clarified concepts, you were still in theoretical mystification. To look at any actual event or area before one had defined an entire theoretical apparatus was, of course, false concreteness. Either you theorised within a fully structuralist terrain or you were still operating within humanism, empiricism, and essentialism. It seemed to call into existence within the domain of theoretical practice what E. P. Thompson called "the thought police," a moment of theoretical terrorism which paradoxically opened the door to a dangerous pull back to empiricism. For those who seemed unable to think properly, there was little choice if they wanted to go on working but to retreat from the difficult questions of overdetermination and relative autonomy and to return to concrete empirical work. Some people used Foucault or Gramsci as warrants for returning to the concrete even if you could not theorise the complex and contradictory relationships.

Unfortunately, it was this particular legacy of Althusser's theoreticism and piety, the centrality of the politics of theory, that allowed Thompson (1978) to do what he did in *The Poverty of Theory*. By then, there were vast numbers of people who had struggled with Althusserianism and come through it without being engulfed by it, who would reject entirely the antitheoretical way in which Thompson tries to resurrect theory, who would object profoundly, as I do, to Thompson's attempt to deny that Althusserianism exists, that Althusser wrote, and that a real break was made. Thompson's practice is a mirror image of Althusserianism at its worst. It is the exact opposite. It uses polemic in exactly the same way: It terrifies people off a particular theoretical space. It says: If you are operating on Althusser's terrain, then you are really a Stalinist! For Thompson, Althusserianism (and its consequences) did not allow people to describe any empirical reality and in a way, this protected the theory, because if it had allowed people to engage with concrete social realities, they would have been able to see that it was false. Thompson's complete rejection led many people to revolt against Althusserianism, against the very things from which they could have learned and advanced. Had it not been so thoroughly dismissive, *The Poverty of Theory* would not be as retrogressive a text as it actually is.

That is not the only reason why *The Poverty of Theory* is what it is. There are other reasons, some public and some silent, why it is Thompson rather than anybody else who takes on Althusser and produces his theoretical mirror image. Thompson breaks with the Stalinism of the Communist Party in 1956 at the moment of the Hungarian Revolution and in the wake of Khrushchev's revelations about Stalinism at the Twentieth Congress and tries to affirm a non-Stalinist Communist tradition. He would say that his current work in the peace movement, which looks at the possibilities for forms of socialist practice on both sides of the Iron Curtain, is nothing but a continuation of that project, the project of the early New Left. After 1956, one of the European parties which refused to break with the Stalinist tradition over the Hungarian Revolution was the French Communist Party, which remains one of the most Stalinist parties in Western Europe, and one of its key intellectual figures was Louis Althusser.

Thompson made the break in 1956 in the name of humanism, the humanist Marx, the historicist Marx, the Marx of political agency, and so on. Those are all characteristic inflections of his work. Althusser's attempt to decenter the subject is a profound scandal and affront both to historicists and historians. After all, the whole project of *The Making of the English Working Class* (Thompson 1963) was precisely to recover and speak for those "men" (mainly) whose agencies and struggles had been neglected in the account given of the history of the past and for whom his work was a kind of testimony. Therefore, to labour as long as Thompson had done to produce *The Making of the English Working Class*, only to be told in another language (though not at another level of abstraction) that his leather stockinger and artisan radical were nothing but the bearers and supports of capitalist social relations which had been lying in wait for them since sometime in the sixteenth century is a rather powerful disruption of one paradigm by another.

Thompson's work continued to develop into the early 1960s around the movement and politics of the New Left, but when the *New Left Review* changed direction, Thompson saw that as the moment when the project of a humanist Communism, of humanist Marxism, of the early New Left was put into cold storage. The "new" *New Left Review* begins its principal intervention in theoretical terms and it is, in fact, in its pages some ten years later that the writings of Althusser are first introduced into British politics and theory. Here Althusser is not only distinguishing himself from old Stalinist positions and interrogating the classical Marxist tradition, but coming forward and being received by the succeeding generations of the New Left as an intellectual and theoretical paragon. And he is advancing into the terrain under the banner of antihumanism. Therefore, the political project that is taken up in the late 1960s and 1970s is increasingly organised in a space defined principally by Althusser, giving rise to a whole range of political movements that claim to be fundamentally antihumanist. That is the sense in which in *The Poverty of Theory* Thompson talks about the Althusserian tradition as not only opposite to the emphases and imperatives of his own work, but as a political project that arises in the space where his project ought to have been. That is why he sees himself fighting a rather personal battle against Althusser and antihumanism. It is a confrontation between two incommensurate Marxist traditions which, by the way they have been articulated historically, have come to be opposed to one another and which therefore present an absolutely exclusive choice, as either one or the other. But that is exactly the same kind of choice in reverse that Althusserians tried to present to people who were hoping to learn from them. Perhaps the only way out of this logic is to recognise that it is impossible to sum up the Althusserian moment without talking about its negative and positive effects, its rich generative possibilities on which so much else has been constructed, and the deformations of both theoretical and political practice that have been its unfortunate legacy.

Let me conclude this lecture, then, by offering some general reflections on and summations of the theoretical gains which flow from Althusser's break with classical Marxism. Althusser persuaded me, and I remain persuaded, that Marx conceptualises the ensemble of relations which make up a whole society—Marx's "totality"—as essentially a complex structure, not a simple one. Hence, the relationship within that totality between its different levels—the economic, the political, and the ideological (as Althusser would have it)—cannot be a simple or immediate one. Thus the notions of simply reading off the different kinds of social contradictions at different levels of social practice in terms of one governing principle of social and economic organisation (i.e., the mode of production) or of reading the different levels of a social formation in terms of a one-to-one correspondence between practices are neither useful nor are they the ways in which Marx, in the end, conceptualised the social totality. Of course, a social formation is not complexly structured simply because everything interacts with everything else—that is the traditional, sociological, multifactorial approach which has no determining priorities in it. Rather, a social formation is a "structure in dominance." It has certain distinct tendencies; it has a certain configuration; it has a definite structuration. This is why the term "structure" remains important. But, nevertheless, it is a complex structure in which it is impossible to reduce one level of practice to another in some easy way. The reaction against both these tendencies to reductionism in the classical versions of the Marxist theory of ideology has been in progress for a very long time. In fact, it was Marx and Engels themselves who set this work of revisionism in motion. But Althusser was the key figure in modern theorising on this question who clearly broke with some of the old protocols and provided a persuasive alternative which remains broadly within the terms of the Marxist problematic. This was a major theoretical achievement, however much we may now, in turn, wish to criticise and modify the terms of Althusser's breakthrough.

Another general advance which Althusser offers is that he enabled me to live in and with "difference." Althusser's break with a monistic conception of Marxism demanded the theorisation of difference: the recognition that there are different social contradictions with different origins; that the contradictions which drive the historical process forward do not always appear in the same place and will not always have the same historical effects. We have to think about the articulation between different contradictions, about the different specificities and temporal durations through which they operate, about the different modalities through which they function. I think Althusser is right to point to a stubbornly monistic habit in the practice of many very distinguished Marxists who are willing, for the sake of complexity, to toy with difference so long as there is the guarantee of unity further on up the road. But the significant advances of this delayed teleology are already to be found in the 1857 "Introduction" to the *Grundrisse* (Marx 1973). There, Marx says, for example, that of course all languages have some elements in common. Otherwise we wouldn't be able to identify them as belonging to the same social phenomenon. But when we have said that, we have only said something at a *very* general level of abstraction: the level of "language in general." We have only begun our investigation. The more important theoretical problem is to think the specificity and difference of different languages, to examine the many determinations, in concrete analysis, of particular linguistic or cultural formations and the particular aspects which differentiate them from one another.

I have to add right away, however, that Althusser allows me to think "difference" in a particular way, which is rather different from the subsequent traditions which sometimes acknowledge their originator. If you look at discourse theory, for example, at post-structuralism, or at Foucault, you will see there, not only the shift from practice to discourse, but also how the emphasis on difference—on the plurality of discourses, on the perpetual slippage of meaning, on the endless sliding of the signifier—is now pushed *beyond* the point where it is capable of theorising the necessary unevenness of a complex unity, or even the "unity in difference" of a complex structure. I think that is why, whenever Foucault seems to be in danger of bringing things together (such as the many epistemic shifts he charts, which all fortuitously coincide with the shift from the ancien regime to the modern in France), he has to hasten to assure us that nothing ever fits with anything else. The emphasis, even when it does not involve an absolute theoretical denial of unity, always falls on the continuous slippage away from any conceivable conjuncture. I think there is no other way to understand Foucault's eloquent silence on the subject of the State. Of course, he will say, he knows that the State exists; what French intellectual does not? Yet he can only posit it as an abstract, empty space—the State as Gulag—the absent/present other of an equally abstract notion of resistance. His protocol says, "not only the State but also the dispersed microphysics of power"; his practice consistently privileges the latter and ignores the existence of State power.

Foucault is quite correct, of course, to say that there are many Marxists who conceive the State as a kind of single object; that is, as simply the unified will of the committee of the ruling class, wherever it is currently meeting today. From this conception flows the necessary "yoking together" of everything. I agree that one can no longer think of the State in that way. The State is a contradictory formation, which means that it has different modes of action, and is active in many different sites: it is pluri-centered and multidimensional. It has very distinct and dominant tendencies, but it does not have a singly inscribed class character. On the other hand, the State remains one of the crucial sites in a modern capitalist social formation where political practices of different kinds are *condensed*. The function of the State is, in part, to bring together or articulate into a complexly structured instance, a range of political discourses and social practices which are concerned at different sites with the transmission and transformation of power. Some of those practices have little to do with the political domain as such, being concerned with other domains which are nevertheless articulated to the State—for example, family life, civil society, gender, and economic relations. The State is the instance of the performance of a condensation which allows that site of intersection between different practices to be transformed into a systematic practice of regulation, rule, and norm, of normalisation, within society. The State condenses very different social practices and transforms them into the operation of rule and domination over particular classes and other social groups. The way to reach such a conceptualisation is not to substitute the difference for its mirror opposite—unity—but to rethink both in terms of articulation. This is exactly the step Foucault refuses.

By "articulation," I mean the form of a connection or link that can make a unity of two different elements under certain conditions. It is a linkage which is not necessary, determined, absolute, and essential for all times; it is not necessarily given in all cases as a law or a fact of life. It requires particular conditions of existence to appear at all, and so one has to ask, under what circumstances can a connection be forged or made. So the so-called unity of a discourse, for example, is really the articulation of different, distinct elements which can be rearticulated in different ways because they have no necessary "belongingness." An articulation has to be positively sustained by specific processes; it is not "eternal" but has constantly to be renewed. It can under some circumstances disappear or be overthrown (disarticulated), leading to the old linkages being dissolved and new connections (rearticulations) being forged. It is also important that an articulation between different practices does not mean that they become identical or that one is dissolved into the other. Each retains its distinct determinations and conditions of existence. However, once an articulation is made, the two practices can function together, not as an "immediate identity" (in the language of Marx's 1857 "Introduction") but as "distinctions within a unity." A theory of articulation, then, is a theory of "no necessary belongingness," which requires us to think the contingent, nonnecessary connections between and among different social practices and social groups.

Hence we have to characterise Althusser's advance, not in terms of "difference" alone—the rallying cry of Derridean deconstruction—but instead in terms of the necessity of thinking unity *and* difference, difference *in* complex unity, without this becoming a hostage to the privileging of difference as such. If Derrida is correct in arguing that there is always a perpetual slippage of the signifier, a continuous "différance," it is also correct to argue that without some arbitrary "fixing" or articulation, there would be no signification or meaning at all. What is ideology but, precisely, this work of fixing meaning through establishing, by selection and combination, a chain of equivalences? That is why, despite all of its faults, I want to bring forward to you, not the proto-Lacanian, neo-Foucauldian, pre-Derridean, Althusserian text—"Ideological State Apparatuses"—but rather, the less theoretically elaborated, but in my view more generative, more original, perhaps because tentative text, *For Marx*; and especially the essay "On Contradiction and Overdetermination," which begins precisely to think about complex kinds of determinacy without reductionism to a simple unity. (I have consistently preferred *For Marx* to the more finished, more structuralist *Reading Capital*, a preference founded not only on my suspicion of the whole Spinozist, structuralist causality machinery which grinds through the latter text but also on my prejudice against the modish intellectual assumption that the "latest" is necessarily "the best.")

I'm not concerned here with the absolute theoretical rigor of *For Marx*; at the risk of theoretical eclecticism, I am inclined to prefer being "right but not rigorous" to being "rigorous but wrong." By enabling us to think about different levels and different kinds of determination, *For Marx* gave us what *Reading Capital* did not: the ability to theorise about real historical events (1917), or particular texts (*The German Ideology*), or particular ideological formations (humanism) as determined by more than one structure, that is, to think the process of overdetermination. I think contradiction and overdetermination are very *rich* theoretical concepts—some of Althusser's happier "loans" from Freud and Marx. It is not the case, in my view, that their richness has been exhausted by the ways in which they were applied by Althusser himself.

The articulation of difference and unity involves a different way of trying to conceptualise the key Marxist concept of determination. Some of the classical formulations of base-superstructure which have dominated Marxist theories of ideology represent ways of thinking about determination which are essentially based on the idea of a necessary correspondence between one level of a social formation and another. With or without immediate identity, sooner or later, political, legal, and ideological practices—they suppose—*will* conform to and therefore be brought into a necessary correspondence with what is mistakenly called "the economic." Now, as is by now de rigueur in advanced post-structuralist theorising, in the retreat from necessary correspondence, there has been the usual unstoppable philosophical slide all the way over to the opposite side; that is to say, the elision into what sounds almost the same but is in substance radically different: the declaration that there is "necessarily no correspondence." Paul Hirst (1979), one of the most sophisticated of the post-Marxist theorists, lent his considerable weight and authority to that damaging *glissance*. "Necessarily no correspondence" expresses exactly the notion—essential to discourse theory—that nothing really connects with anything else. Even when the analysis of particular discursive formations constantly reveals the overlay or the sliding of one set of discourses over another, everything seems to hang on the polemical reiteration of the principle that there is, of necessity, no correspondence.

I do not accept that simple inversion. I think what we have discovered is that there is *no necessary correspondence*, which is different; and this formulation represents a third position. This means that there is no law which guarantees that the ideology of a class is already and unequivocally given in or corresponds to the position which that class holds in the economic relations of capitalist production. The claim of "no guarantee," which breaks with teleology, also implies that there is no necessary non-correspondence. That is, there is no guarantee that, under all circumstances, ideology and class can never be articulated together in any way or produce a social force capable for a time of self-conscious "unity in action" in a class struggle. A theoretical position founded on the open-endedness of practice and struggle must have as one of its possible results an articulation in terms of *effects* which does not necessarily correspond to its origins. To put that more concretely: An effective intervention by particular social forces in, say, events in Russia in 1917, does not require us to say either that the Russian revolution was the product of the whole Russian proletariat, united behind a single revolutionary ideology (it clearly was not), nor that the decisive character of the alliance (articulation together) of workers, peasants, soldiers, and intellectuals who did constitute the social basis of that intervention was guaranteed by their ascribed place and position in the Russian social structure and the necessary forms of revolutionary consciousness attached to them. Nevertheless, 1917 did happen, as Lenin surprisingly observed, when "as a result of an extremely unique historical situation, *absolutely dissimilar currents, absolutely heterogeneous* class interests, *absolutely contrary* political and social strivings . . . merged . . . in a strikingly 'harmonious' manner" (cited in Althusser 1970, 99n19). This points, as Althusser's comment on this passage in *For Marx* reminds us, to the fact that, if a contradiction is to become " 'active' in the strongest sense, to become a ruptural principle, there must be an accumulation of circumstances and 'currents' so that whatever their origin and sense . . . they '*fuse*' into a *ruptural unity*" (1970, 99). The aim of a theoretically informed political practice must surely be to bring about or construct the articulation between social or economic forces and those forms of politics and ideology which might lead them in practice to intervene in history in a progressive way—an articulation which has to be constructed through practice precisely because it is not guaranteed by how those forces are constituted in the first place.

That leaves the model much more indeterminate, open-ended, and contingent than the classical position. It suggests you cannot "read off" the ideology of a class, or even sectors of a class, from its original position in the structure of socioeconomic relations. But it refuses to say that it is impossible to bring classes or fractions of classes, or indeed other kinds of social movements, through a developing practice of struggle, into articulations with those forms of politics and ideology which allow them to become historically effective as collective social agents. The principal theoretical reversal accomplished by "no necessary correspondence" is that determinacy is transferred from the genetic origins of class or other social forces in a structure to the effects or results of a practice. So I would want to stand with those parts of Althusser that I read as retaining the double articulation between "structure" and "practice," rather than the full structuralist causality of *Reading Capital* or of the opening sections of Poulantzas's (1973) *Political Power and Social Classes*. By "double articulation" I mean that the structure—the given conditions of existence, the structure of determinations in any situation—can also be understood, from another point of view, as the result of previous practices. We may say that a structure is what previously structured practices have produced as a result. These then constitute the "given conditions," the necessary starting point for new generations of practice. In neither case should "practice" be treated as transparently intentional: We make history, but on the basis of anterior conditions which are not of our making. Practice is how a structure is actively reproduced. Nevertheless, we need both terms if we are to avoid the trap of treating history as nothing but the outcome of an internally self-propelling structuralist machine. The structuralist dichotomy between "structure" and "practice"—like the related one between "synchrony" and "diachrony"—serves a useful analytic purpose but should not be fetishised into a rigid, mutually exclusive distinction.

Let us try to think a little further the question, not of the necessity, but of the possibility of the articulations between social groups, political practices, and ideological formations which *could* create, as a result, those historical breaks or shifts which we no longer find already inscribed and guaranteed in the very structures and laws of the capitalist mode of production. This must not be read as arguing that there are no tendencies which arise from our positioning within the structures of social relations. We must not allow ourselves to slip from an acknowledgment of the relative autonomy of practice (in terms of its effects) to fetishising practice—the slip which made many post-structuralists into Maoists for a brief moment before they became subscribers to the "New Philosophy" of the fashionable French Right. Structures exhibit tendencies—lines of force, openings, and closures—which constrain, shape, channel, and, in that sense, "determine." But they cannot determine in the harder sense of fix absolutely, guarantee. People are not irrevocably and indelibly inscribed with the ideas that they *ought* to think, the politics that they *ought* to have or not, as if these were already imprinted in their sociological genes. The question is not the unfolding of some inevitable law but rather the *linkages* which, although they can be made, need not necessarily be made. There is no guarantee that classes will appear in their appointed political places, as Poulantzas so vividly described it, with their number plates on their backs. By developing practices which articulate differences into a collective will, or by generating discourses which condense a range of different connotations, the dispersed conditions of practice of different social groups *can* be effectively drawn together in ways which make those social forces not simply a class "in itself," positioned by some other relations over which it has no control, *but also* capable of intervening as a historical force, a class "for itself," capable of establishing new collective projects. These now appear to me to be the generative advances which Althusser's work set in motion. I regard this reversal of basic concepts as an immense theoretical revolution.

Ideology and Ideological Struggle

In this lecture, I want to rethink the nature of ideology and the possibility of struggle on the ideological terrain. I will approach this task indirectly, by returning to Althusser in order to assess his contribution to the reconceptualisation of ideology. Despite my disagreements, Althusser's break with classical Marxism opened up a new perspective on the question of ideology and thus made it possible for me to rethink it as well.

Althusser's critique of ideology follows many of the lines of his critique of general positions in the classical Marxist problematic sketched in the previous lecture. That is to say, he is opposed to class reductionism in ideology—the notion that there is some guarantee that the ideological position of a social class will always correspond to its position in the social relations of production. Althusser here is criticising a very important insight which people have taken from *The German Ideology* (Marx and Engels 1970), the founding text of the classical Marxist theory of ideology: namely, that ruling ideas always correspond to ruling class positions; that the ruling class as a whole has a kind of mind of its own which is located in a particular ideology. The difficulty is that this does not enable us to understand why all the ruling classes we actually know have actually advanced in real historical situations by a variety of different ideologies or by now playing one ideology and then another. Nor does it enable us to understand why there are internal struggles within *all* the major political formations over the appropriate "ideas" through which the interests of the dominant class are to be secured. Nor does it enable us to understand why, to a significant degree, in many different historical social formations the dominated classes have used "ruling ideas" to interpret and define their interests. To simply describe all of that as *the* dominant ideology, which unproblematically reproduces itself and which has gone on marching ahead ever since the free market appeared, is an unwarrantable forcing of the notion of an empirical identity between class and ideology which concrete historical analysis denies.

The second target of Althusser's criticism is the notion of "false consciousness" which, he argues, assumes that there is one true ascribed ideology per class, and then explains its failure to manifest itself in terms of a screen which falls between subjects and the real relations in which subjects are placed, preventing them from recognising the ideas which they ought to have. That notion of "false consciousness," Althusser says quite rightly, is founded on an empiricist relationship to knowledge. It assumes that social relations give their own, unambiguous knowledge to perceiving, thinking subjects; that there is a transparent relationship between the situations in which subjects are placed and how subjects come to recognise and know about them. Consequently, true knowledge must be subject to a sort of masking, the source of which is very difficult to identify, but which prevents people from "recognising the real." In this conception, it is always other people, never ourselves, who are in false consciousness, who are bewitched by the dominant ideology, who are the dupes of history.

Althusser's third critique develops out of his notions about theory. He insists that knowledge has to be produced as the consequence of a particular practice. Knowledge, whether ideological or scientific, is the production of a practice. It is not the reflection of the real in discourse, in language. Social relations have to be "represented in speech and language" to acquire meaning. Meaning is produced as a result of ideological or theoretical work. It is not simply a result of an empiricist epistemology.

As a result, Althusser wants to think the specificity of ideological practices, to think their difference from other social practices. He also wants to think "the complex unity" which articulates the level of ideological practice to other instances of a social formation. And so, using some of the ideas I've identified before and the critique of the traditional conceptions of ideology which he found in front of him, he set to work to offer some alternatives. Let me look briefly at what these alternatives are for Althusser.

The one essay of Althusser's (1971b) with which everybody is familiar is the "Ideological State Apparatuses." Some of his propositions in that essay have had a very strong influence or resonance in subsequent debates. First of all, Althusser tries to think the relationship between ideology and other social practices in terms of the concept of reproduction. What is the function of ideology? It is to reproduce the social relations of production. The social relations of production are necessary to the material existence of any social formation or any mode of production. But the elements or the agents of a mode of production, especially with respect to the critical factor of their labour, have themselves to be continually produced and reproduced. Althusser argues that increasingly in capitalist social formations, labour is not reproduced inside the social relations of production themselves, but outside of them. Of course, he does not mean biologically or technically reproduced only; he means socially and culturally as well. It is produced in the domain of the superstructures: in institutions like the family and church. It requires cultural institutions such as the media, trade unions, political parties, et cetera, which are not directly linked with production as such but which have the crucial function of "cultivating" labour of a certain moral and cultural kind— that which the modern capitalist mode of production requires. Schools, universities, training boards, and research centres reproduce the technical competence of the labour required by advanced systems of capitalist production. But Althusser reminds us that a technically competent but politically insubordinate labour force is no labour force at all for capital. Therefore, the more important task is cultivating that kind of labour which is able and willing, morally and politically, to be subordinated to the discipline, the logic, the culture, and compulsions of the economic mode of production of capitalist development, at whatever state it has arrived; that is, labour which can be subjected to the dominant system ad infinitum. Consequently, what ideology does, through the various ideological apparatuses, is to reproduce the social relations of production in this larger sense. That is Althusser's first formulation.

Reproduction in that sense is, of course, a classic term to be found in Marx. Althusser doesn't have to go any further than *Capital* to discover it; although it should be said that he gives it a very restrictive definition. He refers only to the reproduction of labour power, whereas reproduction in Marx is a much wider concept, including the reproduction of the social relations of possession and of exploitation, and indeed of the mode of production itself. This is quite typical of Althusser—whenever he dives into the Marxist bag and comes out with a term or concept which has wide Marxist resonances, he quite often gives it a particular limiting twist which is specifically his own. In this way, he continually "firms up" Marx's structuralist cast of thought.

There is a problem with this position. Ideology in this essay seems to be, substantially, that of the dominant class. If there is an ideology of the dominated classes, it seems to be one which is perfectly adapted to the functions and interests of the dominant class within the capitalist mode of production. At this point, Althusserian structuralism is open to the charge, which has been made against it, of a creeping Marxist functionalism. Ideology seems to perform the function required of it (i.e., to reproduce the dominance of the dominant ideology), to perform it effectively, and to go on performing it, without encountering any countertendencies (a second concept always to be found in Marx wherever he discusses reproduction and precisely the concept which distinguishes analysis in *Capital* from functionalism). When you ask about the contradictory field of ideology, about how the ideology of the dominated classes gets produced and reproduced, about the ideologies of resistance, of exclusion, of deviation, et cetera, there are no answers in this essay. Nor is there an account of why it is that ideology, which is so effectively stitched into the social formation in Althusser's account, would ever produce its opposite or its contradiction. But a notion of reproduction which is only functionally adjusted to capital and which has no countervailing tendencies, encounters no contradictions, is not the site of class struggle, and is utterly foreign to Marx's conception of reproduction.

The second influential proposition in the "Ideological State Apparatuses" essay is the insistence that ideology is a practice. That is, it appears in practices located within the rituals of specific apparatuses or social institutions and organisations. Althusser makes the distinction here between repressive state apparatuses, like the police and the army, and ideological state apparatuses, like churches, trade unions, and media, which are not directly organised by the State. The emphasis on "practices and rituals" is wholly welcome, especially if not interpreted too narrowly or polemically. Ideologies are the frameworks of thinking and calculation about the world—the "ideas" with which people figure out how the social world works, what their place is in it, and what they *ought* to do. But the problem for a materialist or nonidealist theory is how to deal with ideas, which are mental events, and therefore, as Marx says, can only occur "in thought, in the head" (where else?), in a nonidealist, nonvulgar materialist manner. Althusser's emphasis is helpful here—helping us out of the philosophical dilemma, as well as having the additional virtue, in my view, of being right. He places the emphasis on where ideas appear, where mental events register or are realised, as social phenomena. That is principally, of course, in language (understood in the sense of signifying practices involving the use of signs; in the semiotic domain, the domain of meaning and representation); equally important, in the rituals and practices of social action or behaviour, in which ideologies imprint or inscribe themselves. Language and behaviour are the media, so to speak, of the material registration of ideology, the modality of its functioning. These rituals and practices always occur in social sites, linked with social apparatuses. That is why we have to analyse or deconstruct language and behaviour in order to decipher the patterns of ideological thinking which are inscribed in them.

This important advance in our thinking about ideology has sometimes been obscured by theorists who claim that ideologies are not "ideas" at all but practices, and it is this which guarantees that the theory of ideology is materialist. I do not agree with this emphasis. I think it suffers from a "misplaced concreteness." The materialism of Marxism cannot rest on the claim that it abolishes the mental character—let alone the real effects—of mental events (i.e., thought), for that is, precisely, the error of what Marx (1963) called a one-sided or mechanical materialism (in the "Theses on Feuerbach"). It must rest on the material forms in which thought appears and on the fact that it has real material effects. That is, at any rate, the manner in which I have learned from Althusser's much-quoted assertion that the existence of ideology is material because "ideology always exists in an apparatus, and its practice, or practices" (1971b, 166). Some damage has been done by Althusser's overdramatic and too-condensed formulation, at the close of this part of his argument, that—as he quaintly puts it—"Disappeared: the term *ideas*" (169). Althusser has accomplished much, but he has not to my way of thinking actually abolished the existence of ideas and thought, however convenient and reassuring that would be. What he has shown is that ideas have a material existence. As he says himself, "the 'ideas' of a human subject exist in his [or her] actions" and actions are "inserted into *practices* . . . governed by the *rituals* in which these practices are inscribed, within the *material existence of an ideological apparatus*," which is different (168).

Nevertheless, serious problems remain with Althusser's nomenclature. The "Ideological State Apparatuses" essay, again, unproblematically assumes an identity between the many "autonomous" parts of civil society and the State. In contrast, as we will see, this articulation is at the center of Gramsci's problem of hegemony. Gramsci has difficulties in formulating the state/civil society boundary precisely because where it falls is neither a simple nor uncontradictory matter. A critical question in developed liberal democracies is precisely how ideology is reproduced in the so-called *private* institutions of civil society—the theatre of consent— apparently outside of the direct sphere of play of the State itself. If everything is more or less under the supervision of the State, it is quite easy to see why the only ideology that gets reproduced is the dominant one. But the far more pertinent, but difficult, question is how a society *allows* the relative freedom of civil institutions to operate in the ideological field, day after day, without direction or compulsion by the State; and why the consequence of that "free play" of civil society, through a very complex reproductive process, nevertheless consistently reconstitutes ideology as a "structure in dominance." That is a much tougher problem to explain, and the notion of ideological state apparatuses precisely forecloses the issue. Again, it is a broadly "functionalist" type which presupposes a necessary functional correspondence between the requirements of the mode of production and the functions of ideology.

After all, in democratic societies, it is not an illusion of freedom to say that we cannot adequately explain the structured biases of the media in terms of their being instructed by the State precisely what to print or allow on television. But precisely how is it that such large numbers of journalists, consulting only their "freedom" to publish and be damned, do tend to reproduce, quite spontaneously, without compulsion, again and again, accounts of the world constructed within fundamentally the same ideological categories? How is it that they are driven, again and again, to such a limited repertoire within the ideological field? Even journalists who write within the muckraking tradition often seem to be inscribed by an ideology to which they do not consciously commit themselves and, which instead, "writes them."

This is the aspect of ideology under liberal capitalism which most needs explaining. And that is why, when people say, "Of course this is a free society; the media operate freely," there is no point in responding, "No, they operate only through compulsion by the State." Would that they did! Then all that would be required would be to pull out the four or five of their key controllers and put in a few controllers of our own. In fact, ideological reproduction can no more be explained by the inclinations of individuals or by overt coercion (social control) than economic reproduction can be explained by direct force. Both explanations—and they are analogous—have to begin where *Capital* begins: with analysing how the "spontaneous freedom" of the circuits actually works. This is a problem which the "Ideological State Apparatuses" nomenclature simply forecloses. Althusser refuses to distinguish between state and civil society (on the same grounds which Poulantzas [1973] later spuriously supported—i.e., that the distinction belonged only within "bourgeois ideology"). His nomenclature does not give sufficient weight to what Gramsci (1971) would call the immense complexities of society in modern social formations—"the trenches and fortifications of civil society." It does not begin to make sense of how complex are the processes by which capitalism must work to order and organise a civil society which is not, technically, under its immediate control. These are important problems in the field of ideology and culture which the formulation "ideological state apparatuses" encourages us to evade.

The third of Althusser's propositions is his affirmation that ideology only exists by virtue of the constituting category of the subject. There is a long and complicated story here, only a small part of which I propose to address. As I argued earlier, *Reading Capital* is very similar in its mode of argumentation to Lévi-Strauss and other non-Marxist structuralists. Like Lévi-Strauss (1972), Althusser also talks about social relations as processes without a subject. Similarly, when Althusser insists that classes are simply "bearers and supports" of economic social relations, he, like Lévi-Strauss, is using a Saussurean conception of language, applied to the domain of practice in general, to displace the traditional agent/subject of classical Western epistemology. Althusser's position here is very much in line with the notion that language speaks us, as the myth "speaks" the mythmaker. This abolishes the problem of subjective identification and of how individuals or groups become the enunciators of ideology. But, as Althusser develops his theory of ideology, he moves away from the notion that ideology is simply a process without a subject. He seems to take on board the critique that this domain of the subject and subjectivity cannot be simply left as an empty space. The "decentering of the subject," which is one of structuralism's main projects, still leaves unsettled the problem of the subjectification and subjectivising of ideology. There are still processes of subjective effect to be accounted for. How do concrete individuals fall into place within particular ideologies if we have no notion of the subject or of subjectivity? On the other hand, we have to rethink this question in a way different from the tradition of empiricist philosophy. This is the beginning of a very long development, which begins in the "Ideological State Apparatuses" essay, with Althusser's insistence that all ideology functions through the category of the subject, and it is only in and for ideology that subjects exist.

This "subject" is not to be confused with lived historical individuals. It is the category, the position, where the subject—the "I" of ideological statements—is constituted. Ideological discourses themselves constitute us as subjects for discourse. Althusser explains how this works through the concept, borrowed from Lacan (1977), of "interpellation." This suggests that we are hailed or summoned by the ideologies which recruit us as their "authors," their essential subject. We are constituted by the unconscious processes of ideology, in that position of recognition or fixture between ourselves and the signifying chain without which no signification or ideological meaning would be possible. It is precisely from this turn in the argument that the long trail into psychoanalysis and poststructuralism (and finally out of the Marxist problematic) unwinds.

There is something both profoundly important and seriously regrettable about the shape of the "Ideological State Apparatuses" essay. It has to do exactly with its two-part structure: Part I is about ideology and the reproduction of the social relations of production. Part II is about the constitution of subjects and how ideologies interpellate us in the realm of the Imaginary. As a result of treating those two aspects in two separate compartments, a fatal dislocation occurred. What was originally conceived as one critical element in the general theory of ideology—the theory of the subject—came to be substituted, metonymically, for the whole of the theory itself. The enormously sophisticated theories which have subsequently developed have therefore all been theories about the second question: How are subjects constituted in relation to different discourses? What is the role of unconscious processes in creating these positionalities? That is the object of discourse theory and linguistically influenced psychoanalysis. Or one can inquire into the conditions of enunciation in a particular discursive formation. That is the problematic of Foucault. Or one can inquire into the unconscious processes by which subjects and subjectivity as such are constituted. That is the problematic of Lacan. There has been considerable theorising on the site of the second part of the "Ideological State Apparatuses" essay. But on the site of the first part—nothing. Finito! The inquiry simply halted with Althusser's inadequate formulations about the reproduction of the social relations of production. The two sides of the difficult problem of ideology were fractured in that essay and, ever since, have been assigned to different poles. The question of reproduction has been assigned to the Marxist (male) pole, and the question of subjectivity has been assigned to the psychoanalytic (feminist) pole. Since then, never have the twain met. The latter is constituted as a question about the "insides" of people, about psychoanalysis, subjectivity, and sexuality, and is understood to be "about" that. It is in this way and on this site that the link to feminism has been increasingly theorised. The former is "about" social relations, production, and the "hard edge" of productive systems, and that is what Marxism and the discourse of class are "about." This bifurcation of the theoretical project has had the most disastrous consequences for the unevenness of the development of the problematic of ideology, not to speak of its damaging political effects.

Instead of following either of these paths, I want to break from that impasse for a moment and look at some alternative starting points in Althusser, from which I think useful advances can still be made. Long before he had arrived at the "advanced" position of the "Ideological State Apparatuses" essay, Althusser (1970, 231–236) said, in a short section in *For Marx*, some simple things about ideology which bear repeating and thinking about. This is where he defined ideologies as, to paraphrase, systems of representation—composed of concepts, ideas, myths, or images—in which men and women (my addition) live "their imaginary relations to the real conditions of existence." That statement is worth examining bit by bit.

The designation of ideologies as "systems of representation" acknowledges their essentially discursive and semiotic character. Systems of representation are the systems of meaning through which we represent the world to ourselves and one another. It acknowledges that ideological knowledge is the result of specific practices—the practices involved in the production of meaning. But since there are no social practices which take place outside the domain of meaning (semiotic), are *all* practices simply discourses?

Here we have to tread very carefully. We are in the presence of yet another suppressed term or excluded middle. Althusser reminds us that ideas don't just float around in empty space. We know they are there because they are materialised in, they inform, social practices. In that sense, the social is never outside of the semiotic. Every social practice is constituted within the interplay of meaning and representation and can itself be represented. In other words, there is no social practice outside of ideology. However, this does not mean that, because all social practices are within the discursive, therefore there is nothing to social practice *but* discourse. I know what is vested in describing processes that we usually talk about in terms of ideas as practices; "practices" feel concrete. They occur in particular sites and apparatuses—like classrooms, churches, lecture theatres, factories, schools, and families. And that concreteness allows us to claim that they are "material." Yet differences must be remarked between different kinds of practice. Let me suggest one. If you are engaged in a part of the modern capitalist labour process, you are using, in combination with certain means of production, labour power—purchased at a certain price—to transform raw materials into a product, a commodity. That is the definition of a practice—the practice of labour. Is it *outside* of meaning and discourse? Certainly not. How could large numbers of people either learn that practice or combine their labour power in the division of labour with others, day after day, unless labour was within the domain of representation and meaning? Is this practice of transformation, then, nothing but a discourse? Of course not. It does not follow that because all practices are *in* ideology, or inscribed by ideology, that all practices are *nothing but* ideology. There is a specificity to those practices whose principal object is to produce ideological representations. They are different from those practices which—meaningfully, intelligibly—produce other commodities. Those people who work in the media are producing, reproducing, and transforming the field of ideological representation itself. They stand in a different relationship to ideology in general from others who are producing and reproducing the world of material commodities—which are, nevertheless, also inscribed by ideology. Barthes observed long ago that all things are also significations. The latter forms of practice operate in ideology but they are not ideological in terms of the specificity of their object.

I want to retain the notion that ideologies are systems of representation materialised in practices, but I don't want to fetishise "practice." Too often, at this level of theorising, the argument has tended to identify social practice with social discourse. While the emphasis on discourse is correct in pointing to the importance of meaning and representation, it has been taken right through to its absolute opposite and this allows us to talk about all practice as if there were nothing but ideology. This is simply an inversion.

Note that Althusser says "systems," not "system." The important thing about systems of representation is that they are not singular. There are numbers of them in any social formation. They are plural. Ideologies do not operate through single ideas; they operate in discursive chains, in clusters, in semantic fields, in discursive formations. As you enter an ideological field and pick out any one nodal representation or idea, you immediately trigger off a whole chain of connotative associations. Ideological representations connote—summon—one another. So a variety of different ideological systems or logics are available in any social formation. The notion of *the* dominant ideology and *the* subordinated ideology is an inadequate way of representing the complex interplay of different ideological discourses and formations in any modern developed society. Nor is the terrain of ideology constituted as a field of mutually exclusive and internally self-sustaining discursive chains. They contest one another, often drawing on a common, shared repertoire of concepts, rearticulating and disarticulating them within different systems of difference or equivalence.

Let me turn to the next part of Althusser's definition of ideology: the systems of representation in which men and women *live*. Althusser puts inverted commas around "live," because he means, not blind biological or genetic life, but the life of experiencing, within culture, meaning, and representation. It is not possible to bring ideology to an end and simply live the real. We always need systems through which we represent what the real is to ourselves and to others. That's the first important point about "live." The second important point about "live" is that we ought to understand it broadly. By "live" he means that men and women use a variety of systems of representation to experience, interpret, and "make sense of" the conditions of their existence. It follows that ideology can always define the same so-called object or objective condition in the real world differently. There is "no necessary correspondence" between the conditions of a social relation or practice and the number of different ways it can be represented. It does not follow that, as the neo-Kantians in discourse theory have assumed, that because we cannot know or experience a social relation except "within ideology," therefore it has no existence independent of the machinery of representation: a point already well clarified by Marx (1973) in the 1857 "Introduction" but woefully misinterpreted by Althusser himself.

Perhaps the most subversive implication of the term "live" is that it connotes the domain of experience. It is in and through the systems of representation of culture that we "experience" the world: Experience is the product of our codes of intelligibility, our schemas of interpretation. Consequently, there is no experiencing *outside* of the categories of representation or ideology. The notion that our heads are full of false ideas which can, however, be totally dispersed when we throw ourselves open to "the real" as a moment of the absolute authentication, is probably the most ideological conception of all. This is exactly the moment of "recognition" when the fact that meaning depends on the intervention of systems of representation disappears and we seem secure within the naturalistic attitude. It is a moment of extreme ideological closure. Here we are most under the sway of the highly ideological structures of common sense, the regime of the "taken for granted." The point at which we lose sight of fact that sense is a production of our systems of representation is the point at which we fall, not into Nature but into the naturalistic illusion: the height (or depth) of ideology. Consequently, when we contrast ideology to experience, or illusion to authentic truth, we are failing to recognise that there is no way of experiencing the "real relations" of a particular society outside of its cultural and ideological categories. That is not to say that all knowledge is simply the product of our will to power; there may be some ideological categories which give us a more adequate or more profound knowledge of particular relations than others.

Because there is no one-to-one relationship between the conditions of social existence we are living and how we experience them, it is necessary for Althusser to call these relationships "imaginary." That is, they must on no account be confused with the real. It is only later in his work that this domain becomes the "Imaginary" in a proper Lacanian sense. It may be that he already had Lacan in mind in this earlier essay, but he is not yet concerned to affirm that knowing and experiencing are only possible through the particular psychoanalytic process which Lacan has posited. Ideology is described as *imaginary* simply to distinguish it from the notion that "real relations" declare their own meanings unambiguously.

Finally, let us consider Althusser's use of this phrase, "the real conditions of existence," scandalous (within contemporary cultural theory) because here Althusser commits himself to the notion that social relations actually exist apart from their ideological representations or experiences. Social relations do exist. We are born into them. They exist independent of our will. They are real in their structure and tendency. We cannot develop a social practice without representing those conditions to ourselves in one way or another; but the representations do not exhaust their effect. Social relations exist, independent of mind, independent of thought. And yet they can only be conceptualised in thought. It is important that Althusser affirms the objective character of the real relations that constitute modes of production in social formations, though his later work provided the warrant for a quite different theorisation. Althusser here is closer to a "realist" philosophical position than his later Kantian or Spinozist manifestations.

Now I want to go beyond the particular phrase I have been explicating to expand on two or three more general things associated with this formulation. Althusser says these systems of representation are essentially founded on unconscious structures. Again, in the earlier essay, he seems to be thinking the unconscious nature of ideology in ways similar to those in which Lévi-Strauss defined the codes of a myth as unconscious—in terms of its rules and categories. We are not ourselves aware of the rules and systems of classification of an ideology when we enunciate any ideological statement. Nevertheless, like the rules of language, they are open to rational inspection and analysis by modes of interruption and deconstruction, which can open up a discourse to its foundations and allow us to inspect the categories which generate it. We know the words to the song "Rule Brittania," but we are unconscious of the deep structure—the notions of nation, of the great slabs and slices of imperialist history, the assumptions about global domination and supremacy, the necessary Other of other peoples' subordination, which are richly impacted in its simple celebratory resonances. These connotational chains are not open nor easily amenable to change and reformulation at the conscious level. Does it therefore follow that they are the product of specific unconscious processes and mechanisms in the psychoanalytic sense?

This returns us to the question of how it is that subjects recognise themselves in ideology: How is the relationship between individual subjects and the positionalities of a particular ideological discourse constructed? It seems possible that some of the basic positionings of individuals in language, as well as certain primary positions in the ideological field, are constituted through unconscious processes in the psychoanalytic sense, at the early stages of formation. Those processes could then have a profound, orienting impact on the ways we situate ourselves in later life in subsequent ideological discourses. It is quite clear that such processes *do* operate in early infancy, making possible the formation of relations with others and the outside world. They are inextricably bound up—for one thing—with the nature and development of, above all, sexual identities. On the other hand, it is by no means adequately proven that these positionings *alone* constitute the mechanisms whereby all individuals locate themselves in ideology. We are not entirely stitched into place in our relation to the complex field of historically situated ideological discourses exclusively at that moment alone, when we enter the "transition from . . . biological existence to human existence" (Althusser 1971a, 93). We remain open to be positioned and situated in different ways, at different moments throughout our existence.

Some argue that those later positionings simply recapitulate the primary positions which are established in the resolution of the Oedipus complex. It seems more accurate to say that subjects are not positioned in relation to the field of ideologies exclusively by the resolution of unconscious processes in infancy. They are also positioned by the discursive formations of specific social formations. They are situated differently in relation to a different range of social sites. It seems to me quite wrong to assume that the process which allows the individual to speak or enunciate *at all*—language as such—is the same as that which allows the individual to enunciate him- or herself as a particular gendered, raced, socially sexed, et cetera, individual in a variety of representational systems in definite societies. The universal mechanisms of interpellation may provide the necessary general conditions for language but it is mere speculation and assertion which so far suggests that they provide the sufficient concrete conditions for the enunciation of historically specific and differentiated ideologies. Discourse theory one-sidedly insists that an account of subjectivity in terms of Lacan's unconscious processes is itself *the* whole theory of ideology. Certainly, a theory of ideology has to develop, as earlier Marxist theories did not, a theory of subjects and subjectivity. It must account for the recognition of the self within ideological discourse, what it is that allows subjects to recognise themselves in the discourse and to speak it spontaneously as its author. But that is not the same as taking the Freudian schema, reread in a linguistic way by Lacan, as an adequate theory of ideology in social formations.

Althusser (1971a) himself appeared, earlier in his "Freud and Lacan" essay, to recognise the necessarily provisional and speculative nature of Lacan's propositions. He repeated the succession of "identities" through which Lacan's argument is sustained—the transition from biological to human existence paralleling the Law of Order, which is the same as the Law of Culture, which "is confounded in its *formal* essence with the order of language" (209). But he does then pick up the purely formal nature of these homologies in a footnote:

> *Formally*: for the Law of Culture, which is first introduced as language . . . is not exhausted by language; its content is the real kinship structures and the determinate ideological formations in which the persons inscribed in these structures live their functions. It is not enough to know that the Western family is patriarchal and exoganic . . . we must also work out the ideological formations that

govern paternity, maternity, conjugality, and childhood. . . . A mass of research remains to be done on these ideological formations. This is a task for historical materialism. (211)

But in the later formulations (and even more so in the Lacanian deluge which has subsequently followed), this kind of caution has been thrown to the wind in a veritable riot of affirmation. In the familiar slippage, "the unconscious is structured like a language," has become "the unconscious *is* the same as the entry into language, culture, sexual identity, ideology, et cetera, et cetera, et cetera."

What I have tried to do is to go back to a much simpler and more productive way of beginning to think about ideology, which I also find in Althusser's work though not at the fashionable end of it. Recognising that, in these matters—though our conceptual apparatus is extremely sophisticated and "advanced," in terms of real understanding, substantive research, and progress to knowledge in a genuinely "open" (i.e., scientific) way—we are very much at the beginning of a long and difficult road. In terms of this "long march," *For Marx* is earlier than the flights of fancy, and occasionally of fantasy, which overtake the "Ideological State Apparatuses" essay. It ought not, however, be left behind for that reason alone. "Contradiction and Overdetermination" in *For Marx* contains a richer notion of determination than *Reading Capital*, though not so rigorously theorised. *For Marx* has a fuller notion of ideology than does "Ideological State Apparatuses," although it is not as comprehensive. Again, I prefer the early Althusser to the late Althusser.

The so-called unity of a discourse is really the articulation of different, distinct elements which can be rearticulated in different ways because they have no necessary "belongingness." The "unity" which matters is a linkage between that articulated discourse and the social forces with which it can, under certain historical conditions, but need not necessarily, be connected. Thus, a theory of articulation is both a way of understanding how ideological elements come, under certain conditions, to cohere together within a discourse, and a way of asking how they do or do not become articulated, at specific conjunctures, to certain political subjects. Let me put that the other way: The theory of articulation asks how an ideology discovers its subject rather than how the subject thinks the necessary and inevitable thoughts which belong to it; it enables us to think how an ideology empowers people, enables them to begin to make some sense or intelligibility of their historical situation, without reducing those forms of intelligibility to their socioeconomic or class location or social position.

For example, religion has no necessary political connotation. Anyone interested in the politics of contemporary culture has to recognise the continuing force in modern life of cultural forms which have a prehistory long predating that of our rational systems, and which sometimes constitute the only cultural resources which human beings have to make sense of their world. This is not to deny that, in one historical-social formation after another, religion has been bound up in particular ways, wired up very directly, as the cultural and ideological underpinning of a particular structure of power. That is certainly the case historically. And in those societies, there are powerful, immensely strong, what I would call "lines of tendential force" articulating that religious formation to political, economic, and ideological structures. So that, if you move into that society, it would be idiotic to think that you could easily detach religion from its historical embeddedness and simply put it in another place. Thus, when I say the connections are "not necessary," I don't mean religion is free-floating. It exists historically in a particular formation, anchored very directly in relation to a number of different forces. Nevertheless, it has no necessary, intrinsic, transhistorical belongingness. Its meaning—political and ideological—comes precisely from its position within a formation. It comes with what else it is articulated to. Since those articulations are not inevitable, not necessary, they can potentially be transformed, so that religion can be articulated in more than one way. I insist that, historically, religion has been inserted into particular cultures in a particular way over a long period of time, and this constitutes magnetic lines of tendency which are very difficult to disrupt. To use a geographical metaphor, to struggle around religion in that country, you need to know the ideological terrain, the lay of the land. But that's not to say, "That's how it is, so it always will be so." Of course, if you are going to try to break, contest, or interrupt some of these tendential historical connections, you have to know when you are moving against the grain of historical formations. If you want to move religion, to rearticulate it in another way, you are going to come across all the grooves that have articulated it already.

Nevertheless, as we look across the modern and developing worlds, we see the extraordinary diversity of the roles which religious formations have actually played. We also see the extraordinary cultural and ideological vitality which religion has given to certain popular social movements. That is to say, in particular social formations where religion has become the *valorised* ideological domain, the domain into which all the different cultural strands are obliged to enter, no political movement in that society can become popular without negotiating the religious terrain. Social movements have to transform it, buy into it, inflect it, develop it, clarify it—but they must engage with it. You can't create a popular political movement in such social formations without getting into the religious question, because it is the arena in which this community has come to a certain kind of consciousness. This consciousness may be limited; it may not have successfully helped them to remake their history; but they have been "languaged" by the discourse of popular religion. They have, for the first time, used religion to construct some narrative, however impoverished and impure, to connect the past and the present: where they came from, with where they are and where they are going to, and why they are here.

In the case of the Rastafarians in Jamaica, Rasta was a funny language, borrowed from a text—the Bible—that did not belong to them; they had to turn the text upside down to get a meaning which fit their experience. But in turning the text upside down, they remade themselves; they positioned themselves differently as new political subjects; they reconstructed themselves as blacks in the New World: They *became* what they are. And positioning themselves in that way, they learned to speak a new language. And they spoke it with a vengeance. They learned to speak and sing. And in so doing, they did not assume that their only cultural resources lay in the past. They did not go back and try to recover some absolutely pure "folk culture," untouched by history, as if that would be the only way they could learn to speak. No, they made use of the modern media to broadcast their message: "Don't tell us about tom-toms in the forest. We want to use the new means of articulation and production to make a new music, with a new message." This is a cultural transformation. It is not something totally new. It is not something which has a straight, unbroken line of continuity from the past. It is transformation through a reorganisation of the elements of a cultural practice, elements which do not in themselves have any necessary political connotations. It is not the individual elements of a discourse that have political or ideological connotations; it is the ways those elements are organised together in a new discursive formation.

Let me come to the question of social forces. This ideology, which transforms a people's consciousness and awareness of themselves and their historical situation, although it explodes culturally, does not constitute itself *directly* as a social and political force. It has its limits, as all religious forms of explanation do. But it does become articulated to a social movement, a movement of people. And it functions so as to harness or draw to it sectors of the population who have never been inside that historical bloc before. Is it a class? In the case of the Rastafarian movement, it has at its center the experiences, the position, the determinations of economic life in Jamaican society. It has at its heart a class formation. Is it only a class? No, it could not have become a historical or political force simply reduced to an already unified class. Indeed it never has been a unified class, with a unified ideology already in place. It is crosscut, deeply intersected, by a variety of other determinations and ideologies. In fact, it only *becomes* a unified social force through the constitution of itself as a collective subject within a unifying ideology. It does not become a class or a unified social force until it begins to have forms of intelligibility which explain a shared collective situation. And even then, what determines the place and unity is nothing we can reduce to the terms of what we used to mean by an economic class. A variety of sectors of different social forces, in that moment, become articulated to and within this particular ideology. Therefore, it is not the case that the social forces, classes, groups, political movements, et cetera are first constituted in their unity by objective economic conditions and then give rise to a unified ideology. The process is quite the reverse. One has to see the way in which a variety of different social groups enter into and constitute for a time a kind of political and social force, in part by seeing themselves reflected as a unified force in the ideology which constitutes them. The relationship between social forces and ideology is absolutely dialectical. As the ideological vision emerges, so does the group. The Rastafarians were, Marx would say, as a group in themselves, the poor. But they don't constitute a unified political force *because* they are poor. In fact, the dominant ideology makes sense of them, not as "the poor" but as the feckless, the layabouts, the underclass. They only constitute a political force, that is, they *become* a historical force insofar as they are constituted as new political subjects.

So it is the articulation, the nonnecessary link between a social force which is making itself and the ideology or conceptions of the world which make intelligible the process they are going through, which begins to bring onto the historical stage a new social position and political position, a new set of social and political subjects. In that sense, I don't refuse the connection between an ideology or cultural force and a social force; indeed, I want to *insist* that the popular force of an organic ideology always depends on the social groups that can be articulated to and by it. It is here that one must locate the articulating principle. But I want to think that connection, not as one *necessarily* given in socioeconomic structures or positions, but precisely as the result of *an articulation*.

Let me take a brief, personal example as an indication of how some of the general things I have said about Althusser's general concept of ideology allows us to think about particular ideological formations. I want to think about that particular complex of discourses that implicates the ideologies of identity, place, ethnicity, and social formation generated around the term "black." Such a term "functions like a language." Indeed it does—languages, in fact, since the formations in which I place it, based on my own experience, both in the Caribbean and in Britain, do not correspond exactly to the American situation. It is only at the "chaotic" level of language in general that they are the same. In fact what we find are differences, specificities, within different, even if related, histories.

At different times in my thirty years in England, I have been "hailed" or interpellated as "coloured," "West Indian," "Negro," "black," "immigrant." Sometimes in the street, sometimes at street corners, sometimes abusively, sometimes in a friendly manner, sometimes ambiguously. (A black friend of mine was disciplined by his political organisation for "racism" because, in order to scandalise the white neighborhood in which we both lived as students, he would ride up to my window late at night and, from the middle of the street, shout "Negro!" very loudly to attract my attention!) All of them inscribe me "in place" in a signifying chain which constructs identity through the categories of colour, ethnicity, race.

In Jamaica, where I spent my youth and adolescence, I was constantly hailed as "coloured." The way that term was articulated with other terms in the syntaxes of race and ethnicity was such as to produce the meaning, in effect: "not black." The "blacks" were the rest—the vast majority of the people, the ordinary folk. To be "coloured" was to belong to the "mixed" ranks of the brown middle class, a cut above the rest—in aspiration if not in reality. My family attached great weight to these finely graded classificatory distinctions and, because of what it signified in terms of distinctions of class, status, race, and colour, insisted on the inscription. Indeed, they clung to it through thick and thin, like the ultimate ideological lifeline it was. You can imagine how mortified they were to discover that when I came to England I was hailed as "coloured" by the natives there precisely because, as far as they could see, I *was* "black" for all practical purposes! The same term, in short, carried quite different connotations because it operated within different "systems of differences and equivalences." It is the position within the different signifying chains which "means," not the literal, fixed correspondence between an isolated term and some denotated position in the colour spectrum.

The Caribbean system was organised through the finely graded classification systems of the colonial discourses of race, arranged on an ascending scale up to the ultimate "white" term—the latter always out of reach, the impossible, absent term, whose absent presence structured the whole chain. In the bitter struggle for place and position which characterises dependent societies, every notch on the scale mattered profoundly. The English system, by contrast, was organised around a simpler binary dichotomy, more appropriate to the colonising order: "white/not white." Meaning is not a transparent reflection of the world in language but arises through the differences between the terms and categories, the systems of reference, which classify out the world and allow it to be in this way appropriated into social thought, common sense.

As a concrete lived individual, am I indeed any one of these interpellations? Does any one of them exhaust me? In fact I "am" not one or other of these ways of representing me, though I have been all of them at different times and still am some of them to some degree. But there is no essential, unitary "I"—only the fragmentary, contradictory subject I became. Long after, I encountered "coloured" again, now as it were from the other side, beyond it. I tried to teach my son he was "black," at the same time as he was learning the colours of the spectrum, and he kept saying to me that he was "brown." Of course, he was *both*.

Certainly I am from the West Indies, though I've lived my adult life in England. Actually, the relationship between "West Indian" and "immigrant" is very complex for me. In the 1950s, the two terms were equivalents. Now, the term "West Indian" is very romantic. It connotes reggae, rum and Coke, shades, mangoes, and all that canned tropical fruit salad falling out of the coconut trees. This is an idealised "I." (I wish I felt more like that more of the time.) "Immigrant" I also know well. There is nothing remotely romantic about that. It places one so unequivocally as *really* belonging *somewhere else*. "And when are you going back home?" Part of Mrs. Thatcher's "alien wedge." Actually I only understood the way this term positioned me relatively late in life—and the "hailing" on that occasion came from an unexpected direction. It was when my mother said to me on a brief visit home, "I hope they don't mistake you for one of those immigrants!" The shock of recognition. I was also on many occasions "spoken" by that other, absent, unspoken term, the one that is never there, the "American" one, undignified even by a capital "N." The "silence" around this term was probably the most eloquent of them all. Positively marked terms "signify" because of their position in relation to what is absent, unmarked, the unspoken, the unsayable. Meaning is relational within an ideological system of presences and absences. "Fort! Da!"

Althusser (1971b, 175–176), in a controversial passage in the "Ideological State Apparatuses" essay, says that we are "always-already" subjects. Actually Hirst and others contest this. If we are "always-already" subjects, we would have to be born with the structure of recognitions and the means to position ourselves with language already formed. Whereas Lacan, from whom Althusser and others draw, uses Freud and Saussure to provide an account of how that structure of recognitions is formed (through the mirror phase and the resolutions of the Oedipus complex, et cetera). However, let us leave that objection aside for a moment, since a larger truth about ideology is implied in what Althusser says. We experience ideology as if it emanates freely and spontaneously from within us, as if we were its free subjects, "working by ourselves." Actually, we are spoken by and spoken for, in the ideological discourses which await us even at our birth, into which we are born and find our place. The newborn child who still, according to Althusser's reading of Lacan, has to acquire the means of being placed within the Law of Culture, is already expected, named, positioned in advance by "the forms of family ideology (paternal/maternal/conjugal/fraternal)" (1971b, 176).

The observation puts me in mind of a related early experience. It is a story frequently retold in my family—with great humor all round, though I never saw the joke, part of our family lore—that when my mother first brought me home from the hospital at my birth, my sister looked into my crib and said, "Where did you get this Coolie baby from?" "Coolies" in Jamaica are East Indians, deriving from the indentured labourers brought into the country after abolition to replace the slaves in plantation labour. "Coolie" is, if possible, one rung lower in the discourse of race than "black." This was my sister's way of remarking that, as often happens in the best of mixed families, I had come out a good deal darker skinned than was average in my family. I hardly know any more whether this really happened or was a manufactured story by my family or even perhaps whether I made it up and have now forgotten when and why. But I felt, then and now, summoned to my "place" by it. From that moment onwards, my place within this system of reference has been problematic. It may help to explain why and how I eventually became what I was first nominated: the "Coolie" of my family, the one who did not fit, the outsider, the one who hung around the street with all the wrong people, and grew up with all those funny ideas. The Other one.

What is the *contradiction* that generates an ideological field of this kind? Is it "the principal contradiction between capital and labour?" This signifying chain was clearly inaugurated at a specific historical moment—the moment of slavery. It is not eternal or universal. It was the way in which sense was made of the insertion of the enslaved peoples of the coastal kingdoms of West Africa into the social relations of forced labour production in the New World. Leave aside for a moment the vexed question of whether the mode of production in slave societies was "capitalist" or "precapitalist" or an articulation of both within the global market. In the early stages of development, for all practical purposes, the racial and class systems overlapped. They were "systems of equivalence." Racial and ethnic categories continue today to be the forms in which the structures of domination and exploitation are "lived." In that sense, these discourses do have the function of "reproducing the social relations of production." And yet, in contemporary Caribbean societies, the two systems do *not* perfectly correspond. There are "blacks" at the top of the ladder too, some of them exploiters of other black labour, and some firm friends of Washington. The world neither divides neatly into its social/natural categories, nor do ideological categories necessarily produce their own "appropriate" modes of consciousness. We are therefore obliged to say that there is a complicated set of articulations between the two systems of discourse. The relationship of equivalences between them is not fixed but has changed historically. Nor is it "determined" by a single cause but rather is the result of an "overdetermination."

These discourses therefore clearly construct Jamaican society as a field of social difference organised around the categories of race, colour, and ethnicity. Ideology here has the function of assigning a population into particular classifications organised around these categories. In the articulation between the discourses of class and race-colour-ethnicity (and the displacement effected between them which this makes possible), the latter is constituted as the "dominant" discourse, the categories through which the prevailing forms of consciousness are generated, the terrain within which men and women "move, acquire consciousness of their position, struggle, etc." (Gramsci 1971, 377), the systems of representations through which the people live "the imaginary relationship between them and their real conditions of existence" (Althusser 1970, 234). This analysis is not an academic one, valuable only for its theoretical and analytic distinctions. The overdetermination of class and race has the most profound consequences—some of them highly contradictory—for the *politics* of Jamaica, and of Jamaican blacks everywhere.

It is possible, then, to examine the field of social relations in Jamaica and in Britain, in terms of an interdiscursive field generated by at least three different contradictions (class, race, gender), each of which has a different history, a different mode of operation; each divides and classifies the world in different ways. Then it would be necessary, in any specific social formation, to analyse the ways in which class, race, and gender are articulated with one another to establish particular condensed social positions. Social positions, we may say, are here subject to a "double articulation." They are by definition overdetermined. To look at the overlap or "unity" (fusion) between them, that is to say, the ways in which they connote or summon up one another in articulating differences in the ideological field, does not obviate the *particular effects* which each structure has. We can think of political situations in which alliances could be drawn in very different ways, depending on which of the different articulations in play become at the time the dominant ones.

Now let us think about this term "black" within a particular semantic field or ideological formation rather than as a single term: within its chains of connotation. I give just two examples. The first is the chain black-lazy-spiteful-artful in a specific historical moment: the era of slavery. This reminds us that, though the distinction "black/white" that is articulated by this particular chain is not given simply by the capital-labour contradiction, the social relations characteristic of that specific historical moment are its referent in this particular discursive formation. In the West Indian case, "black," with this connotative resonance, is a way of representing how the peoples of a distinctive ethnic character were first inserted into the social relations of production. But of course, that chain of connotations is not the only one. An entirely different one is generated within the powerful religious discourses which have so raked the Caribbean: the association of Light with God and the spirit, and of Dark or "blackness" with Hell, the devil, sin, and damnation. When I was a child and I was taken to church by one of my grandmothers, I thought the black minister's appeal to the Almighty, "Lord, lighten our darkness," was a quite specific request for a bit of personal divine assistance up the colour chain.

It is important to look at the semantic field within which any particular ideological chain signifies. Marx reminds us that the ideas of the past weigh like a nightmare on the brains of the living. The moment of historical formation is critical for any semantic field. These semantic zones take shape at particular historical periods: for example, the formation of bourgeois individualism in the seventeenth and eighteenth centuries in England. They leave the traces of their connections long after the social relations to which they referred have disappeared. These traces can be reactivated at a later stage, even when the discourses are fragmented as coherent or organic ideologies. Commonsense thinking contains what Gramsci called the traces of ideology "without an inventory." Consider, for example, the trace of religious thinking in a world which believes itself to be secular and which, therefore, invests "the sacred" in secular ideas. Although the logic of the religious interpretation of terms has been broken, the religious repertoire continues to trail through history, usable in a variety of new historical contexts, reinforcing and underpinning more apparently "modern" ideas.

In this context, we can locate the possibility for ideological struggle. A particular ideological chain becomes a site of struggle, not only when people try to displace, rupture, or contest it by supplanting it with some wholly new alternative set of terms, but also when they interrupt the ideological field and try to transform its meaning by changing or rearticulating its associations, for example, from the negative to the positive. Often, ideological struggle actually consists of attempting to win some new set of meanings for an existing term or category, of disarticulating it from its place in a signifying structure. For example, it is precisely because "black" is the term which connotes the most despised, the dispossessed, the unenlightened, the uncivilised, the uncultivated, the scheming, the incompetent, that it can be contested, transformed, and invested with a positive ideological value. The concept "black" is not the exclusive property of any particular social group or any single discourse. To use the terminology of Laclau (1977), the term, despite its powerful resonances, has no necessary "class belongingness." It has been deeply inserted in the past into the discourses of racial distinction and abuse. It was, for long, apparently chained into place in the discourses and practices of social and economic exploitation. In the period of Jamaican history when the national bourgeoisie wished to make common cause with the masses in the fight for formal political independence from the colonising power—a fight in which the local bourgeoisie, not the masses, emerged as the leading social force—"black" was a sort of disguise. In the cultural revolution which swept Jamaica in the later 1960s and 1970s, when for the first time the people acknowledged and accepted their African-slave-black heritage, and the fulcrum or centre of gravity of the society shifted to "the roots," to the life and common experience of the black urban and rural underclasses as representing the cultural essence of "Jamaican-ness" (this is the moment of political radicalisation, of mass mobilisation, of solidarity with black struggles for liberation elsewhere, of "soul brothers" and "Soul," as well as of reggae, Bob Marley, and Rastafarianism), "black" became reconstituted as its opposite. It became the site for the construction of "unity," of the positive recognition of "the black experience": the moment of the constitution of a *new* collective subject—the "struggling black masses." This transformation in the meaning, position, and reference of "black" did not *follow* and *reflect* the black cultural revolution in Jamaica in that period. It was one of the ways in which those new subjects were *constituted*. The people—the concrete individuals—had always been there. But as subjects in struggle for a new epoch in history, they appeared for the first time. Ideology, through an ancient category, was constitutive of their oppositional formation.

So the word itself has no specific class connotation, though it does have a long and not easily dismantled history. As social movements develop a struggle around a particular programme, meanings which appear to have been fixed in place forever begin to lose their moorings. In short, the meaning of the concept has shifted as a result of the struggle around the chains of connotations and the social practices which made racism possible through the negative construction of "blacks." By invading the heartland of the negative definition, the black movement has attempted to snatch the fire of the term itself. Because "black" once signified everything that was least to be respected, it can now be affirmed as "beautiful," the basis of our positive social identity, which requires and engenders respect amongst us. "Black," then, exists ideologically only in relation to the contestation around those chains of meaning and the social forces involved in that contestation.

I could have taken any key concept, category, or image around which groups have organised and mobilised, around which emergent social practices have developed. But I wanted to take a term which has a profound resonance for a whole society, one around which the whole direction of social struggle and political movement has changed in the history of our own lifetimes. I wanted thereby to suggest that thinking that term in a nonreductionist way opens the field to more than an idealistic exchange of "good" or "bad" meanings; or a struggle which takes place only in discourse; or one which is fixed permanently and forever by the way in which particular unconscious processes are resolved in infancy. The field of the ideological has its own mechanisms; it is a "relatively autonomous" field of constitution, regulation, and social struggle. It is not free or independent of determinations. But it is not *reducible* to the simple determinacy of any of the other levels of social formations in which the distinction between black and white has become politically pertinent and through which that whole "unconsciousness" of race has been articulated. The process has real consequences and effects on how the whole social formation reproduces itself ideologically. The effect of the struggle over "black," if it becomes strong enough, is that it stops the society reproducing itself functionally, in *that* old way. Social reproduction itself becomes a contested process.

Contrary to the emphasis of Althusser's argument, ideology does not therefore only have the function of "reproducing the social relations of production." Ideology also *sets limits* to the degree to which a society can easily, smoothly, and functionally reproduce itself. The notion that the ideologies are always-already inscribed does not allow us to think about the shifts of accentuation in language and ideology, which is a constant, unending process—what Volosinov (1973) called the "multiaccentuality of the ideological sign" of the "class struggle in language."

Domination and Hegemony

The topic of this lecture is the organisation of power and the nature of domination in the social formation. In particular, I want to talk about the contribution of Antonio Gramsci to an understanding of the forms of domination and the possibilities for struggle in advanced capitalist democratic societies. I do not intend to give a complete reading of Gramsci's work or even of the many important insights and concepts he has contributed to contemporary Marxist theory and Cultural Studies. In fact, much of the preceding argument has depended on the advances Gramsci offers us. For example, I have used Gramsci to both enrich Althusserian concepts and to define an alternative or limit to Althusser's "hardening of the structuralist categories." I will limit myself in this lecture to those concepts which directly enter our understanding of domination: in particular, the State, ideology, hegemony, and hegemonic politics. First, I will make some preliminary remarks about Gramsci and situate his notion of hegemony in the broader context of his strong anti-reductionist project.

Gramsci was an Italian Marxist intellectual and a militant, one of the founders of the Italian Communist Party. He was born on Sardinia, one of the islands off the Italian coast. He was a socialist journalist, an active figure in the factory struggles in Turin and northern Italy in the period after World War I. He was, therefore, actively engaged in the moment of high proletarian consciousness. It is in the period immediately before and after World War I that one sees an advanced working class—a class actually advanced by capital itself, standing at the forefront of the very processes which contain it—beginning to feel the capacity to make the rest of the world in its image. That moment can be found in many struggles throughout Europe: in labour strikes in Wales and England, in the Hungarian Soviet, in the aborted German revolution, in the mass strikes in France, and in the Turin occupations. When people say that Marx and Engels predicted a revolution in Europe and it didn't happen, I wonder if they realise that it very nearly did happen. It almost happened, although the particular form it took, at least in Britain, France, and to some extent in Spain and the United States, was not the "class consciousness" of classical Marxism but syndicalism. Syndicalist forms of consciousness foregrounded the activity of the proletariat, its capacity to master the scientific and industrial revolution, to know that it had the keys of capitalist production in its hands and to be confirmed in the belief that it could rule. If you read, for example, Gramsci's and others' articles in *Ordine Nuevo* (The New Order), *Avanti* (Forward), and *L'Unità* (Unity), you will see represented a proletariat that believed it could now rule. Of course, it could not; it did not. As it turned out, this was not the final gasp of capitalism but one of its most recuperative periods. It comes out of that series of struggles even stronger and more dominant but only by transforming itself, by giving up its old forms and finding new ones, by articulating itself within new systems of representation. It does this and it pushes back the proletarian advances of the period.

This historical conjuncture—a strikingly condensed and contradictory moment of political struggles, victories, defeats, and transformations—enabled Gramsci to see some very important and profound things about Marxism, about the nature of Western industrial capitalism, and about the nature of proletarian and other forms of social struggle. I think there is a clear relationship between Gramsci as a political militant, the political moment in which he is formed, the forms of consciousness and action to which he relates, and his legacy as a Marxist thinker. Gramsci's thinking in this particular conjuncture is dramatic and original in relation to a number of particular sites. He is not a universal and systematic theorist, but in relation to a number of political and theoretical sites, he develops concepts that represent substantial achievements and advances:

first, in relation to mechanistic and reductive forms of Marxism; second, in terms of confronting the reality and complexity of the State and civil society, and of ideology and the superstructures, in Western capitalist democracies; and third, in confronting the moment of the degeneration of capitalism into Fascism. The latter is crucial of course to understanding Gramsci, given the constraints under which he produced his most important work: He was imprisoned by Mussolini. The *Prison Notebooks* (Gramsci 1971; except where indicated, all page numbers that follow in this lecture refer to this text) owe part of their obscurity to the fact that Gramsci had to speak around the censor. He comes out of prison virtually a broken man and is dead within a few years.

But it must always be kept in mind that Gramsci's project was not that of offering another reading of Marxism or another set of abstract concepts which could define a materialist analysis. Rather, Gramsci understood that Marx's general framework had to be constantly developed theoretically, applied to new historical conditions, related to developments in society which neither Marx nor Engels could have possibly foreseen, and expanded and refined by the addition of new concepts. It is this "sophisticating" work that Gramsci contributed. His work brings into play concepts which classical Marxism did not provide but without which Marxist theory cannot adequately explain the complex social phenomena we encounter in the modern world. Thus, his "theoretical" writing was always developed out of a more organic engagement with real political struggle, and was always intended to serve, not an abstract academic purpose, but the aim of "informing political practice." Gramsci's work uses theory to illuminate concrete historical cases or political questions, what Gramsci called the "conjunctural." Consequently, Gramsci's work often appears almost *too* concrete, too historically specific, too time and context bound, too descriptively analytic. His most illuminating ideas and formulations are typically of this kind. To make more general use of them, they have to be delicately disinterred from their concrete and specific historical embeddedness and transplanted to new soil with considerable care. This is different than both Althusser's and Poulantzas's attempts to "theorise" Gramsci's insufficiently theoretical texts, who rely, I think, on a mistaken perception of the appropriate level of abstraction on which Gramsci is operating.

Gramsci was strongly opposed to the mechanistic interpretations of Marxism that not only survived but were still canonised in both theoretical and political forms (through the Second International and the ideas and practices of Lenin and Stalin). Gramsci emphasised instead the importance of the relationship between the structure (the term he used instead of the base) and the superstructure. He substitutes for the reductionist approach which would "read off" political and ideological developments from their economic determination, a far more complex and differentiated type of analysis. This is based, not on a "one-way determination," but on the analysis of "the relations of force" which aims to differentiate (rather than to collapse as identical) the "various moments or levels" in the development of such a conjuncture. Only through rather complex processes can one extend one's analysis from the description of the base relationships of a capitalist social formation through what he calls "the decisive passage from the structure to the sphere of the complex superstructures" (181). Although he is still using the language of base and superstructure, he sees an integral and irreversible relationship between structure and superstructure. Once the contradiction of classes is elaborated in any particular society at the level of economic, political, ideological, and cultural formations, there is no way those complex forms of articulation can be squeezed back into the base from which they arose. That is to say, Gramsci can only think the relationship between structure and superstructure in terms of the effects which their interrelationship have in the end; or in my own terms, whether or not they effectively reproduce the social and political conditions for the real expansion and development of the capitalist mode. Although Gramsci himself takes his philosophical orientation from a "Marxism of praxis" (which bears close relations to the culturalism of Williams and Thompson), I would argue that he thinks the questions of determinacy and of the effects of different practices for the reproduction of capitalism in a structuralist way.

Gramsci has little tolerance for, and often wrote quite satirically about, the attempt to impose an instrumental Marxism, an economic or class reductionism, on that complexity. Such theories satisfy only the Marxism of exposure, which seeks to expose evil capitalists operating behind the scenes. It substitutes an analysis based on the assumption of "immediate class interests" (in the form of the question, who profits directly from this?)—as if every class interest were intrinsic to the social position and inscribed upon each member's back—for a fuller, more structured analysis of "economic class formations . . . with all their inherent relations" (163). On every particular occasion, it asks, how much of the capitalist class has been paid off in profits? That, Gramsci says, is a vulgar economic question. The functioning of the capitalist mode frequently requires that no fractions of the capitalist class are paid off; it often requires the power of the State to impose the terms of concession on capital as the price for its continued existence. So the idea that you can undo and ignore all the complexities of economic, class, political, social, and cultural relations and struggles, simply by looking for someone who profited financially from a particular event, merely undercuts the realities of the situation; it only *appears* to be materialist and scientific. The notion that one can understand history as a series of rip-offs, by various fractions of the capitalist class, of various fractions of the working class, receives only scorn from Gramsci; it has nothing to do with the processes by which a mode of production reproduces itself. Does this mean that the economic plays no part in the development of historical crises and conditions? Not at all, but its role is rather to "create a terrain more favourable to the dissemination of certain modes of thought, and certain ways of posing and resolving questions involving the entire subsequent development of national life" (184). In short, until one has shown how "objective economic crises" actually develop, through the changing relations in the balance of social forces, into crises of the State and society, and are taken up in ethico-political and ideological struggles influencing the conception of the world of the masses, one has not conducted a proper kind of analysis, rooted in the decisive and irreversible "passage" between structure and superstructure. This is what he meant by saying that the relationship between "structure" and "superstructures," or the "passage" of any organic historical movement right through the whole social formation, from economic "base" to the sphere of ethico-political relations, was at the heart of any nonreductionist or noneconomistic type of analysis. To pose and resolve that sort of question demanded an analysis of the complex relationships of overdetermination between the different social practices in any social formation. (Here you can see the strong Gramscian influence in Althusser.)

This is the protocol Gramsci (1959) pursued in "The Modern Prince" where he outlined his characteristic way of "analysing situations." The details are complex and cannot be filled out in all their subtlety here, but the bare outlines are worth setting out, if only for purposes of comparison with both a more reductionist approach and a more rigorously structuralist approach. He considered this effort "to establish the various levels of the relations of force . . . an elementary exposition of the science and art of politics—understood as a body of practical rules for research and of detailed observations useful for awakening an interest in effective reality and for stimulating more rigorous and more vigorous political insights" (175–176)—an effort, he added, which must be *strategic* in character.

First of all, he argued, one must understand the fundamental structure—the objective relations—within society or "the degree of development of the productive forces," for these set the most fundamental limits and conditions for the whole shape of historical development. From them arise the major lines of force or tendencies which might be favourable to this or that line of development. The error of reductionism is then to translate these tendencies and constraints *immediately* into their absolutely determined political and ideological effects or, alternatively, to abstract them into some "iron law of necessity." In fact, they structure and determine only in the sense that they define the terrain on which historical forces move; they define the horizon of possibilities. But they can neither in the first nor last instance fully determine the content of political and economic struggles, much less objectively fix or guarantee the outcomes of such struggles.

The next move in the analysis is to distinguish between "organic" historical movements, which are destined to penetrate deep into society and be relatively long lasting, and more "occasional, immediate, almost accidental movements." In this respect, Gramsci reminds us that a "crisis," if it is organic, can last for decades. It is not a static phenomenon but rather one marked by constant movement, polemics, contestations, et cetera, which represent the attempt by different sides to overcome or resolve the crises and to do so in terms which favour their own long-term interests. The theoretical danger, Gramsci argues, lies in "presenting causes as immediately operative which in fact only operate indirectly, or in asserting that the immediate causes are the only effective ones" (178). The first leads to an excess of economism; the second to an excess of ideologism. (Gramsci was preoccupied, especially in moments of defeat, by the fatal oscillation between these two extremes, which in reality mirror one another in an inverted form.) Far from there being any "law-like" guarantee that will inevitably convert economic causes into immediate political effects, Gramsci insisted that the analysis only succeeds and is "true" *if* those underlying causes become a new reality. The substitution of the conditional tense for positivistic certainty is critical.

Next, Gramsci insisted on the fact that the length and complexity of crises cannot be mechanically predicted, but develop over longer historical periods; they move between periods of relative "stabilisation" and periods of rapid and convulsive change. Consequently, periodisation is a key aspect of the analysis; it parallels his concern with historical specificity. "It is precisely the study of these 'intervals' of varying frequency which enables one to reconstruct the relations on the one hand, between structure and superstructure, and on other between the development of organic movement and conjunctural movement in the structure" (180). There is nothing mechanical or prescriptive for Gramsci about this study.

Having thus established the groundwork of a dynamic historical-analytic framework, Gramsci turns to the analysis of the movements of historical forces—the "relations of force"—which constitute the actual terrain of political and social struggle and development. Here he introduces the critical notion that what we are looking for is not the absolute victory of this side over that side in the relations of force, nor the total incorporation of one set of forces into another. Rather, the analysis is a relational matter—i.e., a question to be resolved relationally, using the idea of an "unstable balance" or "the continuous process of formation and superceding of unstable equilibria." The critical question (not to be converted into an explanation) is "the relations of forces favourable or unfavourable to this or that tendency." This critical emphasis on "relations" and "unstable balance" reminds us that social forces which lose out in any particular historical period do not thereby disappear from the terrain of struggle; nor is struggle in such circumstances suspended. For example, the idea of the "absolute" and total victory of the bourgeoisie over the working class or the total incorporation of working-class demands into the bourgeois project are totally foreign to Gramsci's notion of domination (and even more so to his notion of hegemony)—though this is often misunderstood in scholarly and political commentary. It is always the tendential balance in the relations of force which matters.

Gramsci then differentiates the "relations of force" into its different moments. He assumes no necessary teleological evolution between these moments. The first has to do with an assessment of the objective conditions which place and position the different social forces. The second relates to the political moment—the "degree of homogeneity, self-awareness and organization attained by the various social classes" (181). The important thing here is that so-called class unity is never assumed, a priori. It is understood that classes, while sharing certain common conditions of existence, are also crosscut by conflicting interests, historically segmented and fragmented in this actual course of historical formation. Thus the "unity" of classes is necessarily complex and has to be produced—constructed, created, articulated—as a result of specific economic, political, and ideological practices. It can never be taken as automatic or "given." Coupled with this radical historicisation of the automatic conception of classes lodged at the heart of classical Marxism, Gramsci elaborates further on Marx's distinction between "class in itself" and "class for itself." He notes the different stages through which class consciousness, organisation, and unity can—under the right conditions—develop. There is the "economic corporate" stage, where professional or occupational groups recognise their basic common interests but are conscious of no wider class solidarities. Then there is the "class corporate" moment, where class solidarity of interest develops, but only in the economic field. Finally, there is the moment of "hegemony," which transcends the corporate limits of purely economic solidarity, encompasses the interests of other subordinate groups, and begins to "propagate itself throughout society—bringing about not only a unison of economic and political aims, but also intellectual and moral unity," and "posing all the questions around which the struggle rages . . . thus creating the hegemony of a fundamental social group over a series of subordinate groups" (181–182). It is this process of the coordination of the interests of a dominant group with the general interests of other groups and the life of the State as a whole that constitutes the "hegemony" of a particular historical bloc. It is only in such moments of "national popular" unity that the formation of what he calls a "collective will" becomes possible. Gramsci reminds us, however, that even this extraordinary degree of organic unity does not guarantee the outcome of specific struggles, which can be won or lost on the outcome of the decisive tactical issue of the military and politico-military relations of force. He insists, however, that "politics . . . must have priority over its military aspect and only politics creates the possibility for manoeuvre and movement" (232). I want to say more about the notion of hegemony, but first it is necessary to make some brief remarks about Gramsci's conception of the State and his theory of ideology.

The question of the role of the State had been, at best, marginal within classical Marxism (with the exception of Lenin). The centrality which has been given to the State in contemporary Marxist debates is largely due to Gramsci and those who have learned from him. The State is a new kind of structuring force which often interposes itself between the direct play of economic or class forces and the relationships of culture. Consequently, in advanced democratic capitalist societies, the domains of culture and ideology have to be understood as much in relation to the State as to the mode of production. The State is frequently what Gramsci would call the instance which organises the terrain of civil society. It is the point where the rule of an economic class is converted into political power; it is where it becomes centralised and condensed, invested with the power and authority of the State itself.

Moreover, the State is frequently the primary agency through which cultural relations are organised and reorganised. One need only think of the relations between the ideological fields of public or popular opinion and the institutions of civil society—newspapers, the mass media, educational institutions, and the church—in terms of access both to the technology and to the means of the formation of people's identities, to realise that it is the State which regulates many of the forms in which cultural and ideological production take place. Gramsci's recognition of the importance of the State's regulatory function—as the agent of the regulation of social relations, as the instance of law and of rule—is a crucial insight which prior to Gramsci was not a part of Marxism's common vocabulary for thinking about the relationship between culture, ideology, and other domains of social practices.

Gramsci undermines the classic Marxist-Leninist language of the State as simply a coercive instrument of the ruling class. The State in advanced industrial capitalist societies is not simply coercive, nor are its noncoercive activities simply a disguise or cover for the real apparatuses of coercion. Gramsci insists that the State is also educative: It enlarges social and cultural possibilities; it enables people to enter new terrains. It is necessarily a contradictory site on which concessions have been won. Without this double-sidedness of the State, how could one possibly understand the importance of the introduction of the welfare apparatus—through legislation—throughout Western industrial capitalism? One would have to argue, as some Marxists indeed have, that this is really just a ruse of the capitalist class, in spite of the fact that millions of people struggled for it, struggled to win from the State what was owed them, and continue to engage in political struggles to enlarge that aspect of the State. What sense can be made of these struggles if we talk about welfare as if it were just a clever way in which the capitalist class continues to exploit workers? It is impossible to define the State in that simple way, as if it had only an instrumental coercive role, which is not to say that the State does not have a coercive role.

It is sometimes through coercive measures, sometimes through educative and regulative measures, and most frequently through a combination of these, that the State attempts to mobilise cultural and ideological consent. Part of the object of the State's concern is public opinion in the sphere of civil society, which it cannot take hold of and manufacture directly, but which it organises. This leads us to recognise that the State, while always a contradictory instance, is articulated to the dominant social forces, the dominant ideological systems, and the dominant class positions in the economy. But it is not, by virtue of that, simply controlled by the capitalist class; its relations to that class are not already "wrapped up" and guaranteed. It is, as Lenin began to understand, an instance which requires its separation from the capitalist class. It is often the State in advanced industrial capitalist societies which brings about the unity of the capitalist class, which unites those fractions of capital which are unable to unite themselves in their ordinary economic dealings; it frequently proposes to those fractions the political program on which they can become more united. But the State requires a degree of separation, specificity, and relative autonomy from the direct play of classical class contradictions if it is to perform its many and diverse functions.

Gramsci adopts what, at first, may seem a fairly traditional definition of ideology, by beginning with "any conception of the world, any philosophy which has become a cultural movement, a 'religion,' a 'faith,' any that has produced a form of practical activity or will in which the philosophy is contained as an implicit theoretical 'premiss'" [*sic*]. "One might say," he adds, "'ideology' here, but on condition that the word is used in its highest sense of a conception of the world that is implicitly manifest in art, in law, in economic activity and in all manifestations of individual and collective life" (328). This is followed by a clear statement of the problem ideology addresses or its basic function: "that of preserving the ideological unity of the entire social bloc which that ideology serves to cement and unify" (328). However, even this definition is not as simple as it looks, for it makes the essential link between the philosophical nucleus or premise at the centre of any distinctive ideology or conception of the world, and the necessary elaboration of that conception into a practical and popular form of consciousness, which affects the broad masses of society in the form of a cultural movement, political belief, faith, or religion. Gramsci is *never* only concerned with the philosophical core of an ideology; he always addresses *organic* ideologies, which "organise human masses, and create the terrain on which men move, acquire consciousness of their position, struggle, etc." (377).

This is the basis of Gramsci's critical distinction between "philosophy" and "common sense." Ideology consists of these two, distinct "floors." The coherence of an ideology often depends on its specialised philosophical elaboration. But this formal coherence cannot guarantee its organic historical role. That can only be found when and where philosophical currents enter into, modify, and transform the practical everyday consciousness of the masses. The latter is what he calls "common sense." Common sense is not coherent; it is usually "disjointed and episodic," fragmentary and contradictory. In it the traces and "stratified deposits" of more coherent philosophical systems have sedimented over time without leaving any clear inventory. It represents itself as the "traditional wisdom or truth of the ages," when in fact, it is deeply a product of history, "part of the historical process." Why then is it important? Because it is the terrain of conceptions and categories on which the practical consciousness of the masses of the people is actually formed. It is the already formed and "taken-for-granted" ground on which more coherent ideologies and philosophies must contend for mastery, the ground which new conceptions of the world must contest and even transform, if they are to shape the conceptions of the world of the masses and in that way become historically effective:

Every philosophical current leaves behind a sedimentation of "common sense": this is the document of its historical effectiveness. Common sense is not rigid and immobile but is continually transforming itself, enriching itself with scientific ideas and with philosophical opinions which have entered ordinary life. . . . "Common sense" creates the folklore of the future, that is as a relatively rigid phase of popular knowledge at a given place and time. (326n5)

It is this concern with *popular thought* which distinguishes Gramsci's treatment of ideology. Thus, he insists that everyone is a philosopher or an intellectual insofar as they think, since all thought, action, and language is reflexive, contains a conscious line of moral conduct, and thus sustains a particular conception of the world (although not everyone has the specialised function of "the intellectual").

In addition, a class will always have its spontaneous, vivid, but not coherent or philosophically elaborated, instinctive understanding of its basic conditions of life and the nature of the constraints and forms of exploitation to which it is commonly subjected. Gramsci described the latter as its "good sense." But it requires a further work of political education and cultural politics to renovate and clarify these confused constructions of popular thought—common sense—into a more coherent political theory or philosophical current. This "raising of popular thought" is part and parcel of the process by which a collective will is constructed, and requires extensive work of intellectual organisation—an essential part of any hegemonic political strategy. Popular beliefs, in this sense, Gramsci argues, are not an arena of struggle which can be left to look after itself. They "are themselves material forces" (165).

Gramsci's thinking on this question also encompasses novel ways of conceptualising the *subjects* of ideology. He altogether refuses any idea of a pregiven unified ideological subject—for example, the proletariat with its "correct" revolutionary thoughts or the blacks with their already guaranteed antiracist consciousness. He recognises the "plurality" of selves or identities of which the so-called subject of thought and ideas is composed, and that this multifaceted nature of consciousness is not an individual matter but a consequence of the relationship between "the self" and the ideological discourses which compose the cultural terrain of a society.

"The personality is strangely composite," he observes. It contains "Stone Age elements and principles of a more advanced science, prejudices from all past phases of history . . . and intuitions of a future philosophy" (324). Often, there is a contradiction in consciousness between that conception of the world which manifests itself, however fleetingly, in action, and those conceptions which are affirmed verbally or in thought. This complex, fragmentary, and contradictory conception of consciousness is preferable to the explanation by way of "false consciousness," which is nothing more than an explanation in terms of self-deception, which he rightly regards as inadequate.

Similarly, though Gramsci recognises that questions of ideology are always collective and social, not individual, he is aware of the complexity and interdiscursive character of the ideological field. There is never any one, single, unified, and coherent "dominant ideology" which pervades everything. "There co-exist many systems and currents of philosophical thought." The object of analysis here is not the single stream of "dominant ideas" into which everything and everyone has been automatically absorbed, but rather an analysis of the different discursive currents, their points of juncture and break: in short, an ideological complex, ensemble, or discursive formation. The question is, "how they are diffused, and why in the process of diffusion they fracture along certain lines and in certain directions" (327).

I believe it clearly follows from this line of argument that, though the ideological field is always, for Gramsci, articulated to different social and political positions, its shape and structure do not precisely mirror, match, or "echo" the class structure of society. Ideas, he argues, "are not spontaneously 'born' in each individual brain: they have a centre of formation, of irradiation, of dissemination, of persuasion" (192). They are not psychologistic or moralistic in character "but structural and epistemological." Consequently, they are not transformed or changed by replacing one, whole, already formed, conception of the world with another, so much as by "renovating and making 'critical' an already existing activity" (331). The multiaccentual, interdiscursive character of the field of ideology is explicitly acknowledged by Gramsci when, for example, he describes how an old conception of the world is gradually displaced by another mode of thought and is internally reworked and transformed:

What matters is the criticism to which such an ideological complex is subjected. . . . This criticism makes possible a process of differentiation and change in the relative weight that the elements of the old ideologies used to possess. What was previously secondary and subordinate . . . becomes the nucleus of a new ideological and theoretical complex. The old collective will dissolves into its contradictory elements since the subordinate ones develop socially. (195)

This is an altogether more original and generative way of perceiving the actual process of ideological struggle—and obviously the ground from which I was able to reread Althusser. It includes such ideas as the existing cultural ground, structured by previous history, on which all "new" philosophical and theoretical currents work and with which they must come to terms; the given structure or determinate character of that terrain; the complexity of the process of deconstruction and reconstruction by which alignment can be effected between elements in different discourses; the gradual disarticulation of one mode of thinking from another, and the rearticulation of that mode to a different set of social practices and political positions.

For Gramsci, classes are formed in relation to the State; they do not appear before the State, already unified, with their program in hand. The State is not an empty instrument or conduit merely carrying out that program through its coercive powers. It is perhaps comforting to think that our society is ruled by that kind of transitive domination, but Gramsci's conception of hegemony radically challenges any such simple notion of domination. Although many contemporary Marxists use hegemony and domination as interchangeable, they are importantly different. When we use terms like domination, cultural domination, or incorporation, we are immediately simplifying what Gramsci means by hegemony. It is useful then to begin to explain hegemony by describing what Gramsci did not mean by it. Then we can appreciate the ways in which he was suggesting a much more open and enlarged notion of the nature of rule, of politics, and of domination. And we can appreciate as well that his analysis centered on the real circumstances and conditions of politics as we know them in advanced mass industrial capitalist societies.

He did not mean hegemony to suggest that everyone is incorporated into the existing system because they are mesmerised by the ideological forms and media. There is no more reductionist, instrumentalist, class-delusionary position than to assume that the extraordinary complexities of the society in which we live are really held together by the cement of the media's messages. As crude as this may sound, a large part of the Marxist literature which tries to explain how Western societies are held together consensually—how the consensus is constructed, why it is that the working class is not revolutionary, and why it is that history is not following the punctuating rhythm of class struggle—relies on that position. Hegemony is not ideological mystification. Nor is it merely cultural domination as total incorporation, as if all the contradictory and oppositional forces and practices simply were engulfed and disappear, forever lost to history. While that may happen on some occasions, the actual establishment of domination in hegemony is more that of having the capacity to actively contain, educate, and reshape oppositional forces, to maintain them in their subordinate places. The work of subordination is what Gramsci emphasises in hegemony rather than the achievement of total incorporation.

Nor does hegemony refer to either the coercive power of the State or simple instrumental rule by an economic class. Hegemony does not mean rule by an economic class. Gramsci was interested in the variety of political formations and political class fractions through which the bourgeoisie has ruled. He takes nineteenth-century Britain as exemplary; it was a society becoming bourgeois in its relations while the actual system of rule was still predominantly in the hands of a landed capitalist class rather than a merchant, industrial, or commercial one. What interested him is the capacity of a particular form of economic (class) domination to exercise itself politically through a variety of other mediations—through particular political parties and through the formation of a particular historical bloc. This is how Gramsci thinks the nonreductive relationship between economic contradictions and political forms. When hegemony is established as a form of political rule, it does not involve whole classes but the formation of a historical bloc which provides the political, social, and economic underpinnings of a period of hegemony. Such a bloc combines the leading section of the dominant class with subaltern and subordinate sections of other classes, of the middle classes and the petty bourgeoisie, as well as of the popular classes which have been drawn into the matrix or configuration of power. That is to say, hegemony refers to the way in which those elements that rule politically and dominate ideologically (in the rule of a particular State) do so by having the capacity to mobilise popular forces in support; by mobilising, colonising, incorporating, grasping, circumventing, or containing those elements necessary to pull into and hold to itself the support of sections of the popular classes. Hegemony entails the formation of a bloc, not the appearance of a class. It is precisely the establishment of the ascendency of a particular historical bloc or formation over the society as a whole that constitutes hegemony, and this can only be accomplished if that bloc is able to generalise the interests and the goals of a particular group so that they come to command something like popular recognition and consent. The political project of rule in that sense has been changed completely by Gramsci's terminology and concepts. Many political formations have established rule without the capacity to establish hegemony. Only hegemony enables the leading bloc to constitute a set of historical tasks for the society as a whole, to begin to make a variety of different social groups and institutions conform to and cooperate with that particular task. Sometimes it is the overcoming of a particular crisis; sometimes it is the setting of a new goal for the social formation, having the society undertake some new historical venture. Hegemony thus involves the way in which political forces are able to win or mobilise popular support for historic tasks.

Hegemony does not obliterate the difference between those who rule and those who do not. It does not erase the line separating the subordinate classes and those who are in the dominant position. On the contrary, it precisely allows for the space in which subordinate and excluded peoples develop political practices and social spaces of their own. Hegemony does not mean that they have to be driven out of existence or brutalised into acquiescence. They can maintain their own space as long as they are constantly contained within the horizon of political practices and ideological systems of representation which place them always in the subordinate position. It is perfectly compatible with a moment of hegemony to have a substantial area of working-class life, organisations, and institutions. It is only necessary to contain the forms of class consciousness and struggle that emerge around the ideological distinction between us and them. The position of a subordinate group—"We are of course of a different class. We don't belong up there. We have our own spaces. Come down to our communities, come down to our clubs, come down to working-class culture. See us in our own space."—can perfectly well be a subordinated space over which hegemony is exercised. Subordination remains alive, as real social practices, political spaces, and genuine institutions that allow a class to elaborate its life always do so in a language spoken by others, always in a political space defined by others. That is the way in which the hegemony of one group is established over another. Hegemony is about leadership and not only about domination.

Nor does hegemony ever function without opposition, because it cannot overcome all of the fundamental contradictions within the structure of the society in which it is established, and it cannot totally contain all of those elements which are not part of the historical bloc. But it is capable of taking the leading, defining position. It is capable of a certain mastery of the terrain. It is capable of generalising its rule across the society, of becoming the "taken for granted," that is, of establishing the point at which the conversation begins, the scale within which the calculations are made. The place from which a society begins to move is the point of a certain balance of power, a balance of forces across a number of key domains, and that is the point at which one can recognise hegemonic formations.

Of course hegemony is never without coercion; no State has attempted to lead and establish its authority while abolishing its police force. The fact that consent is often the leading instance through which hegemony is generated does not mean that there isn't coercion. Consent is always supported, reinforced, and underpinned by the capacity— when necessary—to enforce the terms of consensus and domination over others. But the moment of hegemony is never a moment of pure coercion. The moment of pure coercion is clearly a moment of relative instability for a dominant or ruling group. The point at which you have to call upon what Althusser (1971b) called the "repressive State apparatuses" to get people into line behind you is a moment of greater exposure than the point at which you can appeal to the people's right to a free election and a secret ballot which somehow always tends to deliver a victory to those already in power. The moments of coercion and consent are always complementary, interwoven, and interdependent, rather than separated elements. Most systems of exploitation are maintained by the double modalities of coercion and consent; they are both always present. Coercion functions as what Gramsci called "the support system," even when power is functioning principally through consensual modes. But we must also recognise that there are important shifts in the tempo or rhythm by which societies structured in dominance maintain and reproduce their dominance. Hegemony points, not to the overthrow of one modality in favor of the other, but to the movement from the coercive to the consensual pole. For example, there is a moment in recent British history, as the 1970s advance, where, while the existing political forces are still in command of the State—electorally and in every other way—there is nevertheless an important shift in the balance between coercion and consent. As the consensual becomes more difficult to sustain, as the material conditions which allow consensual mechanisms to operate become more fragile and increasingly contested, one finds the coercive elements of the State and social institutions playing an increasingly important role in maintaining the mode of domination. That is the moment in which the law, the practices of the "policing of society," and authoritarian discourses become more pronounced in their capacities to discipline and regulate the society.

Hegemony is leadership which is in control, and that is what hegemony means: mastery. It means continually exercising the mastery of a situation. It entails forms of domination, if you will, that are not explicitly repressive. The notion that once hegemony is established it goes on forever is also quite foreign to Gramsci's conception. Hegemony is difficult work. It always has to be won. A dominant bloc has to constantly work for the establishment and continuation of its hegemony. It has to occupy the spaces which are required to reproduce its authority in the society. And what it gains is leadership and the containment of alternative forces. It need not incorporate or destroy them. It has enormous space within it for those who cannot live within the system. It is perfectly capable of tolerating marginals and deviants. It boxes them in, partly by the iron fist and partly by the velvet glove. But the fact that those open spaces exist is a testimony to its capacity to rule.

In Gramsci's view, it is only in such hegemonic moments of leadership that a historical bloc can get hold of society and shape it to meet the new conditions required to establish, develop, and expand the power of a particular bloc and its economic forms. A historical bloc is genuinely hegemonic—morally, intellectually, culturally, politically, *as well as* economically—when it can reshape the social formation and bring it into line with those forms of social and political practice and ideological representation which are the conditions for a new historical task, for the development of something different, or for the power to deal with a crisis. It is important to notice that Gramsci arrived at the conception of hegemony because he thought it had never been achieved in Italy. This cannot be explained by appealing to the lack of a ruling class but rather to the fact that there are two constantly fighting with one another: one, based in the south, was still powerfully attached to a feudal mode of production; the other, based in the north, was built upon a mixed although largely modern economic system. Therefore, it was not the case that Italy was not under the determining influence of particular modes of production. But there had been no Italian force capable of establishing an identity between the capitalist project and the project of the people as a whole, on the terrain of what Gramsci calls the "national popular." The lack of hegemonic rule in Italy was then due to the failure to work on the terrain of the common sense of ordinary people, outside of the direct imposition of State constraint, in order to create the necessary ground on which capitalism can develop as a national project. This is where the moment of hegemony operates to create the conditions—cultural, economic, moral, and political—which are required for modes of production to genuinely expand, to change direction significantly, or to resolve a particular crisis.

It follows that hegemony can only be conceived as a historical process, not as a thing achieved. But on the other hand, it is not merely the ongoing maintenance of rule and domination. It has to be specified "empirically" if the power of the ruling class or the dominant bloc is in fact a moment of hegemony. Additionally, because hegemony is the establishment of the leading position on a variety of sites of social and political struggle, it includes domains that are usually ignored by Marxists, like the discourses of morality. Anybody who wants to command the space of common sense, or popular consciousness, and practical reasoning has to pay attention to the domain of the moral, since it is the language within which vast numbers of people actually set about their political calculations. The Left has rarely talked about that space in which the difference between the "good" and the "bad" is defined; it has rarely attempted to establish the language of a socialist morality. Consequently, it is left entirely in the keeping of religious and moral entrepreneurs, of the churches and the moral majority. For Gramsci, failing to recognise the importance of giving people the capacity to make the necessary calculations—in their own idioms, languages, and everyday life—of moral judgments (as well as of social, political, and intellectual ones) simply means that a particular political force (e.g., the Left) has abstained from engaging on a front where it ought to be present. Consequently, the subordination of the cultural field in the effort to construct a hegemonic politics—the notion that it is merely a matter of whim whether you enter into it, that it is someplace that you can get into or not as you like—would be ludicrous.

Consider the question of Britain at the end of the nineteenth century, the period in which the modern British State is formed, the period of mass democracy, the period of the establishment of a particular form of working-class socialism ("labourism") which gets institutionalised in the Labour Party. It is also the period of the collapse of a genuinely hegemonic formation from the past, namely, of liberalism. In the previous period, liberalism was the leading philosophy, the leading political formation, the one which was able for a long period of time to contain the working-class organisations. It is in the leading position even when the Conservatives are in power; it defines the ideas with which people thought about their project in the world, the way in which they came to understand what British society was like, what its achievements were, what its historical destiny was, as well as the nature of British politics and culture. The formation of liberalism was able to contain, for a very long time, the trade union movement, working-class socialism, and the representations of working people. It was a formation in which everybody could find their place, a "mansion with many rooms" as it were. Thus, radicals did not have to position themselves within the established parties or political alternatives. There were spaces for everybody in the *same* house, and one knew what the leading elements which defined the formation were. It is when those key elements begin to be challenged, both in terms of material practices—its economic conditions of existence (e.g., the decline of Britain in competition with the United States, Japan, and Germany)—and of ideological representations, that there is a real disintegration of that particular hegemonic formation.

And then there is a struggle to construct a new hegemony; and that struggle is particularly interesting because, in part, all of the different sides understood that the relationship between the individual and the society had to be constructed differently from its articulation within the liberal formation. Consequently, it is a period when the individualism of liberalism is broadly challenged under the banner of what I call collectivism. Whether on the Right, the Middle, or the Left, one finds attempts to articulate forms of collectivism: There is a socialist collectivism, a conservative collectivism, and a collectivism of those people who are involved in enunciating a new era of national efficiency and imperial destiny. All operate under some notion of collectivism because they all have to come to terms with the destruction of the hegemony of that conception of the State embodied in liberalism, although they all attack it from different points. It is only out of the struggle itself that one begins to get the elements which might lead to a new hegemony. And the results of the particular ways in which those struggles are conducted are very important in defining, not only what happens in the 1920s and 1930s, but what has happened ever since. That is the period in which a particular form of social democracy, a particular kind of labourism, is generated. It wins out over a whole range of other kinds of socialism which were active in the labour movement during that period (e.g., Fabianism, which has survived as a kind of permeating middle-class socialism; and syndicalism), movements which were struggling for new ways of representing the emergent interests of working people in the new industrial classes and, indeed, of wider social categories. This is, not coincidentally, the period of the struggle for women's rights. You cannot understand this period as if there was a single ruling class with its one ideology which had repressed and incorporated all opposition and difference. It is only out of an ongoing and continuous struggle in which different groups ascend and descend that the actual configuration of new forms of hegemony are generated.

This example raises important ambiguities in Gramsci's use of the concept of hegemony. It is, on the one hand, as I have suggested, a very particular, historically specific, and temporary moment in the life of a society. It is rare for such a degree of unity to actually be achieved. On the other hand, later in his work, Gramsci expands the notion beyond that of the formation of a particular class alliance and suggests that it is at least a strategy of all ruling classes, that it applied to the formation of all leading historical blocs. But that distinction is complicated by a historical question. Gramsci connects hegemony to the distinction between "East" and "West" formations; the distinction is a metaphor for a particular historical shift which took place in the Western capitalist nations after 1870, a shift characterised by the internationalisation of capital, the emergence of modern mass democracy, the complexification of the role and organisation of the State, and an unprecedented elaboration in the structures and processes of civil society. One could equally well point to other significant changes that mark the transition into modern capitalism. But the decisive point for Gramsci was that these changes marked the increasing diversification of social antagonism and the dispersal of power. Consequently, forms of domination were required to ground their power more and more in an increasingly complex and autonomous civil society, in the processes of winning consent within the voluntary institutions of civil society. Thus, according to Gramsci, hegemony is a specific formation of domination with particular conditions of existence and, hence, a specific historical location. But it is unclear whether Gramsci continues to hold to this historical specificity, or whether we are obliged to take the fruitful historical example as necessary and constitutive of hegemony.

Gramsci's conception of hegemony entails, not only a different notion of domination, but also a different notion of political, cultural, and ideological struggle. Gramsci identifies three different moments of political struggle; he does not—as he has often been misread—divide politics into two exclusive types as if one had then to choose one or the other. These are the "war of maneuver" (or movement), "underground warfare," and the "war of position" (229–239). The "war of maneuver" occurs when there is a genuine division of society, not only between classes, but more generally, between the oppressed and the oppressors. In such profound moments of rupture, society is split by a mass mobilisation of the popular forces against the power bloc, of the people against those who command power. The two sides or forces can be clearly isolated and identified, and there is a direct contestation or confrontation of power. The moment of "underground warfare" exists where there are already pertinent sites of political and economic struggle in the society, and the contestation cannot be head-on. It is not class against class or people against the power bloc; it is the development of raiding parties which strategically attack the strongholds of power of a particular class. It is, for Gramsci, the beginning of mass or popular mobilisation. Finally, a "war of position" can only exist in societies that have a fully formed mass democracy, in which the working classes and other popular democratic forces have already engaged in successful struggles to win particular economic, political, and civil rights and powers. These are societies of extraordinary social and political complexity; within them, civil society does not have the kind of simple structure which would permit the State to overwhelm it instantly and easily. Civil society has developed a great deal of autonomy and independence from the direct mediations of State power and it includes institutions which have been developed to some degree outside of the immediate purchase of the dominant or ruling classes. Consequently, the direct confrontation between the excluded and the included classes, or between the powerless and the powerful, is now subject to the extraordinarily diverse and often displaced forms of political struggle that are common in parliamentary and democratic regimes. In those societies, politics will be conducted through a war of position much of the time, although not all of the time. Struggle will be differentiated, conducted in what Gramsci calls the "'trenches' and . . . fortifications" (243) of civil society (culture, language, ideology, and morality), as well as in direct confrontations with the condensed power of the State or with the economic power guaranteed in capitalist class relations.

Gramsci's opening of Marxism to the possibility, indeed the necessity, of differentiated forms of political struggle grounds a useful effort to adapt the forms of class struggle to the historically emerging conditions of capitalism between the two world wars. Once the "high proletarian moment" described above had ebbed and the capitalist social formations went on, the new formations began to acquire a degree of hegemony. They reorganised themselves both politically and economically. It is not simply that the struggle had been defeated and turned back, but rather, that its very form and nature have had to change. It has had to adapt to a new kind of terrain on which new and diverse forms of mass politics are demanded.

The only politics capable of confronting a hegemonic position is a hegemonic politics, a war of position. Only a hegemonic politics is capable of the degree of organisation which can confront bourgeois ideology on the terrain of common sense. A hegemonic politics operates in the cultural apparatuses, the discourse of moral languages, in the economic struggle, in the political space (including electoral struggles as well as other forms). It tries to occupy each and every front and understands that victory is not the great battle which ends with the final collapse of the enemy. Victory is the seizing of the balance of power on each of those fronts of struggle. It is commanding the balance of political, social, and ideological forces at each point in the social formation. That is a lesson which few on the Left have understood, but one which the bourgeoisie (especially in its contemporary forms) absolutely understands. They do not leave the cultural, intellectual, and moral spaces alone. They do not ignore the academies because there are relatively few people involved. They do not refuse to do battle on the terrain of sexual, social, and religious problems because that is not the domain of politics and power. They know that if they are to make a difference in history, they are going to have to make a difference on all those fronts.

When Thatcherism emerged in England, it entered the struggle on every single front on which it calculated it could advance itself. You know that their project is to be hegemonic when, for example, the minister for education takes the time to propose changing the name of the body which gives grants to higher education from the Social Science Research Council to the Social Studies Research Council. After all, since 1968, everyone knows that sociology is not a science: That is working on the ground of common sense. That is a formation which means to contest every single idea, to have a theory for every single arena of human life, a definition for every single social position. It means to contest Keynesianism, in its simple and its most advanced forms. It intends to tell you how to bring up your children, how a teacher should act and appear, what languages to use at various times, and so on. It means to occupy and define a dominant space at every single point. It separates itself from those forms of paternalist conservatism which would accommodate themselves to corporatism and social democracy—the "wets" [old-style conservatives] who borrow from and accommodate to oppositional formations—because they are not fighting for a real victory. Thatcherism understands that hegemony requires you to block out the spaces and to define the new reference points for the entire social landscape. It has the capacity to operate hegemonically, at one and the same time, in the most advanced theoretical language and in the idioms of ordinary language. For example, it elaborates monetarism as an economic theory (if you can believe that possible) at the same time that it presents the complexities of monetary supply in the idioms of ordinary language: for example, comparing the national economy to running a domestic family budget—"You can't spend what you don't have." The ordinary commonsense wisdom of the people, forged often in historical confrontation with those dominant forces, generated in the subordinate spaces of society, can be won, colonised, turned around, and made to speak in the idioms in which hegemony is produced. The hegemonic bloc is always a radical bloc. It seeks to cut the ground from under the previous forms of hegemony, settlement, and consensus. It wants to reverse the historical trends and make a new common sense. It needs to insert itself into the pores of the practical consciousness of human beings. And the notion that this has nothing to do with culture, is outside of ideology, or is really dictated by their position in the class structure, is absolutely absurd.

Culture, Resistance, and Struggle

In this lecture I want to elaborate on the notions of resistance, opposition, and struggle that I have been using, continuing to focus on cultural and ideological rather than political forms of resistance. The most important point I want to make, the point I have been making from the very beginning, is that cultural struggle is not reducible to other areas of determination. You cannot predict the contents, forms, or particular groupings that will be attached to particular areas of cultural resistance simply by attempting to read them off from either the political or economic forms of practice in a society. The domain of culture has its own specificity, modality, and relative autonomy or independence from the other levels of the social formation. That does not mean that it is outside of their structuring influence nor that it does not have, as its conditions of existence, forms of social practices and relations other than cultural. Culture is not, and can never be, outside of the structuring field of the central contradictions that give shape, pattern, and configuration to a social formation, that is, contradictions around class, ethnicity, and gender. It is not outside of them, but it is not reducible to them.

Two consequences of this attempt to think a Marxist theory of cultural struggle in a noneconomic and non-class-reductionist way are worth emphasising at the outset, and I shall do so by remaining within the domain of ideological struggle as discussed in the previous lecture. The first involves the relationship between particular elements within the ideological terrain as sites of struggle and their relationship to class formations; the second involves the relations among the different contradictions that structure the social formation. The position I have presented is sometimes mistakenly taken as denying that there are class forces in play within ideological struggles. I am not denying the existence of class-articulated ideologies, of the very clearly and well-established articulation of certain ideological elements of discourses to particular class positions—for example, the relationship between particular ideological formations and the emergence of the bourgeoisie as a historical force. It is nevertheless an attempt to say that the field of ideological discourse, the systems of representation which articulate the terrain of ideology, are neither organised by nor directly reducible to economic class positions.

While that proposition is widely supported when put in general terms, its more specific exemplifications are often less enthusiastically received. So let me place the following example—the question of rights—before you. The emergence of a political language of rights—of natural rights, of individual rights, and of a conception of the State as predicated on the defense of such rights—is a moment crucial to the formation of bourgeois ideology. Whenever one sees that language appear in the ideological field, one has to be quite careful about the persistence of its articulation to certain bourgeois positions. However, it must be clear—I would hope—that the language of rights cannot belong *only* to the bourgeoisie. The demand for civil rights, and the movements which it organises, may be ultimately limited and contained in their reach by the ground on which they often end up; but they are, nevertheless, in many of their historical appearances, real and effective movements of protest, resistance, and struggle.

A particular elaboration of the language of rights can only be understood within a complex field, as a set of connections between the language of rights, particular conceptions of human nature, definitions of the market, ideals of freedom, and ideas of subject and subjectivity (e.g., possessive individualism). It is a specific configuration, a nexus of ideas and discourses. Ideologies do not exist as or within single terms or concepts. In fact many of the elements within the so-called language of rights existed before their appearance in the seventeenth and eighteenth centuries within the ideological positions of the bourgeoisie, but they did, in that context, connote a new set of meanings in relation to the appearance of a rising class, to the fundamental break of old patterns of economic development and organisation, to the formation of a market society, and to the emerging dominance of these relations. That is of course a critical historical moment in the formation of ideologies, the point where a class or class fraction engages a particular system of representations in order to understand its emerging place in the world, to define what those relations are and how they are different from those of the previous epoch. Only by defining the new emerging economic and social reality in terms of that system of representations can they make sense of and normalise the emerging values and forms of collective action. And after such a critical moment of historic formations, it is impossible to enter that particular field of ideological articulations without mobilising the whole chain of connotations that have articulated it into bourgeois positions. That is the dialectical formation of a class and of what one might call an organic ideology.

Nevertheless, it cannot follow that all the elements of that ideology belong exclusively to the bourgeoisie. The elements are themselves open to being reconnotated through ideological struggle in exactly the same way as Western socialists in the 1980s have to struggle over the meaning of "democracy." Democracy, although it has been implicated in a particular bourgeois parliamentary political discourse, cannot be, as it were, given to the other side. Though elements of ideologies are historically constructed and powerfully stitched into a particular location in relation to class and other social forces, they remain a field of potential—and often real—ideological struggle. The language of bourgeois rights, even in the way it was articulated by Thomas Hobbes and later by John Locke, helped both to secure the position of a particular bourgeois class and to open the possibility for classes which had been excluded by the ways in which that ideology functioned, to claim the universality of such rights. Those excluded others could struggle to place themselves within a language which claimed to speak of *human* rights. It takes an enormous political struggle to articulate the notion of rights within liberalism to practice, because those forces attached to a particular definition of freedom in liberal discourse forcefully resist the attempts of classes (like the working class in the nineteenth century) and other social groups (which may not have a clear class belongingness, like women in the suffrage struggle) to claim those rights. Even though they had been articulated in a universalising discourse in order to mobilise mass political popular support for them, the early bourgeois formation delivered their effects only to a particular class. That becomes a site of potential struggle, a point around which the working classes organise and struggle for their enfranchisement. It is certainly true, as critics have objected, that the franchise is eventually won in a form which, while allowing them access to political power, also individualises and fragments their political representation (one person, one vote). And this in turn makes it difficult for them to mobilise around another form of democratic power, one defined in opposition to the deeply rooted, individualised organisations of power structuring the parliamentary forms of the democratic process. This is the containment of more radical definitions of democracy by articulating them to, stitching them into place within, ideologies of liberalism. The result is no longer liberalism alone or democracy; it is a particular form of liberal democracy. Yet this was clearly the site of one of the most sustained struggles entered into by the working classes in the nineteenth century. At this site, it staked a claim to political power and set certain popular limits on the capacity of the bourgeois class to determine what they were and would be. It made important gains and advances at the same time that it was itself constrained. And of course, the meanings of all of these terms, and the struggles organised around them, changed from the seventeenth to the nineteenth and into the twentieth century. The same terms refer to different realities. They can even represent different interests, different demands, different sites of struggle, as the historical conditions in which they are mobilised, the social forces to which they are attached, change.

The same case can be made using E. P. Thompson's (1975) discussion of the rule of law. In the first instance, "the rule of law" is put forward by a class that does not yet have full political power—the bourgeoisie—against the forms of power practiced by the gentry and the aristocracy. It is an emergent and a progressive demand, one which limits and constrains existing forms. It is then installed as one of the key bourgeois rights by which the new emergent landed bourgeoisie articulates its interest in law and excludes other interests. And yet, by the end of the eighteenth century, it is exactly the point around which the popular demand for the extension of justice is raised. People who were being excluded, whether the working classes, the poor, women, servants, et cetera, did not need another term; they needed *that* term, the term which the bourgeoisie already understood, in order to conduct the struggle. It is simply not possible to understand the crucial struggles which marked the emergence of the bourgeoisie, and the challenges raised against its power by the working classes and by women, if we assume that the key ideological concepts around which these central struggles were organised have always been, and remain essentially, bourgeois. The fact that these struggles were stitched into a fabric of ideas which were bourgeois in origin does not guarantee that they always remain inscribed in just this way. This is as true of the present as of the past.

The point I am trying to make is not only theoretical but has serious political implications. Before we simply and finally ascribe the rule of law only to the bourgeoisie, we need to acknowledge that, for many of the oppressed and subordinated populations in our world, the rule of law would be an important and real advance. The idea that notions of the law cannot belong to the socialist project because they are a part of the ideology through which the bourgeoisie established its domination rests upon an oversimplified and reductionist theory of the relation between ideologies and classes. It constructs the field of social forces as if it were composed of monolithic classes, "as if," in Poulantzas's terms, ideologies "were 'political' number-plates worn by social classes on their backs" (1973, 202). It assumes that entire configurations of ideas are permanently stitched into simple class positions: The bourgeoisie inevitably and solely possesses the ideas of rights, liberties, democracies, freedom, et cetera, and hence, they cannot belong to us. That position leaves the field of potential ideological intervention as an empty space, and while we wait for the great war between the two classes, we ignore the endless possibilities for struggling with and contesting the dominant definitions of ideological terms in order to disarticulate them from their current class positions and rearticulate them in some new way.

The second issue I want to expand upon, continuing the discussion of ideological struggle, involves the question of the primacy of class over other contradictions or, perhaps more accurately, the relations among the different contradictions in any conjuncture, since I do not think one can abstractly hierarchise their importance. It is necessary, however, to acknowledge the irreducibility of one contradiction to another. Different contradictions have different effects in the social field, and it is the tendency to reduce one to the other that is the theoretical problem. For this reason, the suspension of the capitalist mode of production in a particular society will not guarantee the liberation of blacks, women, or subordinate classes. The primacy which Marxism has given to the capital-class contradiction is in fact a problem. It is implicit in, albeit not necessary to, its logic that, in the end, the principal contradiction not only structures every other contradiction but is their truth as well. Consequently the capital-class contradiction not only has political priority, but it often serves as a master key which can unlock all the secrets of the social formation. It is essential, both theoretically and politically, that we face the consequences of the difficult fact that one could move from the capitalist mode of production and see the continuation of the domination, not only of one race by another and especially of one gender by another, but also of one class by another.

The only alternative is a Marxist politics which recognises the necessary differentiation of different struggles and the importance of those struggles on different fronts, that is to say, a Marxist politics which understands the nature of a hegemonic politics, in which different struggles take the leading position on a range of different fronts. Such an understanding does not suppress the autonomy and specificity of particular political struggles, and it rejects reductionism in favor of an understanding of complexity in unity or unity through complexity. The reality of this complexity is not merely a local problem of organising but the theoretical problem of the noncorrespondence of the mode of production and the necessary relative autonomy of different political and ideological formations. The mode of production does not command every contradiction; it does not find them all at the same place or advanced to the same degree—neither within our political organisations nor within the formations of capitalism and socialism in the Western industrial world.

This is, after all, the site of the emergence of Cultural Studies: that we have lived through a succession of periods in the Western world when nonproblematic forms of the class struggle and the class belongingness of ideologies have simply refused to appear. There are only two responses to this situation: Either continue to use theory to guarantee that somewhere down the road such correspondences will appear, or undertake the exceedingly difficult task of bringing theory into line with the complexities of the empirical problems you have to explain. A contemporary

Marxism that does not place the apparent containment of the most advanced industrial working classes in the world at the center of its problematic is no longer facing up to the real world of people; and even more important, it cannot help us understand how it is that the vast masses of working people in the most advanced industrial capitalist civilisations of the world *are* contained and constrained by forms of political reformism. Unless we have a better grasp of the hold which reformist political ideologies have exerted over men and women and over the potential revolutionary agencies within capitalism, we are not using the theories to address the political issues that demand our attention. We are using them to create illusory scenarios which cheer us up.

I want to make a similar point about the illustration I gave in an earlier lecture (lecture 6), because thinking about the ideological articulation of "black" clearly demands that we recognise its relations to issues of class, class ideologies, and class struggles, but in ways that do not reduce the specificity of race, of racist concepts and practices, as well as of antiracist struggles as a potential field of ideological contestation. I tried to demonstrate that such an understanding requires us to move beyond the obvious: that it is a field or site of discrimination; that it is the source of negative identities. By understanding that "black" works within a variety of chains of connotation, we can begin to acknowledge that different groups in specific historical situations have been able to identify with different terms within this complex network. Each identification helps define and constitute the position of the group in the field of ideology and excludes other possibilities. Each appropriation, each positioning of the black subject in relation to terms like West Indian, immigrant, Negro, black, Afro-Caribbean, all of which are possible in the field of ideology, is different. Each requires a different ideological position. A different set of political practices follows from each and each is dependent on a different set of historical conditions.

Further, there is absolutely no way you could reduce the systems of representations of race in any social formation—say, South Africa—to a matter of class. It will not be explained away in relation to the capital-labour contradiction. It is perfectly clear that black and white labour in South Africa is exploited by capital. In relation to race, it is perfectly clear that, in addition, black races are exploited differently from white races in relation to capital. Black labour is positioned differently in social, economic, and ideological relations. There are two contradictions operating politically and ideologically, and while they work in the same space, they refuse to be identical. To assume their supposed correspondence is simply politically ineffective, because the two fields are constantly intersected and bifurcated from different directions. Race and class are powerfully articulated with one another but they are not the same and, consequently, each is likely to both unite and divide. A black labouring class, exploited by capital, is able to begin to constitute its political unity, partly through the categories of class, but more significantly through the categories of race in this particular political situation. One can see this only by recognising the necessary autonomy of the different movements in the South African political scene, and the capabilities of developing a common political struggle through the possible articulation of those elements, without assuming their necessary correspondence. Otherwise one will go on assuming or hoping that that scene will resolve itself in ways which are historically impossible. Notions of articulation, over-determination, and the specificity of the different contradictions within the ideological field are important, then, not only for an adequate general theory of ideology but for the analysis of a particular political situation as well.

Cultural resistance can have many and varied forms and effects, although often we do not know how to identify these differences or how to theorise them. Consider, for example, the so-called cultures of survival, which particular groups may require if they are not to be totally overwhelmed by alternative definitions of their identity and history, if they are to have any sense of solidarity or identity at all. But such cultures of survival neither guarantee nor necessarily generate the basis of a culture of hegemony. Groups can survive without the slightest chance of being in the leading position at the moment. And although forms of culture that arise in response to the need for survival are not necessarily even strong enough to negotiate with hegemonic formations, the ability to survive is most certainly one of the conditions of possibility for such negotiation. Despite the "reformist" ring of "negotiation," if a group is to enter into important cultural negotiation with the dominant ideological or cultural forms of a society, it must have a good deal of persistence and strength. It has to have achieved a certain degree of organisation; it has to have achieved a level of self-reflexivity which makes it capable of formulating projects. You cannot enter into negotiation without knowing the ground you are working on and the possibilities and potential sites of victory, however small they may be. The moment of negotiation is also a moment of struggle and resistance. The fact that the other side is not going to be overthrown does not mean that important concessions and gains cannot be won.

E. P. Thompson (1963) describes just such a moment, in the period after Chartism, when the British labour movement had, for all practical purposes, lost its capacity to define the world in its own image. But one could not give an account of the history of that class, its culture, its political and ideological institutions, without acknowledging what Thompson demonstrates: that at that moment, the labour movement turned back on its own social and cultural forms, developing and providing them with a necessary warrant. It negotiated spaces and found ways of keeping people off its terrain. It developed institutions which were more organically connected to its material conditions and to the lives of labourers and their families; through these, it penetrated into myriad areas of working-class life. It established in that period what we now think of as traditional working-class culture. The fact that it remains, partly as a result of these developments, a subordinate and incorporated class throughout its history does not negate the fact of the intense internal corporate strength which these changes also produced.

The strengths and contributions of that culture are always contradictory; it has positive and negative features, progressive and conservative effects. It is this I want to insist upon, that cultural forms and practices are always contradictory. The culture that holds the traditional working class together and allows people to identify the difference between "us and them" is also the very same culture that maintains particular forms of masculinity inside working-class political organisations and renders that culture in some ways blind to the contradictions of gender. Precisely one of the ways that culture unites diverse groups in the working class depends upon its capacity to define and resist the "other," the alien, the person from another culture; and this of course has rendered it in some ways blind to the contradictions of race and ethnicity. It is not a question of simply celebrating that cultural formation—one cannot do it—but rather of recognising that such cultures of survival are required for resistance, for opposition, for negotiation, for the kinds of upheavals you find in rebellion and revolution, and, perhaps even more important, for counterhegemonic formations. They are required for the construction of new kinds of societies. But every such formation, every struggle for change, has contradictory effects as well as limits. One cannot ignore the negative side in defending the positive contributions it advances, but one cannot ignore the gains that are made while condemning its defeats.

We have to think of both domination and resistance as processes. We need to look at the way in which forms of cultural and ideological resistance by particular groups or classes provide the space for interventions. Intervention can deepen the forms of cultural resistance by working on them, dislocating them, or disarticulating them from the ways in which they are constantly held in subordinate places. But this requires us to recognise the strengths and the weaknesses of those forms and one can only do that by entering into their spaces, beginning to work with them as well as on them. One is then involved in the process of strengthening and deepening the oppositional elements of already existing cultural forms and not of inviting people to abandon the forms in which they are involved and to suddenly move over to a different place, into a different formation. The latter strategy is not only unlikely to persuade anybody to move, it is also deeply self-delusory. It suggests that we have ourselves clarified and cleansed our own cultural positions, that we have rendered them transparent to our own critical gaze, and that they are free of all residues and attachments to older, more problematic cultural forms. It suggests that we no longer collaborate in those illicit pleasures we derive from the many cultural practices which we do or should know are ideologically impure, which may even belong to the "other side." To approach people as if everything is perfectly clarified—the forms over there belong to the terrain of delusion, false consciousness, illicit pleasures, and mere consumerism, while these over here belong entirely to the ideologically pure pursuit of the truly revolutionary consciousness—is a strategy that is unlikely to bring people on from position to position. You will not enable people to deepen those elements which separate them from the dominant formations, to resist the attachments that stitch them into the existing system, and to begin the difficult process of articulating themselves into another set of positions. While cultural politics and ideological struggle are not sufficient in themselves to restructure the social formation, there can be no sustained establishment of counterhegemonies without their articulations in culture and ideology. Cultural politics and ideological struggle are the necessary conditions for forms of social and political struggle. Those political and social forces that are actually attempting the difficult task of intervening in the actual social formations and beginning to transform them into some new image or at least in some new direction—and not merely to go on resisting—cannot avoid the need to open the possibility of new political subjects and subjectivities. The domain of culture and ideology is where those new positions are opened and where the new articulations have to be made. And in that domain, people can change and struggle.

But if we cannot guarantee in advance what either the determinations or the political effectivities of a cultural form are, can we at least describe their historical relations to each other? Can we, for example, make use of Williams's (1977) distinction between dominant, residual, and emergent elements or forms of culture as a way of beginning to map the cultural terrain? Although I suggested earlier that this was a quite useful schema, it is clear that there is no point in trying to assign each of the forms of particular cultures to one of those categories, because those forms are never pure and their identities are never entirely inscribed upon their surface apart from their articulation into particular contexts. Thus, we find that residual forms are reworked in an emergent situation and become precisely the forgotten languages in which people speak of their new projects. And practices whose identity seemingly depends upon their status as "avant-garde" rapidly emigrate to the arts review pages where they become, if not part of the dominant, certainly no longer part of a strongly resistant cultural formation. And perhaps most significantly, we also find that the dominant has the capacity not only to speak its own language, but to speak through the fact that it grants many other languages the possibility of speaking. As I suggested earlier, hegemonic leadership need not incorporate or dissolve all but the dominant cultural forms; it can even enable the subalterns to take on their own formations. It is perfectly capable of devolving cultural leadership to other groups. It need not secure the absolute cultural power of one delegated group of organic intellectuals. It allows many inorganic intellectuals to function in the field, recognising, representing, celebrating, and even supporting their diversity, at least to the extent of guaranteeing that the medley of voices will be sustained. Hegemony entails precisely this capacity to continually command a central position within an apparently open plurality of voices. When power is exerted in the cultural field through the censorship or repression of that plurality, then hegemony has not yet been secured. Consequently, I want to resist the notion that one can permanently ascribe cultural forms to particular positions. Hence I reject that type of formal analysis of cultural fields which sorts the world into progressive and nonprogressive forms because I am struck by the number of non-progressive forms that actually progress and the number of progressive forms that do not seem to progress anywhere. The progressiveness of a particular form or practice is not given within the culture itself. I will illustrate this with some examples of the interplay of both residual and emergent moments within the cultural field, and of the play of domination in between, as it were.

Some of the best-known work of the Centre for Contemporary Cultural Studies was in the area of the succession of youth cultures, often identified with particular styles of music and dress which emerged largely in the 1960s and seventies in the wake of the period of affluence of the 1950s. Some of that work is collected in *Resistance through Rituals* (Hall and Jefferson 1976). In that body of work, we tried to find ways of describing the relationship between class and youth cultures without reducing youth cultures to class. On the one hand, it was clear to us that there was no way the field of postwar youth social movements could be reduced to the structure of the fundamental classes or even to the questions of class contradictions. On the other hand, there was no way one could understand what was going on in the waves of movements among young people which have marked out that terrain in Britain since the early 1950s outside of the structuring determinations of class. Classes play in and across the field of those movements in complex and often indirect ways.

We suggested, for example, that in many of the forms of cultural differences between two of the leading forms of such movements in the late 1950s and early 1960s (the Mods and the Rockers), one could see the shadow as it were, not of the distinction between the middle and the working class, but the perhaps equally crucial distinction between an upwardly mobile fraction and a downwardly mobile fraction of the working class. I say "shadow" because it is not the case that the class affiliations of the groups corresponded that exactly; many members in fact were not working class in their precise social or economic origins. But the Mods, for example, did tend to be kids who were on an upward trajectory, perhaps out of their class, or transitionally within their class. They also tended to have more years of education and to be better educated than others; and of course, education in England is a crucial signifier of class. But there is no way you could define the intrinsic forms that generated the Mods' style, taste, and culture simply in terms of those class elements or their class position. Nevertheless, certain very important things about the ways in which they lived in the world and saw their own difference are, I would say, "shadowed" by class.

While such movements provided new identities and subjectivities for young people, and engaged the youths themselves in this production, the movements were not at all politicised. Neither did they engage directly with questions of economy and labour: There are no messages about work. The culture was suspended in the space of the good time, which is not work. It was defined by and within "not work time." Kids who had to work throughout the day lived their relation to their real conditions of working through the imaginary relations of being a Mod. It was precisely an alternative subjectivity or identity.

Moreover, if you look at the meanings that were becoming dominant within these youth cultures, you will see that they were defined generationally. The generational contradiction between older and younger people or fractions is very important. One can identify within the culture of these movements "the parental class culture." But this generational contradiction cannot be isolated from either the particular class fractions from which the different formations were drawn or from the larger structures of the culture as a whole. After all, youths—even Mods—have to grow up and find out how to be adult workers, spouses, and parents. And there were very few messages in The Who about any of that! Even if one wants to celebrate the Mod style as a moment of resistance, one has also to think about the life trajectory, within particular class fractions, of people whose new subjectivities were being formed in these cultural spaces. Although it could not be predicted, it is important to look at the question in relation to the fraction of the class from which they came and to which they were likely to be consigned. And that is articulated onto a much wider cultural frame. The ways in which all those adult identities were taken up will make a difference, but they are not self-sufficient in themselves; they are part of a larger configuration.

Similarly, when we talked about the middle-class subcultures—the countercultures of the sixties and early seventies—we noted the complex relations that they had to class identities and political possibilities. The countercultures often operated within cultural fields marked by intense generational and political differences, and a whole range of symbolisms were mobilised to generate new subjectivities. And yet, there were strong relationships between those divisions and the divisions within the middle class. The great cultural split and the different ways in which the countercultures of the younger generations developed were framed by important divisions within the class itself. It was not simply a question of the middle versus the working class. It had as much to do with the internal differentiations which were opening up against the background of the rhythms of a new economic period. One of the key cultural divisions in the middle classes in that period in Britain was the distinction between what we call the "progressive" and the "provincial" middle class. Those in the progressive middle class—regardless of generational identity—adopted the ethic of consumption. They understood how it worked, moved with it, and took advantage of it. They did not feel that their lives would collapse if the Protestant ethic weakened its boundaries a bit. Indeed they found pleasure in the rapid movements in and out of more conventional bourgeois positions. The parental generation was obviously not able to live their children's lives, but they did seem to be trying to catch up as rapidly as possible. In that very default, other fractions of the middle class felt attacked and increasingly "squeezed" into a narrow set of cultural possibilities: attacked from below by rising Mods and Rockers and from above by the "cosmopolitan middle class's" desertion of traditional bourgeois positions. What were they to do? They were neither the propertied class nor the dominant class; their whole identity, and their future as well, was invested in their position as keepers of the bourgeois consciousness, defending the virtues of saving and thrift and the respectable life. They had made great sacrifices for that, and they expected their place in the cultural sun, even if it was a subordinate one. Interestingly, this division penetrates very deep into the way that sexual ideologies were mapped onto the cultural field of the middle class. Out of the progressive middle class has come a certain kind of liberal progressive feminism. Out of the provincial middle class has come our version of the moral majority.

In making such arguments, we were trying to maintain the relative autonomy of the ways in which those new youth subcultural identities were generated. Rather than denying the importance of what you might call the secondary contradictions around gender and race, we wanted to argue that you could not develop an adequate understanding of youth subcultures until you located them within the framework of a class structuring of the society, a structuring which is deep and penetrative across its whole future. The subcultural work of the Centre was accused of class reductionism: of reducing the Rockers to their working-class position and of consigning the Mods to their petty bourgeois project. There is, unfortunately, some truth to that. We did not get the balance of the determining effects of the different contradictions quite right. But the work is important for having raised the project of trying to think about the non-reductiveness of cultural formations to class formations without pulling them so apart that they fall into totally autonomous positions.

I also want to offer a subcultural illustration of the way in which cultural forms themselves may open up and structure possibilities without going completely over to the position that claims that those possibilities and their politics are intrinsic to the forms. If political tendency alone will not organise, as Benjamin (1970) suggested in "The Author as Producer," I want to add that cultural forms alone will not guarantee. There is no guarantee of the intrinsically progressive or regressive nature of particular cultural forms. This was very clear in the era of the Skinheads in England, after the Mods and Rockers. It occurred in different economic conditions. The principal forms of this subculture were articulated against the middle-class forms of the 1960s; therefore, they stressed and amplified their proletarian symbols. That is, Skinhead culture revalorised a relationship to some working-class cultural elements on the ideological terrain of the need to mount an effective opposition to the dominant middle-class-related symbolism. This can be seen in the way the Skinheads dressed (short hair as opposed to long hair, jeans as opposed to flowing Indian robes) and in the affirmation of the increasing importance of territoriality. The most important thing about the Mods was that they were all attached to Italian scooters and could go anywhere: Their very style affirmed mobility. The very fact of being able to leave the East End where one lived most of one's life and set out in large numbers for a weekend in Brighton (which is not very far away, but is very different) was a sign of the acquisition of new cultural space. But the Skinheads were as deeply imbricated in their localities as any football team and its fans. They denied the reasons for leaving one's locale by affirming that, as it were, the whole world is in a particular area of Liverpool.

Despite their mixed social composition, the Skinheads revalorised certain elements of the working-class culture as a whole and reworked them in generational, musical, visual, and stylistic terms. Many people who had found it difficult to come to terms with the implications of the politics of the previous phase hailed the movement as a more hard-edged, realistic, proletarian cultural moment. But this was also the moment in Britain of the rise in the National Front as an active political organisation. Racism was becoming more overt and organised as a political and ideological position, and for a time, there was an absolutely crucial struggle to attach the cultural associations and affiliations of young people in these new styles to the fascist movement itself. The effort was very effective because the subcultural formation revalorised certain proletarian elements that have a strongly masculine, aggressive edge to them. The struggle to attach those kids to a fascist political position worked through the culture of football (soccer) where there is already a structured violence organised around the territoriality of supporters' relation to a particular team. The attempt was made to articulate together elements of Skinhead culture—proletarian identification and strong support for particular clubs, including the violence that followed from that occasionally—directly into a youth fascist movement. There were about eighteen months when it was absolutely uncertain whether that culture would be the first indigenous young working-class fascist movement in Britain. It was suddenly clear that the progressive possibilities of rock—exaggerated perhaps by the explicit politics of the middle-class countercultures—did not stem from the intrinsic progressiveness of rock's cultural forms. At that moment, rock looked like anything but a potentially progressive form; in fact, it looked like an opening into a kind of mindless race-gender-class identification, which would have created a trajectory among young people right into the hands of the National Front.

This articulation to the right was not stopped by the intrinsic cultural and political value or content of the cultural forms but by an alternative cultural practice, which began with the formation of a group and then an organisation: Rock Against Racism. It began by attempting to win over those musical groups that already had visible and leading positions in the culture and convince them to adopt overt political positions. Its project was, then, to constitute in the minds of the supporters the notion that being in that culture—being young, being a football supporter, et cetera—might go along with being antiracist. Antiracism could then become something fashionable and explicit. Rock Against Racism is one of the few real political-cultural interventions in recent times. More typically, the Left watches the growth of cultural forms and, intuiting their oppositional tendencies, hopes that a socialist youth movement, rocking and opposing as it goes on, will come out of them. We have rarely found, or even searched for, an actual cultural practice that would articulate these things together. Instead, many progressive people romanticise the deviant by mistaking the moment of opposition for the moment of rebellion. It is true that the members of the various subcultures were not exactly "inside the big system," but the problem is precisely how to work on that disavowal in order to constitute other subject positions. It does not happen on its own. Left on its own, virtually everything and anything can and did happen: Some were politicised, some depoliticised, some moved to the right, most moved to the middle, and a few moved to the left. The oppositional relationship to parental cultures and the dominant culture was maintained across the field of effects. It was still youth running wild, but youth could run wild to the right as well as to the left. Youth could run wild against Pakistanis as well as with them. The fact that rock was a progressive form of music, that it broke with many of the dominant musical forms, did not guarantee its political space and social content. That can only be guaranteed by articulating the forms of subjectivity it opens to particular political positions. The importance of Rock Against Racism is not undermined by the fact that it has declined. It was a moment in which the Left developed a practice for the contradictions of the moment, realistically recognised both the positive and negative aspects of the forms it had to work with, and inserted itself into a language which was capable of being heard. It was able in this case to find a language which could establish a system of equivalence between the values of its own cultural formation and particular political and social positions outside. It established an articulation. Although it did not win white British youth for antiracism, as if there were some final battle, it stopped a particular moment of racism dead in its tracks.

The example serves my general point: Cultural forms themselves are important. They create the possibility of new subjectivities, but they do not themselves guarantee their progressive or reactionary content. They still require social and political practices to articulate them to particular political positions. That is a formal practice that requires the utmost sensitivity to the nature of the complexity and nuanced quality of the cultural period in which you are working. If you simply enter the space of a concert by The Clash to give a political speech, you will fail. Who wants to hear a political speech in the middle of The Clash? But there are ways of working with the oppositions that are already implicit in that music and deepening their political content by associating them with positions that are linked to an alternative or oppositional content. A politics of cultural resistance that neglects the internal and intrinsic forms of the cultural field in which it operates is not likely to create alternative subjectivities, but those forms of cultural politics that are satisfied with working only at the levels of forms, as if that will guarantee their necessarily progressive nature or content, are likely to be frequently if not forever disappointed.

I want to turn to an example of emergent forms—emergent forms of music, emergent forms of social movements, emergent forms of cultural practices, and emergent forms of subjectivity—that operate within and upon the context of residual forms. There is, after all, nothing so residual as religion. Although the vast majority of the people involved in the contemporary black movement in Britain are not Rastafarians, it is the accessibility of the new subjectivities inside Rastafarianism and of its music (essentially reggae, but other associated musical forms as well) that have given a cultural articulation to that movement. Without that articulation, the movement would have even less shape and direction than it currently has, and we would presumably be in more trouble than we already are. Rastafarianism has a long history which I will not develop here, but I do want to say something about the cultural skills which it built upon and offered us.

There is something which all slaves learned (although as I suggested at the beginning of this lecture, it is certainly not confined to slave or ex-slave culture): the importance of cultural resistance by negotiation. It is not possible to be in the position of the slave in a society and not learn how important it is to maintain the difference between yourself and the other in the moments between the points where you can resist openly. All those things that supposedly describe the "simple-mindedness" of blacks—their inability to speak the language properly, their fondness for imitation and mimicry (which is supposed to be a very primitive element), their overdeveloped physical properties, and underdeveloped intellectual ones—are all ways in which slaves learned how to remain people in a culture which denied them that possible subjectivity. A slave must learn the difference between how one can operate both outside the dominant culture and inside its spaces. For example, in Jamaica, African drumming has been maintained somewhere about ten miles from the window of the room in which I grew up. It was a continuous voice in the night when I was a child, as I imagine it still is. It never died out, although people outlawed it for a variety of reasons (e.g., to stop the killing of the animals from which the drums are made). Nevertheless, people went on being able to drum *outside* the dominant culture. But if you are in a slave society, it is not possible to remain outside of the dominant culture for very long. So we understood how to maintain and keep Africa alive *inside* the Christian religions, both Catholic and Protestant.

I used to live next door to a black Baptist church where they sang British, Baptist, and nonconformist hymns. They sang them for hours. As time passed and the rhythms became slower (and you thought you'd never get to the end of a line, let alone the end of the hymn), someone—the person who was hoping to preach—would begin to fill the space allowed by the slow rhythms, reminding people of the lines. And suddenly, you could hear this traditional religious music and language—a part of the dominant culture—being subverted rhythmically from underneath. Where did this other rhythm come from, this other language preserved inside the forms of religious music? How is this subversion from within possible? Slaves develop a set of skills by which they can conform perfectly—they meet the requirements, speak the language, honor the gods, sing the songs, learn the Bible, and so on—but adapt the forms in such a way that something is secured, some advance is made, maintained, and continued. Forms remain contradictory in spite of their manifest meanings. That is a skill learned a long time ago, and although slavery has been gone for quite a long while, it is a cultural skill that survives. It becomes crucial in a certain period in Jamaica that I want to describe briefly, a period in which religion and the musics associated with it came to play an absolutely central role in Jamaican politics.

In the period after Jamaican independence (in 1962), it was no longer acceptable for our music to be a residue from other cultures. Nations need their own music and musical forms. So we were given one by a Jamaican anthropologist trained in the U.S.A. from a middle-class Lebanese family. Edward Seaga, the prime minister from 1980 to 1989, argued that this music had to be truly Jamaican, free of the many musical forms that had been assimilated, and he proposed a music called "ska." Ska is, like all cultural forms, very contradictory in relation to the legitimated musics of the period. It is a bizarre mixture of North American blues and Third World authenticity. It does retain and bring to the surface many of the African rhythms. It is not only slow but deliberately retarded so that the repetitive, simple, rhythmic base can be heard again by a population looking for national cultural identities. Its form presents itself to be heard as a black music. At the same time, it is impressed on the population by the most advanced commercial advertising techniques. There are records on how to learn ska and dance clubs where you can learn to do the ska (a dance) and so on. Ska not only became very popular, it was frequently used to organise particular groups politically. It is the music associated with the early phases of Jamaican nationalism.

This appropriation of ska has to be understood in a larger field of struggle. One of the central aspects of Jamaican nationalism, as in all such nationalist movements, is the attempt to constitute a new subjectivity: the Jamaican identity. Having been for so long a part of the British Empire and suddenly becoming an independent country, there had to be ways of being and feeling Jamaican. The unity of Jamaican society is in fact constructed on top of a very complicated system of color distinctions. My grandmother, who must have learned something from slavery, could detect at least eight different lines. When nationalist Jamaica first had its beauty contest, it could only deal with the real differences in the color spectrum by having a range of different beauty contests for the different color groupings. You could be Miss Mahogany, or Miss Majo, or Miss Pine, and so on. And these differences were intersected by others: differences of class and education. Those provided the classifications that my mother and grandmother operated with in the crucial questions of life—for example, in questions of kinship. It was a schema which Lévi-Strauss would have understood as soon as you unfolded it. If you were Majo but well educated, you could marry in a certain way. Certain affiliations were permitted and others were not. Identity was then an arena of difference, of antagonism, of actually whom this nation belonged to. That unity had to be created and constituted. It doesn't really exist in the society, which is actually riven with all kinds of differences: color, race, class, politics, geography, and religion. You have to constitute the subjective possibility of unity out of this, and one of the languages for doing so is music. Ska was supposed to be the music that could appeal to everyone. Everyone can join in it because it affirms the national unity of the people, despite their differences. Everyone could dance to ska to celebrate their independence.

However, just as some people wanted to use the combination of religious and musical forms to constitute a new unity, others wanted to reconstitute the difference. They wanted to say that within this unity that is Jamaica, there are some who are more Jamaican than others, and differences are also partly expressed in, partly constituted through, music and religion. Rastafarianism was, in my childhood, a tiny religious sect connected with Marcus Garvey's Pan-African movement and thus affiliated with Africa. It represented a small part of the population which was constantly oppressed by various social powers but who had clearly learned the sorts of skills of negotiation that I described earlier. They needed a language to tell them who they were but they had only one book: the Bible. So they made that say what they needed to hear it say. They reread the Bible by entirely turning it on its head, in terms of the persecution of black people. They reread the exodus from Egypt as the exodus of black people from slavery. They went on to say that they are still, as they were then, in Babylon; they looked forward to a new moment of promise, release, and liberation. So they adapted the language of the Bible, as blacks have adapted the language of Christianity to their own situations, and they began to articulate that. The internal complexities of the forms of Rastafarianism are perhaps less important than the fact that it became an alternative language for speaking about what Jamaica is. It made the African connection overt and alive in a way that many of the other ideologies and cultures of independence could not. It had the capacity to construct new subjectivities because it operated in the religious field in a society in which religion is an absolutely central bearer of meanings.

It is impossible to move in Jamaican society without encountering the traces of religious language and thought because it was one of the few spaces allowed to the slaves. If you look at the cultures of Jamaica, religion is imprinted in everything. It is in every political and cultural position. You cannot begin to articulate the culture without encountering the language of religion. Very close to where I lived was another church which only operated at night. It was essentially for domestic servants, the black underclass that was locked into the kitchens of the black and brown middle class until after dinner, which was usually rather late. After being allowed to go back to their homes in downtown Kingston, they would stop in at the church and sing about being oppressed, about being at the end of one's rope. It was a very different sound than that of the church I described before. Yet that form enabled the women to walk every day from one world into the other and to work. They could not possibly have done it without some compensation. It was the opium of the oppressed. But it was also their means of survival, a moment of pure survival. It was not a moment from which new identities could be constructed, nor a moment from which opposition could come. Later on this group—and their daily movement—became very important, but only when women who worked in that way in Jamaica were much fewer and better organised. But in this moment religion kept them in their place, but it also enabled them to survive a certain kind of life.

Does this mean that one celebrates the role of religion? One has to recognise the negative effects as well as the positive purchase it may have given people on their lives. Religion is largely the reason why Jamaica remains an anticommunist society. Those very forms of religious consciousness that enabled people to open doors and speak new languages about themselves also had limits and shut some doors. It was possible within its terms to counterpose God and capitalism to communism. As deeply oppressed as you felt, you never felt so oppressed as those living under and trying to flee the devil of communism. That is, you could generate in the very symbolism of religion a hatred for the "other." So religion in Jamaica is a form of consciousness which is effective in different ways at different levels: It helps people to survive; it helps them to constitute a false notion of unity; and it helps them to distinguish themselves from false representations of themselves. It permeates the society and it also establishes its own kinds of limits. That is one of the functions that Rastafarianism came to play, and people who could not become Rastafarian in their religious beliefs became "cultural Rastas." They wanted to identify the core of what it was to be Jamaican with those things that had never been spoken openly in the culture before: the African connection, the slave connection, the trench town connection, and the yard connection. They said, "That is what Jamaica really is."

The politics of Jamaica has to be understood in terms of that project of producing a cultural definition of the people, of helping to constitute what the people are. Although politics has to function on the terrain of the popular, the people and the popular are themselves constituted through discourses, collective practices, and cultural forms. There is no Jamaican people "out there." There are many peoples and they can be constituted in many different ways. In the crucial election between Michael Manley and Edward Seaga in the early 1970s, Seaga's party was substantially supported by the lower classes and in the towns, largely through affiliations to certain kinds of music and to certain religious sects. The Pentecostal and other fundamentalist Baptist black sects and churches have always strongly supported that particular party. Undoubtedly, one of the main reasons why Manley was able to acquire political power at that time was that the Rastafarians "gave him the rod." He was suddenly identified with Rastafarianism, even though Manley is the son of an English mother and a high Majo Jamaican father, a Jamaica brown, very high classed and refined. How this articulation happened is less important than the fact that it did. Nor is it important whether Manley was in some sense Rastafarian, but that this was the moment of the articulation between a particular cultural definition of the country—and of what it would mean to be a Jamaican in that sense—and a particular political position. It was the recognition that there might be a politics that could construct Jamaica in that way. That is, in Jamaican politics, politicians are often forced to follow the cultural definitions of what Jamaica is and of what it is to be. Politics becomes endowed with very special—almost intrinsic—cultural and religious significance.

That is Rastafarianism in one place. But of course many of the people involved in its forms are not in Jamaica at all; they are in some other place: in London, in Birmingham, in Bradford, and so on. They are young people who can hardly speak patois. They are, after all, second- or third-generation West Indians. They are suffering from the problems of the alienation of a population that had identified itself with the possibilities that immigration opened for them and find that they are treated as second-class citizens. And they are suffering as well from the problems of increasing unemployment among blacks, especially black youths. They are, of course, a potential part of the unskilled or semiskilled sector of the working class. Black immigrants do the most menial and unskilled tasks in the society as a whole. There are occupations in Britain, just as there are in the United States, that have acquired a clear ethnic or race identity, whether cleaning, or ticket taking, or food service. That is the situation that increasing numbers of young black people face at that point: their insertion into the labour process in terms of their race.

Although their class position is crucially important, it is through the categories and structures of race that they become conscious of the complexities of the systems of exploitation of which they are the object. It is there that they begin to become conscious of their position and start to fight it out. They are overwhelmed by the threat to their identity or by the possibility of having no identity at all, of being denied an identity in the educational and cultural apparatuses of society which seem to want the generations of British-born blacks to be as their parents were obliged to be: invisible, not present. What was required of us when I first came to England was not to appear, not to trouble anybody by being too much "out there," living what I call the "lace curtain syndrome," as we stayed inside, pulled the curtains, and watched England go by "out there." A trip to a pub in the 1950s was like going into unknown territory. You didn't know the language or the mores; you didn't know whether somebody was going to throw you out or not; you knew nobody would talk to you. The first generation of immigrants lives in a foreign territory, but the third generation has no other place to go; it has no other sense of itself than what is offered it within that foreign territory. But in fact it has developed another sense of itself, a sense of itself as other, a sense of itself that is very substantially related to the cultural forms that had been generated by Rastafarianism. The language that it speaks is largely that of reggae, which has been the musical carrier of its religious forms and concepts.

Young black people in Britain today are actually worse off economically and politically than their parents were when they first emigrated. But they are better off in at least one respect: They have a sense of themselves in the world; they have a pride of their place; they have a capacity to resist; they know when they are being abused by the dominant culture; and they have begun to know how to hold it at bay. But above all, they have a sense of some other person that they really are. They have become visible to themselves. One of the manifestations of this is that they speak a deeper patois than their fathers and mothers ever did. Jamaican patois has deepened in England in the fourth generation. That has become possible only because of the music and music shops. And that opens onto questions about the difficulties in establishing a black record shop and the commercial exploitation of the black culture. But nevertheless, out of the exploitation of black culture and the music business back home, and out of some very politically tainted sources, has come the possibility of a black subjective identity for these young people in the new world; they are going to make their own that which emerged in the old world to which they no longer have real connections. They have transformed the language from something that refers to the Kingston yard to that which refers to Handsworth or Brixton. They use a language which grew out of and resists one form of oppression to translate and to begin to articulate another form. That would not be possible without the music and the religion. Their music and religion cannot guarantee their success; they cannot say if they will win, or when, or how. There are limits imposed on them by the fact that their language, and the identity it constructs for them, take a religious form. Yet without that form, no black political movement would be possible today. Are those limits the product of some essential irrationality at the heart of religious cultural forms? No. But what other cultural practice do you offer black kids who are not satisfied with definitions of identity and politics which, built on their relations with the police, construct them as criminals who are either beaten up or fight back?

You have to acknowledge the irrationality of religious forms, but also you have to recognise that all cultures, including religious ones, have very different logics. Consider the following illustration of that. I was in Jamaica in the late 1970s when the truth was being revealed about Ethiopia (the land to which Rastafarianism looks) and Haile Selassie's regime. Many of us thought that the revelations about the actual history and conditions of Ethiopia under his rule as emperor (1930–1974), followed by his eventual death, seemed to undermine many of the Rastafarians' core beliefs (including that Selassie, as the first black king, was the incarnation of God or "Jah") and might signal its end. It does, after all, make very explicit and visible the limits of a highly irrational culture. I challenged this very old, very distinguished, and very religious Rastafarian: It did now appear that Ethiopia was not such a wonderful place for blacks and that it was in fact in turmoil. And Haile Selassie did not seem to rule quite as well as one might have hoped God to do. And besides, bringing out my final rationalist key, how could he be God if he's dead? The Rastafarian's response was quite simple and yet elegant: "When was the last time you heard the mass media tell the truth about the Son of God?" I had to confess that it wasn't the Word that was on the lips of BBC announcers or in the newspaper headlines. Within the logic of his discourse, the media were certainly no evidence for his death. But it need not have mattered that he was dead, just as it did not matter that some of them actually did go to Ethiopia and did not like it. Ethiopia is a place in the mind or, perhaps more accurately, in a language. It is a place they need because it is somewhere other than where they are. It is where people are free because here they are oppressed. They know about Ethiopia because they know about Babylon.

People have to have a language to speak about where they are and what other possible futures are available to them. These futures may not be real; if you try to concretise them immediately, you may find there is nothing there. But what is there, what is real, is the possibility of being someone else, of being in some other social space from the one in which you have already been placed. As I said before, nothing in the cultural forms of Rastafarianism guarantees the success of the black movement, but it is its necessary condition at the current moment. It is the necessary condition within which black politics, black alternatives, black struggles, and black resistance are developing and will develop.

In this lecture, I have tried to demonstrate, at least by example, that although emergent cultural forms do not contain their own guarantees, they do contain real possibilities. Also, although they cannot be thought of as self-sufficient and outside of the structuring effects of the contradictions that deeply penetrate and organise the social formation, they cannot be reduced to them either. Their progressive or nonprogressive content cannot be read off from the cultural level alone. And I have tried to talk about the way in which residual cultural forms are constantly appropriated, expropriated, and reworked. Sometimes the forms people appropriate may not look like they have any potential for struggle, resistance, negotiation, or even survival, but nevertheless generate them for people who are able to discover in them a language within which alternative subjective possibilities are made available. But this appropriation is always limited and partial; after all, we cannot all be Rastafarians and the politics of contemporary black struggles cannot be entirely Rastafarian. Finally, considering both emergent and residual forms, I have tried to suggest that we understand resistance as a process. Rather than reserving the notion of class struggle only for the moment of the barricades, we need to see resistance as the continual practices of working on the cultural domain and opening up cultural possibilities. This is perhaps not the most glamorous political work but it is the work we need to do. The conditions within which people are able to construct subjective possibilities and new political subjectivities for themselves are not simply given in the dominant system. They are won in the practices of articulation which produce them.

REFERENCES

Abrams, Mark, and Richard Rose. 1960. *Must Labour Lose?* Harmondsworth: Penguin.

Althusser, Louis. 1970. *For Marx.* Translated by Ben Brewster. New York: Random House.

Althusser, Louis. 1971a. "Freud and Lacan." In Althusser 1971c, 189–219.

Althusser, Louis. 1971b. "Ideology and Ideological State Apparatuses (Notes towards an Investigation)." In Althusser 1971c, 127–186.

Althusser, Louis. 1971c. *Lenin and Philosophy and Other Essays.* Translated by Ben Brewster. New York: Monthly Review.

Althusser, Louis, and Etienne Balibar. 1970. *Reading Capital.* Translated by Ben Brewster. London: New Left.

Arnold, Matthew. (1869) 2014. *Culture and Anarchy: An Essay in Political and Social Criticism.* Originally published London: Smith, Elder, and Co. Accessed as etext September 17, 2014. http://www.gutenberg.org/cache/epub/4212/pg4212/html.

Bell, Daniel. 1960. *The End of Ideology: On the Exhaustion of Political Ideas in the Fifties.* Glencoe, IL: Free Press.

Benjamin, Walter. 1970. "The Author as Producer." *New Left Review* 62: 83–96.

Blackstone, William. 1776. *Commentaries on the Laws of England.* London: His Majesty's Law Printers.

Coleridge, Samuel Taylor. 1817. *A Lay Sermon Addressed to the Higher and Middle Classes, on the Existing Distresses and Discontents.* London: Gale and Fenner. Accessed March 3, 2016. https://archive.org/details/blessedareyethat00cole.

Crosland, Anthony. 1956. *The Future of Socialism.* London: J. Cape.

Durkheim, Émile. 1947. *The Elementary Forms of the Religious Life: A Study in Religious Sociology*. Glencoe, IL: Free Press.

Durkheim, Émile. 1951. *Suicide: A Study in Sociology*. New York: Free Press.

Durkheim, Émile. 1982. *The Rules of Sociological Method and Selected Texts on Sociology and Its Method*. Edited by Steven Lukes, translated by W. D. Halls. New York: Free Press.

Durkheim, Émile, and Marcel Mauss. 1963. *Primitive Classification*. Translated by Rodney Needman. Chicago: University of Chicago Press.

Eliot, George. 1859. *Adam Bede*. Edinburgh: William Blackwood and Sons.

Eliot, George. 1860. *The Mill on the Floss*. Edinburgh: William Blackwood and Sons.

Eliot, T. S. 1949. *Notes toward the Definition of Culture*. New York: Thomas Sterns.

Freud, Sigmund. 1938. *The Basic Writings of Sigmund Freud*. New York: Modern Library.

Goldmann, Lucien. *The Hidden God: A Study of Tragic Vision in the Pensées of Pascal and the Tragedies of Racine*. London: Routledge and Kegan Paul.

Gramsci, Antonio. 1959. *Modern Prince and Other Writings*. New York: International.

Gramsci, Antonio. 1971. *Selections from the Prison Notebooks*. Translated by Quintin Hoare and Geoffrey Nowell Smith. New York: International.

Hall, Stuart, and Tony Jefferson, eds. 1976. *Resistance through Rituals: Youth Subcultures in Post-War Britain*. London: Hutchinson.

Hirst, Paul. 1979. *On Law and Ideology*. London: MacMillan.

Hoggart, Richard. 1951. *Auden: An Introductory Essay*. London: Chatto and Windus.

Hoggart, Richard. 1957. *The Uses of Literacy: Aspects of Working-Class Life with Special References to Publications and Entertainments*. London: Chatto and Windus.

James, Henry. 1881. *The Portrait of a Lady*. London: Macmillan.

James, Henry. 1903. *The Ambassadors*. London: Methuen.

Joyce, James. (1934) 1990. *Ulysses*. New York: Random House.

Lacan, Jacques. 1977. *Ecrits: A Selection*. Translated by Alan Sheridan. London: Routledge.

Laclau, Ernesto. 1977. *Politics and Ideology in Marxist Theory*. London: New Left.

Leavis, Queenie Dorothy. 1932. *Fiction and the Reading Public*. London: Chatto and Windus.

Lévi-Strauss, Claude. 1955. "The Structural Study of Myth." *Journal of American Folklore* 68 (270): 428–444.

Lévi-Strauss, Claude. 1969a. *Mythologiques*, vol. 1: *The Raw and the Cooked*. Translated by John Weightman and Doreen Weightman. New York: Harper and Row.

Lévi-Strauss, Claude. 1969b. *Totemism*. Translated by Rodney Needham. Harmondsworth: Penguin.

Lévi-Strauss, Claude. 1972. *Structural Anthropology*. Translated by C. Jacobson and B. G. Schoepf. London: Penguin.

Lévi-Strauss, Claude. 1974. *Mythologiques*, vol. 2: *From Honey to Ashes*. Translated by John Weightman and Doreen Weightman. New York: Harper and Row.

Lévi-Strauss, Claude. 1978. *Mythologiques*, vol. 3: *The Origin of Table Manners*. Translated by John Weightman and Doreen Weightman. New York: Harper and Row.

Lévi-Strauss, Claude. 1981. *Mythologiques*, vol. 4: *The Naked Man*. Translated by John Weightman and Doreen Weightman. New York: Harper and Row.

Lévi-Strauss, Claude. 2004. "The Story of Asdiwal." In *The Structural Study of Myth and Totemism*. Edited by Edmund Leach, translated by Nicholas Mann, 1–48. New York: Routledge.

Marx, Karl. 1961. *The Economic and Philosophic Manuscripts of 1844*. Moscow: Foreign Languages.

Marx, Karl. 1963. *Early Writings*. Translated by Tom B. Bottomore. London: C. A. Watts.

Marx, Karl. 1970. *A Contribution to the Critique of Political Economy*. Translated by Maurice Dobb. London: Lawrence and Wishart.

Marx, Karl. 1973. *Grundrisse: Foundations of the Critique of Political Economy (Rough Draft)*. Translated by Martin Nicolaus. London: Penguin.

Marx, Karl. 1977. *Capital: A Critique of Political Economy*, vol. 1. Translated by B. Fowkes. New York: Vintage.

Marx, Karl. 1978a. *Capital: A Critique of Political Economy*, vol. 2. Translated by David Fernbach. London: Penguin.

Marx, Karl. 1978b. *The Eighteenth Brumaire of Louis Bonaparte*. In *The Marx-Engels Reader*, 2nd ed. Edited by Robert C. Tucker. London: W. W. Norton.

Marx, Karl, and Friedrich Engels. 1934. *Karl Marx and Friedrich Engels: Correspondence, 1846–1895: A Selection with Commentary and Notes*. London: M. Lawrence.

Marx, Karl, and Friedrich Engels. 1964. *The Communist Manifesto*. New York: Simon and Schuster.

Marx, Karl, and Friedrich Engels. 1970. *The German Ideology*. Translated by C. J. Arthur. London: Lawrence and Wishart.

Parsons, Talcott. 1967. *The Structure of Social Action*. New York: Free Press.

Poulantzas, Nicos. 1973. *Political Power and Social Classes*. Translated by T. O'Hagan. London: New Left.

Ricoeur, Paul. 1968. "Structure, Word, Event." *Philosophy Today* 12: 114–129.

Shils, Edward A. 1961. "Centre and Periphery." In *The Logic of Personal Knowledge: Essays Presented to Michael Polanyi on His Seventieth Birthday*, 117–130. London: Routledge and Kegan Paul.

Thompson, Edward P. 1961. "The Long Revolution Parts I and II." *New Left Review*. Part I, no. 9: 24–33; Part II, no. 10: 34–39.

Thompson, Edward P. 1963. *The Making of the English Working Class*. New York: Random House.

Thompson, Edward P. 1967. "Time, Work-Discipline, and Industrial Capitalism."
Past and Present 38: 56–97.

Thompson, Edward P. 1974. "Patrician Society, Plebeian Culture." *Journal of Social
History* 7: 382–405.

Thompson, E. P. 1975. *Whigs and Hunters: The Origin of the Black Act.* New York:
Pantheon.

Thompson, Edward P. 1978. *The Poverty of Theory and Other Essays.* London:
Monthly Review Press.

Volosinov, V. N. 1973. *Marxism and the Philosophy of Language.* Translated by L.
Matejka and I. R. Tutunik. New York: Seminar.

Williams, Raymond. 1958. *Culture and Society: 1780–1950.* London: Chatto and
Windus.

Williams, Raymond. 1961. *The Long Revolution.* London: Chatto and Windus.

Williams, Raymond. 1971. "Literature and Sociology: In Memory of Lucien Goldmann." *New Left Review* 67: 3–18.

Williams, Raymond. 1973a. "Base and Superstructure in Marxist Cultural Theory."
New Left Review 82: 3–16.

Williams, Raymond. 1973b. *The Country and the City.* New York: Oxford University Press.

Williams, Raymond. 1977. *Marxism and Literature.* Oxford: Oxford University Press.

Williams, Raymond. 1979. *Politics and Letters: Interviews with New Left Review.*
London: New Left Books.

38–39, 41–43, 51–52; history as discipline, 37, 41–43, 48; literary critical tradition, English, 8, 9–10, 12–14, 27–32; and structuralism, 45–46, 72–73; Western Marxism and, 21, 43–46. *See also* Thompson, E. P.; Williams, Raymond

cultural resistance, 180, 187–89. *See also* ideological struggle

Cultural Studies: moment of emergence, 185–86; as political project, 5, 7–8, 11

cultural transformations: contestation in, 49–50; rearticulation, 152–54; rearticulation in, 144–48; struggle in cultural change, 40–41; Thompson on, 41–43. *See also* "black" as ideological formation; Rastafarianism; subcultures

culture, concepts of: anthropological, 15, 33–34; community and communication, 32–34, 52; cultures of survival, 187–89; dominant cultures, 44, 190–91; Eliot, T. S., 40–41; elite culture, 13–15; emergent and residual, 49–50; emergent cultures, 44, 197; experience as, 28, 32–33, 52; Frankfurt School, 16–17; Leavis, F. R., 10, 12–15; literature and art, 28–29; lived culture, 8–10, 15, 33–34; norms and values, 17–18; oppositional, 30; power in, 18–19; residual cultures, 44, 49–53; in sociology, 16–19; struggle in, 29–32, 180

Culture and Society (Williams): absence of struggle in, 29–32; critique of dominant cultural traditions, 29; literary criticism as social analysis, 27–28

deep structure, 63

Derrida, Jacques, 122

determinacy: base/superstructure, 23–24, 75, 80; cultural resistance and, 180; in *The Eighteenth Brumaire*, 95; in *For Marx*, 124–25, 142; Gramsci on, 160; interdetermination (Williams), 34, 38–39, 51–52; in late Marx, 86, 89; levels of abstraction and, 90–91; in Marxist structuralism, 81, 106–9, 112; relative autonomy and, 108–11; strong, 24; structural causality, 111–12; structuralist,

71; technological, 78. *See also* correspondence; overdetermination

deviance, 58–59

difference, relations of, 88–89, 119–22, 149–53

discourse, 72–73. *See also* ideology, theories of

discourse theory, 114, 135, 136–37, 141

displacement, 107–8, 111

Durkheim, Émile, 19, 55–59

Economic and Philosophical Manuscripts (Marx), 23, 39

The Eighteenth Brumaire (Marx), 77, 93–96, 106

elite culture, 13–15, 30–32

emergent cultures, 49–50, 197

empiricism: Althusserian critique, 112–16, 134; in British sociology, 16; English empirical mode of thought, 3; epistemology in, 128

Engels: on base/superstructure, 22, 85–86; on determinacy, 106; on history, 85–86; legal systems, 110

equivalence, systems of, 149–50

ethnography, 10

exchange, relations of, 88–89

exclusion, 31, 47–48, 58–59, 182–83

experience: as culture, 28, 31, 32–33, 52; ideologies and, 83–84, 137; vs. theoretical abstractions, 47–48

Factory Acts, 102–3, 109–10

false consciousness, 83–84, 128

fascism, 16–17, 157, 195–96

feminism, 135, 193–94

Fiction and the Reading Public (Q. D. Leavis), 13

force, relations of, 158–60

formalist methodology, 69

For Marx (Althusser), 107, 115, 122–24, 135–42

Foucault, Michel, 120–21, 135

Freud, Sigmund, 107, 141, 148

functionalism: Althusserian, 109–10, 130, 132–33; structuralist, 60–61 gender: articulation to the State, 121; and capital-class contradition, 180; contradictions of, 185, 188; economic determinacy and, 75; and mode of production, 93; overdetermination and, 150; subjectivity and, 39, 141

The German Ideology (Marx), 75, 77, 83, 100, 127–28

Goldmann, Lucien, 35, 44

Gramsci, Antonio: civil society, 132–33; concept of base/superstructure, 158–60; ideology, 164–68; influence on Williams, 44–45; methodology, 159–63; political engagement, 155–57; on political struggle, 176–77; relations of force, 158–60; on subjectivity, 166–68; on theory, 157. *See also* hegemony

Great Britain: "American phase," 6; Labour Party, 5–7, 174; liberalism, 174–75; post-Second World War, 5–7

Grundrisse (Marx), 75, 81, 112–13, 137

Hegelianism: being and consciousness, 23; culturalism and, 39, 158; Marxist, 22–23, 98, 104; Marxist inversion of, 75, 84–86, 113–15; theoretical abstractions, 47, 104

hegemonic politics, 177–79

hegemony, 162–63, 168–79; consent, 169, 170, 172; containment, 183–84, 190–91; historic blocs, 169–72; negotiations with, 187–88; political struggle within, 176–77, 189–90; resistance, 187–90; subordination, 169–71; war of position, 176–78

Hirst, Paul, 123, 148

historical-analytical methodology, 159–63

historical materialism, 75–76, 84–85, 141–42

historicism, 117–18; Althusser on, 112–15; concept of theory, 112; explanation of myth, 65; in Marx, 104

history: and Cultural Studies, 37, 41–43; Gramsci on, 160–63; vs. structure, 71, 72

Hoggart, Richard, 8–12

homologies, 35

Horkheimer, 16–17

humanism, 39, 46–48, 70, 72–73

idealism, 75, 84–85

identities, 140–42

ideological formations: experience and, 83–84; language in, 144–48; rearticulation, 181–84; social class, 83; as systems of representation, 181–82

ideological practices, 128–32, 136–37

"Ideological State Apparatuses" (Althusser), 129–35

ideological struggle, 174–79; class formations and, 181; containment, 183–84, 190–91; Gramsci on, 159, 167–68; rearticulation, 152–54, 182–84, 194–97

ideology, theories of: in Althusser, 109–11, 129–41; articulation in, 142, 153–54; civil society and, 132–33; in classical Marxism, 79; collective norms as, 58; common sense, 137–38, 165–66; in discourse theory, 141; in *The Eighteenth Brumaire*, 94–96; "end of," 7; as field of struggle, 153–54; Gramsci on, 164–68; interdiscursivity, 166–68; and language, 131; materialist theory, 131–32; modes of production, 79, 127–28, 143, 158–59; philosophy and, 165–66; positionality, 140; reproduction, 129–30, 132–33, 153–54; and the State, 163–65; structure in dominance, 132–33; as systems of representation, 135–37; traces, 151–52; unconscious structures, 139–40. *See also* subjectivity

incorporation, 50

industrial capitalism: *Culture and Society*, 28–30, 29–30; dominant ideologies of, 29

interpellation, 134, 141

key terms, 28, 35

Labour Party, 5–7, 174

Lacan, Jacques, 65–66, 134, 135, 141–42, 148–49

Laclau, Ernesto, 152

language: and class, 10; and ideology, 131, 154; positionality, 140–41; as primary symbolic system, 59–61; structuralist paradigm, 63–65; Volosinov, 45–46, 154. *See also* linguistic paradigm

langue, 62–63

law, systems of: and base/superstructure metaphor, 46; Engels on, 110; in the political terrain, 94; and the State, 163, 172; as systems of collective representations, 57–56

leadership, hegemony as, 171, 172–73

Leavis, F. R.: concept of culture, 13–15; Marxist literary criticism and, 19–20; methodology, 12–15

Leavis, Q. D., 13

Lenin, Vladimir, 107

Lévi-Strauss, Claude, 45, 59–73; critique of functionalism, 60; effect on Marxist structuralism, 110, 111, 133–34; on the plurality of cultural logics, 60–61, 70; on social contradictions, 67–68; unconscious codes, 62–63, 65, 71–72, 139–40; use of linguistic paradigm, 61–63

liberalism (Great Britain), 174–75, 182–83

linguistic paradigm, 61–63, 63–65, 72, 105, 107, 133–34, 141–42

linguistics, structural, 61–63

literary critical tradition, English, 8, 9–10, 12–14

literary criticism: Marxist, 19–21; as social analysis, 8–9, 12–15, 27–32

lived culture, 8–10, 15, 33–34

The Long Revolution (Williams), 32–43; class formations, 35–37; concepts of culture, 32–34; determination in, 34, 38–39; experience as culture, 32–33; methodology, 34–35; social formations, 38–39; structure of feeling, 35–37; Thompson on, 40–42

The Making of the English Working Class (Thompson), 31, 42–43, 117

Mao, Zedong, 107–8

Marx, Karl: determinacy, 95–96; the economic, 78; Hegelianism, 84–85, 98; on history, 75–76; human praxis, 101; on materialism, 131; method, 88; methodology, 95–96, 102–3, 112–13; representation, 95–96; on reproduction, 129–30; as

structuralist, 98–101, 107–8, 112–13, 115; subjectivity, 103; on theory, 89

Marxism, classical: base/superstructure, 22; concept of change, 79–81; consciousness, 79; Hegelian influences, 39, 47; historical materialism, 75–76, 84–85, 141–42; indirect engagement with, 21; models of determinacy, 80–81, 86; relations of production, 77–79; social classes, 82, 86–87; social contradictions, 81–82; social relations, 76–77; the State, 76–77; structural forces, 75–76; structure, 78; on technology, 78

Marxism, humanist, 39, 98, 116–18

Marxism, structuralist. *See* Althusser, Louis; structuralism, Marxist

Marxism, Western, 43–45

Marxism and Literature (Williams), 44–52

Marxism and the Philosophy of Language (Volosinov), 45–46

mass culture, 6, 11, 13, 18

mass media, 132–33, 136–37

mass society, 6, 13

Mauss, Marcel, 19, 55–56

meaning: and practices, 136–37; production of, 128; signifying chains, 144–48; in social formations, 42–43; in structural analysis, 65; in structuralism, 66–67; struggle over, 152–54; Volosinov, 45–46

migration, 26, 148

"The Modern Prince" (Gramsci), 159

morality, 173–74

myth. *See* Lévi-Strauss, Claude

New Left, 8, 21–22, 22

New Left Review, 8, 27, 44, 117–18

norms, 57–58

organic ideologies, 165

originality, 68–69

overdetermination, 107–8, 111, 122–23, 149–51, 159

parole, 62–63

Parsons, Talcott, 17–18, 55–56

periodisation, 161

pluralism, 17–18

policing, 172

political economy, 35–36

political formations, 169–70, 172–73

political practices, 105, 121, 159, 160–61

political struggle, 176–77, 189–90

politics, language of, 93–96

Poor Laws, 36, 40, 41–42

popular culture, 13, 30–32

popular knowledge, 165–66

popular literature, 13

positionality, 140–41

poststructuralism, 134

Poulantzas, Nicos, 99, 133, 184

The Poverty of Theory (Thompson), 47, 78–79, 116–18

practices: in *Capital*, 101; discourse and, 136–37; *The German Ideology*, 77; ideology and, 136–37; interrelation of, 51–52, 74, 77–78; of knowledge production, 128; materiality of, 136–37; relative autonomy, 108–11; as semiotic, 72–73; in social formations, 39, 77–78, 105; specificity of, 105–6, 108–9, 136–37. *See also* ideological practices

The Prison Notebooks (Gramsci), 157

production, modes of, 38; as abstraction, 89; as combinatories, 100, 103; determinacy in, 80–81; displacement, 110–11; noncorrespondence, 75–76, 84–85, 141–42, 185; and social contradictions, 101–2

production, social relations of, 77–79, 88–89

productive forces. *See* production, modes of

psychoanalysis, 134, 135, 140–41

race, 146–51, 186–87

Rastafarianism, 144–45, 152

rationalist logic, 60–61

Reading Capital (Althusser and Balibar), 99, 133–35

reading culture, 8–9, 27–29

rearticulation: of cultural forms, 194–97; in cultural transformations, 144–48,

152–54; in ideological struggles, 181–84; of working-class cultures, 195–96

reductionism, 20, 76; Althusser on, 96–98, 119, 122, 127–28; class, 82, 83, 127–28, 183–87, 194; economic, 82–83, 158–59, 160; Gramsci's critique, 158–60

relative autonomy, 107, 108–11, 185

religion: articulation of, 143–45, 151–52, 197–205; as residual culture, 49, 197–205; as symbolic systems, 59

representation: collective, 56–57; in *The Eighteenth Brumaire*, 95–96; experience and, 137; systems of, 135–37. *See also* norms

reproduction, 108–9; Althusser on, 111, 129–30, 135; in civil society, 132–34; contestation in, 152–54; Gramsci on, 159; Marx on, 129–30

residual cultures, 44, 49–50; and emergent cultures, 197–205; rearticulation of, 190–97

resistance. *See* ideological struggle

Resistance through Rituals (Hall and Jefferson), 191–97

rights, language of, 181–82

Rock Against Racism, 196–97

The Rules of Sociological Method (Durkheim), 56

Saussure, Ferdinand de, 45, 61–63, 148

science: vs. ideology, 112, 115; linguistic paradigm as, 61–63; positivist, 55–57; rationalist logic in, 60

semiotics, 45, 71–73, 131, 136

sexuality, 135

Shils, Edward, 18

signifying chains, 134, 146–53

signifying systems, 63–65, 70, 72–73

social class: in *Capital*, 101–3; classical Marxism, 83; in *The Eighteenth Brumaire*, 93–96; Gramsci on, 162–63, 168; ideologies and, 83; race and, 186–87

social formations: Althusser on, 104–6; in classical Marxism, 77; culture in, 180; hegemony in, 177–79; humanist concept of, 39; as interactive totalities, 46; practice in, 39; structure in dominance, 118–19; transformations in, 42–43

social movements, 96, 124, 144–46, 153–54, 160–61

social order, 57–58

social relations: historical structure, 77–78; ideology and, 138–39; as interdiscursive fields, 150–51; Marx on, 76–77; and productive forces, 82. *See also* production, modes of

sociology, 16–19, 56

the State: capitalist mode of production and, 96; civil society and, 131–33; Gramsci on, 163–65, 168; ideology and, 163–65; limits on capitalism, 159; Marx on, 76, 82, 95–96; theorisation, 120–21

state capitalism, 96

structural analysis, 63–65, 71

structural causality, 111–12

structuralism: agency in, 72; concept of change, 68–69, 70; culturalism vs., 72–73; formalist methodology in, 69; functionalism in, 60–61; vs. humanism, 70, 72–73; internal systems, 67–68; linguistic paradigm, 61–65; meaning in, 66–67; and the plurality of cultural logics, 70; and social contradictions, 67–68; on subjectivity, 133–35; symbolism, 66–70; systems of rules, 61–65, 70. *See also* structuralism, Marxist

structuralism, genetic, 35, 44

structuralism, Marxist, 97–126; antihistoricism, 104–5; concept of theory in, 89; determinacy in, 81, 106–9, 107–8, 111, 112, 122–23; functionalism of, 109–11, 132–33; vs. Hegelianism, 86, 104, 115–16; vs. humanist Marxism, 71–72, 116–18; ideology in, 109–11, 112, 127–28, 130–32, 133–35; levels of social formation in, 105–6; Marx as structuralist, 98–101, 107–8, 112–13, 115; overdetermination, 85, 111, 116, 122–23; relative autonomy, 107, 108–11; scientific Marxism, 86; social relations, 138–39; structural causality, 111; structure in dominance, 118–19; subjectivity in, 77–79, 100–101, 103, 107–8, 111, 115, 117, 133–35;

use of linguistic paradigm, 65–66, 101. *See also* Althusser, Louis

structural linguistics, 61–63

structure of feeling, 34–37, 44, 50–51

struggle: counterhegemonic, 187–90; in cultural analysis, 31; in cultural change, 40–41; in cultural formations, 31; differentiation of, 185–87; Gramsci on, 44–45, 160–61, 166; Thompson on, 29–32, 40–43

subcultures: countercultures, 193–94; Mods and Rockers, 191–93; norms and, 58–59; relative autonomy, 193–94; Skinheads, 194–97

subjectivity: "always-already" interpellated, 148–49; articulation and, 144–48; collective, 145, 152; decentered, 77, 100–101, 103, 117, 133–34, 134–35; and discourse, 134–35; Gramsci on, 166–67; and ideology, 133–35, 140–43; Marx on, 77–79; new, 144–48, 191–97; positionality, 140; psychoanalysis, 135

symbolic classifications, 59–73

symbolic interaction theory, 19

syndicalism, 156

Thatcherism, 178–79

theory, concepts of: Althusser, 112–15, 128; empiricist, 112–13; experience vs. abstraction, 47–48; Gramsci, 157; levels of abstraction in, 89–93, 101–3, 113; Marx on, 89, 112–13; theoreticism, 115–16; Thompson on, 46–48, 113, 116–18; Williams on, 33–34, 50–51, 113

Thompson, E. P.: base/superstructure, 46; consciousness, 79; critique of *Culture and Society*, 29–32; critique of *The Long Revolution*, 40–42; cultural resistance, 188; experience as culture, 33; Gramsci and, 158; on history, 41–43; on popular struggle, 40–43; *The Poverty of Theory*, 116–18; rule of law, 183–84; on theory, 46–48, 116–18

totality: culturalist, 51–52; humanist, 38–39; Marx, 38–39, 89; Marxist structuralism, 104

underground warfare, 176–77
University of Birmingham. *See* Centre for Contemporary Cultural Studies
The Uses of Literacy (Hoggart), 8–11

Volosinov, V. N., 145–46, 154

war of maneuver, 176
war of position, 176–78
Weber, Max, 19
welfare state, 6, 37, 164
Williams, Raymond, 25–53, 40–43; concept of struggle in, 40–43, 44–45; concept of totality, 38–39, 51–52; concepts of culture, 28, 29, 38, 49–50, 190; critical literary analysis, 27–32; critique of base/superstructure metaphor, 34, 38–39, 44–46, 51–52, 79; critique of structuralism, 45–46; cultural change, 49–50; on determination, 51–52; dominant cultures, 50; forms of culture, 190–91; humanism, 39, 47–48; influence of E. P. Thompson, 45–46; influence of Gramsci, 44–45; Leavis tradition, 20–21, 28–29; on social formation, 38–39; on structuralism, 35, 44, 45–46; structure of feeling, 34–37, 44, 50–51; on theory, 45–48; and Western Marxism, 43–46
working-class cultures, 9–10, 25–26, 155–56, 188, 195–96

youth subcultures, 191–95, 194–95, 196–97